# WORLD WAR II
# 1945
## THE FINAL VICTORIES

# TIME LIFE BOOKS

## TIME INC. BOOKS

**Publisher** Margot Schupf
**Associate Publisher** Allison Devlin
**Vice President, Finance** Terri Lombardi
**Executive Director, Marketing Services** Carol Pittard
**Executive Director, Business Development** Suzanne Albert
**Executive Publishing Director** Megan Pearlman
**Associate Director of Publicity** Courtney Greenhalgh
**Assistant General Counsel** Simone Procas
**Assistant Director, Special Sales** Ilene Schreider
**Assistant Director, Finance** Christine Font
**Assistant Director, Production** Susan Chodakiewicz
**Senior Manager, Sales Marketing** Danielle Costa
**Senior Manager, Category Marketing** Bryan Christian
**Manager, Business Development and Partnerships** Stephanie Braga
**Associate Production Manager** Kimberly Marshall
**Associate Prepress Manager** Alex Voznesenskiy

---

**Editorial Director** Stephen Koepp
**Art Director** Gary Stewart
**Senior Editors** Roe D'Angelo, Alyssa Smith
**Managing Editor** Matt DeMazza
**Project Editor** Eileen Daspin
**Copy Chief** Rina Bander
**Design Manager** Anne-Michelle Gallero
**Assistant Managing Editor** Gina Scauzillo
**Editorial Assistant** Courtney Mifsud

---

**Special thanks:** Allyson Angle, Katherine Barnet, Brad Beatson, Jeremy Biloon, Ian Chin, Rose Cirrincione, Pat Datta, Assu Etsubneh, Alison Foster, Erika Hawxhurst, Kristina Jutzi, David Kahn, Jean Kennedy, Hillary Leary, Amanda Lipnick, Amy Mangus, Robert Martells, Melissa Presti, Danielle Prielipp, Kate Roncinske, Babette Ross, Dave Rozzelle, Ricardo Santiago, Divyam Shrivastava, Larry Wicker

ISBN 10: 1-61893-402-3
ISBN 13: 978-1-61893-402-4

We welcome your comments and suggestions about Time Inc. Books. Please write to us at:

Time Home Entertainment books, Attention: Book Editors,
P.O. Box 361095, Des Moines, IA 50336-1095

If you would like to order any of our hardcover Collector's Edition books, please call us at 800-327-6388, Monday through Friday, 7 a.m.–9 p.m. Central Time.

## Created by Contentra Technologies
**Project Manager** Phyllis Jelinek
**Advisors** Gordon Clarke, John Perritano
**Designer** Sandy Kent
**Maps & Illustration** Paul Brinkdopke
**Special Thanks** Sharon Luster, Lisa Slone

CONTENTRA
TECHNOLOGIES

# CONTENTS

# Introduction

Almost every major country in the world, 20 in all, became embroiled in World War II (1939–1945), the deadliest conflict in history. By the war's end, much of Europe and Asia lay in ruins and more than 60 million people had lost their lives.

Today, 1945 endures as the most transformative period of the twentieth century. During this time, national borders were reshaped; new countries emerged, while old ones crumbled and disappeared from the postwar map. The year gave rise to a new multinational organization, the United Nations, and the United States became the world's first superpower. It also led to a nuclear arms race and a new conflict that would dominate the globe for nearly 50 years—the Cold War.

As 1945 dawned, Adolf Hitler's Third Reich was on the brink of defeat. Allied troops had already landed in Normandy, France, and were poised to crush Hitler's last offensive in the west—the Battle of the Bulge—and gut what remained of Nazi forces in western Europe.

British, American, Canadian, and French forces then crossed the Rhine River and pushed deep into Hitler's Reich. As those troops moved east, the Soviets marched west toward Berlin. With each footfall, the full extent

## Path to the End

As 1945 dawned, six long years of war was ending. The Allies squeezed Germany from two sides, while the fighting in the Pacific became even more savage.

▲ **JANUARY 17** Soviet forces liberated Poland's capital city, Warsaw, opening the path for the Russians to move south into Germany.

**JANUARY 25** The Battle of the Bulge, Hitler's last major offensive on the Western Front, ended in a decisive victory for the Allies.

**FEBRUARY 4** Allied leaders met at Yalta, a city on the Black Sea, to discuss the surrender of Germany and Japan and to plan for the postwar world.

▲ **MARCH 7** U.S. troops crossed the Rhine River at Remagen in western Germany, paving the way for soldiers to move into Germany's heartland.

**MARCH 26** U.S. forces completed the capture of the island of Iwo Jima, about 760 miles southeast of Tokyo, which would serve as a strategic American air base as they moved toward the Japanese home islands.

**JANUARY** • • • • **FEBRUARY** • • • • **MARCH** • • • • **APRIL** •

of the Nazi atrocities became apparent. Allied armies liberated hundreds of concentration camps, where only a fraction of those imprisoned had survived. By May 9, Hitler was dead and Germany was defeated and buried in rubble.

But even after the fighting in Europe ended, Japan, seeking to dominate Asia and the Pacific, stubbornly held on. The country's collapse finally came in August, at a terrible cost, when two U.S. atomic bombs obliterated the cities of Hiroshima and Nagasaki. Those earthshaking blasts marked the decisive end of World War II.

This book, *World War II—1945: The Final Victories*, examines this critical year. It explores the key battles and strategies that finally brought the war to an end, as well as world leaders' motivations and political actions. Each chapter reveals compelling new turning points. There is brave resistance to occupiers by ordinary civilians in Poland and Italy. There is the Soviet Union trying to outmaneuver Western democracies in a land grab in eastern Europe. There are U.S. Marines in the Pacific, facing the tenacity of the Japanese in the Philippines, Iwo Jima, and Okinawa. Throughout, you'll also find fascinating firsthand accounts and stunning photographs.

*World War II—1945: The Final Victories* is a story of remarkable courage, sacrifice, dreams fulfilled and failed, and the triumph of righteousness. It illustrates how today's world emerged from the events of this pivotal year—and how 1945 changed the lives of generations to come.

MAY 7 Germany surrendered to the Western Allies.

▲ MAY 9 Germany surrendered to the Soviets, bringing the war in Europe to a close.

AUGUST 6 Determined to end the war in the Pacific, the United States dropped an atomic bomb on Hiroshima, Japan.

▲ AUGUST 9 The United States dropped a second atomic bomb on Nagasaki, Japan.

SEPTEMBER 2 Japan surrendered, formally ending World War II.

# 1 | THE WESTERN FRONT

AS 1945 DAWNED, MOST GERMANS KNEW THAT THEIR COUNTRY WAS ON THE BRINK OF COLLAPSE. FOR MANY, SURVIVING THE ALLIED ONSLAUGHT WAS THE ONLY THING THAT MATTERED.

American officers stopped to inspect a disabled tank during the Battle of the Bulge in Belgium. While the Americans were at first on the losing side of the battle, they would, in the end, triumph over the enemy.

"We are determined that before the sun sets on this terrible struggle our flag will be recognized throughout the world as a symbol of freedom on the one hand and of overwhelming force on the other."

—General George C. Marshall

▲ Allied soldiers and sailors arrived in England in 1945 following a tour of duty. They would soon be deployed back to the continent to wage war against Nazi troops.

# The New Year

GERMANY FOUND ITSELF FACING AN INSURMOUNTABLE FOE.

The Allies had much to cheer about as they celebrated the New Year in January 1945. The invasion of Normandy, France, the previous summer had finally put the Nazis on the run, and the Allies—the United States, Great Britain, and the Soviet Union—could see that Germany was on the brink of collapse. Along both the Eastern and Western Fronts of Germany, though, there were brutal battles to wage and to win if the Allies were to succeed. Nazi leader Adolf Hitler believed that his country could still triumph, but many of his generals no longer shared this optimistic view.

In Berlin, Allied bombing raids—American during the day and British at night—took a heavy toll. People crowded into air-raid shelters and basements. They wrote messages on walls of gutted buildings to sons and husbands returning from the front, letting them know their families were safe, at least for the moment, and living elsewhere. Berliners were short on food, water, and sanitation facilities. "*Heil Hitler!*" had been the prevailing everyday greeting and rallying cry; now, Berliners declared, "*Bleib übrig!*"—Survive!

The Russians compounded Germans' misery as they advanced north from Hungary and west through East Prussia. The Red Army showed no mercy to captured military or to civilians. Murder, rape, and looting became common tactics of the Soviet forces. Germans faced their situation with a dark humor: "Be practical," they quipped at Christmastime. "Give a coffin."

## Europe 1945

When World War II began, Axis powers lined up behind the Nazis, but by 1945 Germany was surrounded by enemy forces.

Axis Powers: Germany, Italy, Hungary, Romania, Bulgaria, Japan

Allied Powers: United States, Britain, USSR, Australia, Belgium, Canada, China, Denmark, France, Greece, Netherlands, New Zealand, Norway, Poland, South Africa, Yugoslavia, Brazil

▲ Germany's prized panzer tanks played a key role in the Battle of the Bulge, December 16, 1944, to January 25, 1945.

# The Battle of the Bulge

WITH THE ALLIES SQUEEZING GERMANY FROM THE EAST AND WEST, HITLER PROPOSED A DARING PLAN.

In the fall of 1944, Hitler developed a strategy that he hoped would turn the war in the western regions of Europe to his favor and halt the advancing American and British troops. He wanted to seize Antwerp, Belgium, a key port city on the Atlantic coast, which would split the American and British armies fighting in the heavily wooded Ardennes Forest in Belgium. He named the plan Operation Autumn Mist, but it became known as the Battle of the Bulge for the

effect the maneuver had on the Allied front lines. If the plan succeeded, Hitler believed American president Franklin Roosevelt and British prime minister Winston Churchill would be forced to the negotiating table.

Hitler's military advisers complained that the scheme was overly ambitious. The Nazi army lacked fuel, tanks, replacement parts, guns, and artillery shells for such an aggressive campaign. In addition, they noted that German soldiers had begun to

**Driving a Wedge Between the Western Allies**

German forces pierced the American and British front lines in the Ardennes region of Belgium and Luxembourg.

▲ In the first days of fighting, Nazi soldiers, part of the SS, moved quickly through the Ardennes Forest.

# Moving on the Western Front

A handful of key events forced Germany to its knees and wreaked havoc on the country.

**1945 JAN**

**JANUARY 1** Germany conducted a raid against Allied airfields, destroying more than 450 planes.

**JANUARY 25** Battle of the Bulge ended.

**FEB**

**FEBRUARY 3** Allies began bombing Berlin.

**FEBRUARY 13** Dresden bombing created a firestorm that reduced the city to ashes.

**MAR**

**MARCH 7** U.S. forces crossed the Rhine River at Remagen, Germany.

**APR**

**APRIL 12** President Franklin Roosevelt died, and Harry Truman became president.

**APRIL 26** American and Soviet armies met at the Elbe River in Germany.

**APRIL 30** Adolf Hitler committed suicide.

surrender en masse and that five years of heavy combat had so depleted the rank and file that most of the fighting was being done by young boys and old men. Hitler was unswayed by these arguments and pushed preparations forward.

A cornerstone of the offensive strategy was the creation of a new armored tank group, the Sixth Panzer Army, which was placed in the hands of Josef "Sepp" Dietrich, Hitler's friend and adviser. The Fifth Panzer Army, led by General Hasso von Manteuffel, who had gained fame for his battle strategies on the Eastern Front and in North Africa, also played an essential role. The offensive's success hinged on the element of surprise.

Allied code breakers, however, were one step ahead of the Germans. They intercepted a message sent by the Japanese ambassador in Berlin to government and military officials in Tokyo. The revealing missive described the massing of "a million" Nazis on the Western Front. In addition, the Allies learned that the *Luftwaffe*, the German air force, was stockpiling fuel and ammunition in the west and that Nazi officers were seeking soldiers who spoke "the American dialect" to disrupt Allied troop movement and spread confusion among the ranks.

But instead of providing the Allies with a strategic advantage, the advance information made Allied commanders overconfident. This deadly battle began early on December 16, 1944, when artillery guns lit up the winter sky in what would be one of the last great German offensives of World War II. For many American troops, it would be their first battle and their last.

### General Sepp Dietrich: A Privileged Tank Commander

Josef "Sepp" Dietrich (1892–1966) joined the Nazi Party in 1928, and in 1929 became Hitler's chauffeur and bodyguard. Dietrich rose quickly through the ranks of the SS, the elite corps of combat troops that served as Hitler's personal guard and as special security forces within Germany and its occupied territories.

Because Hitler had such a close relationship with Dietrich, he allowed the tank commander to question some of his decisions—a privilege extended to very few in Hitler's inner circle. In late 1944, Dietrich was named commander of the Sixth Panzer Army, Germany's renowned tank force, and during the Battle of the Bulge, he began to challenge Hitler's military strategies and methods of conducting battles and the war itself, yet he continued to follow the Führer's orders.

In March 1945, Dietrich was transferred to Hungary, where he unsuccessfully faced off against the Soviets in the Battle for Budapest. This last major Nazi offensive of the war was an ill-fated attempt to retake the oil fields of Hungary. In the wake of that defeat, Dietrich retreated north to Vienna to prepare for a final stand against the Russians.

◄ Adolf Hitler (left) with Sepp Dietrich

### NOVEMBER 30, 1874–JANUARY 24, 1965

# WINSTON CHURCHILL

*A statesman and inspiring orator, Churchill led the British during their darkest hours. "I have nothing to offer but blood, toil, tears and sweat," he told the House of Commons in his first speech as prime minister.*

Born into a life of privilege, Winston Churchill graduated from the Royal Military College at Sandhurst in 1894 and served in India, the Sudan, and South Africa. He entered politics at age 25, when he successfully ran for Parliament, and later held several government jobs. In 1904, he switched allegiance from the Conservative Party to the Liberal Party, realizing that his beliefs fit better with the Liberals.

When the Liberal Party won the 1905 national election, Churchill assumed the post of under-secretary of state at the Colonial Office. He continued to rise in the government and in 1911 became First Lord of the Admiralty, in charge of the British navy. He applied his energies to strengthening the navy, but during World War I, he lost this position due to naval failures.

After the war, Churchill served in various administrative government positions, eventually shifting back to the Conservative Party in 1924. With the defeat of the Conservative government in 1929, he turned to composing articles, speeches, and biographies, and became one of the highest-paid British writers of the 1930s. As the Nazis rose to power in 1933, Churchill became a persistent voice speaking out about the perils of German nationalism.

When Hitler invaded Poland in September 1939, Prime Minister Neville Chamberlain was swept from office due to his policy of appeasement toward Hitler; Churchill took Chamberlain's place in 1940. "I have nothing to offer but blood, toil, tears and sweat," Churchill told the House of Commons on his first speech as prime minister.

During the early years of the war, Churchill's leadership inspired the British people and helped keep his country strong as it alone sought to stymie Nazi Germany. In late 1940, Churchill and Roosevelt signed what became known as the "Lend-Lease" agreement, under which the United States would "lend" war supplies to Britain, in exchange for long-term leases to territory for air and naval bases. As prime minister, Churchill also worked closely with Soviet premier Joseph Stalin to create a unified campaign against the Axis.

**"We shall not fail or falter; we shall not weaken or tire. . . . Give us the tools and we will finish the job."**

## FACES *of* WAR

**JANUARY 30, 1882–APRIL 12, 1945**

# FRANKLIN DELANO ROOSEVELT

*Born to a wealthy family, Roosevelt led America out of the Depression and through World War II. He became a champion of everyday Americans and a staunch supporter of the nation's military troops.*

> "We can gain no lasting peace if we approach it with suspicion and mistrust or with fear. We can gain it only if we proceed with the understanding, the confidence, and the courage which flow from conviction."

When Franklin Delano Roosevelt became president in 1933, the Great Depression was in full force, and throughout the country, Americans were suffering. Within his first 100 days in office, Roosevelt pushed through Congress his signature "New Deal" legislation creating 42 new agencies designed to produce jobs, regulate banks, and provide unemployment insurance.

Roosevelt also led the nation through World War II, managing the effort as an active commander in chief. He became known for working closely with his military advisers to develop strategies and for choosing field commanders. When FDR passed away in April 1945, victory in Europe had not been achieved, and the United States still faced months of fighting in the Pacific.

Roosevelt was one of the most beloved, and also one of the most hated, presidents in American history. Some called him a savior of the nation for his efforts during the Depression and World War II; others criticized his

▲ Franklin Roosevelt

expansion of the federal government and limitations on free-market capitalism. His legacy as one of the nation's great presidents endures.

▲ Roosevelt speaking to a joint session of Congress, March 1, 1945

> "We . . . are passing through a test. It is a test of our courage—of our resolve—of our wisdom—our essential democracy. If we meet that test—successfully and honorably—we shall perform a service of historic importance. . . ."

◄ The Americans were well armed and fought back with heavy-duty shells fired from howitzers.

▲ Americans soldiers managed to cross the Meuse River as enemy shells exploded around them.

## "Forward to and over the Meuse!"

Hitler gave this order during the Battle of the Ardennes, expecting German troops and tanks in France to surround the Allied forces stationed on the other side of the Meuse River.

One of Europe's more important navigable waterways, the Meuse flows some 600 miles from Saint Mihiel and Verdun north through Belgium and the Netherlands to empty into the North Sea. In France, the river's valley served as part of the natural barriers helping to protect the Paris Basin from attacks coming from the east.

## Penetrating Allied Lines

German field marshal Gerd Von Rundstedt, assigned to lead the attack in the Ardennes, was a trusted, experienced commander who had served in World War I. Although he was pessimistic about the offensive and knew he did not have enough troops for a decisive victory, he lined up his men along a 60-mile front that stretched from southern Belgium to Luxembourg. "Your great hour has struck," he told his men. "You bear in yourselves a divine duty to give everything and to achieve the superhuman for our Fatherland and our Führer."

A frigid winter challenged U.S. tanks and troops advancing to counter German forces in the Ardennes Forest.

As the assault began, 250,000 German soldiers, accompanied by infantry and tanks, charged rapidly through the Ardennes. Within nine days, the Germans had penetrated the American and British front lines, creating a 70-mile-wide and 50-mile-deep "bulge" in the Allied defensive positions.

The stunned Allies retreated, and the advancing Germans captured thousands of soldiers. The Nazis executed many and held others as prisoners of war. Germans disguised as American GIs moved behind the Allied lines, cutting communication lines and seizing vital bridgeheads.

### Hardened Troops

By December 20, four days after the start of Operation Autumn Mist, the Germans had surrounded American forces stationed in Bastogne, Belgium, a strategically important town where the Ardennes region's main roads converged.

### Old Blood and Guts

General George Patton (1885–1945) was as audacious as he was abrupt, a soldier who always kept his men moving across the battlefield. Patton also relished combat. He earned the nickname "Old Blood and Guts," prompting his troops to joke, "Our blood, his guts." He helped lead Allied troops in their successful invasion of Sicily, the island off the southern tip of Italy, and later led the Third Army as it swept across France in 1944. He was never a diplomat, however, and his bosses, especially General Dwight Eisenhower, the supreme commander of the Allied forces in Europe, were often critical of him.

◄ Wary American troops fighting in St. Vith, Belgium, watched for German snipers as they sought to capture the village.

Running short on ammunition, besieged U.S. troops fought valiantly but gave up ground hour after hour while sustaining heavy losses from enemy bombardment. Still, they managed to hold on, and when the Germans demanded that the Americans surrender on December 22, the U.S. commander refused.

Finally, on December 26, the U.S. Third Army, led by General George Patton, broke through the German lines and relieved Bastogne's beleaguered defenders. When the Nazis were running out of fuel and ammunition, and unable to push Patton's troops back, Fifth Panzer Army general von Manteuffel asked for permission to withdraw. Hitler denied the request, and the panzers remained mired in the conflict.

## One-Word Reply: Nuts!

When U.S. Army general Anthony McAuliffe (1898–1975) received a written demand from the Germans on December 22 ordering him to surrender at Bastogne, the U.S. position was dire. McAuliffe's troops had been surrounded for days and had sustained heavy casualties. Nevertheless, McAuliffe's now-famous response was "Nuts!" Officers under his command tried to come up with suitable, official language to rephrase the answer, but in the end decided to let the one-word reply stand. It would become one of the most famous quotes of the war.

A graduate of West Point, McAuliffe was artillery commander of the 101st Airborne Division when he parachuted into Normandy on D-Day. Six months later, he was acting commander of that division during the siege of Bastogne. On December 30, 1944, McAuliffe received the Distinguished Service Cross, the second-highest military award that can be given to a member of the army. After the Battle of the Bulge, McAuliffe was given command of the 103rd Infantry Division, a position which he held until the end of the war.

▲ American soldiers used occasional lulls in the Battle of the Bulge to recover from the bitter cold.

In the days after Bastogne, the battle for the Ardennes continued, but the tide of war had changed. Patton moved his men north, successfully attacking the southern German lines. British field marshal Bernard Montgomery and his soldiers, moving south on January 3, struck on the northern flank of the "bulge." Four days later, the U.S. VII Corps cut off a main German supply road, depriving the Nazis of an important route to transport ammunition, fuel, and other crucial equipment to the troops. With the Battle of the Bulge lost, the weary German soldiers retreated to the east, toward the German heartland.

While Churchill called the Battle of the Bulge "undoubtedly the greatest American battle of the war," troops paid a heavy price for the victory. Close to 21,000 Allied soldiers were killed. Another 43,000 men were wounded, and over 23,000 were captured or reported missing in action. German losses were horrific as well: 15,000 killed, 41,000 wounded, and 27,000 captured or missing. The Germans also lost 600 tanks and 1,600 aircraft. In the end, Hitler's costly grand scheme only delayed the Allied march into Germany by about six weeks. Moreover, the Allies had destroyed the Germans' ability to hold a line in the west.

# FACES *of* WAR

**JUNE 20, 1925–MAY 28, 1971**

# AUDIE MURPHY

*Dashing, fearless, and handsome, this second lieutenant became a decorated hero for killing over 240 Germans and wounding and capturing many others. He was honored both in the United States, where he earned a Congressional Medal of Honor, and in Europe.*

After recovering from wounds sustained in an October 1944 German mortar attack, U.S. second lieutenant Audie Murphy rejoined his platoon in the Colmar region of France in mid-January 1945.

Within days, Murphy and the men of Company B of the Third Infantry Division found themselves in a dangerous position, near the town of Holtzwihr, France, one of the last Nazi strongholds in the country. On the cold afternoon of January 26, 1945, Company B was facing heavy enemy fire. With only 19 of his men remaining, Murphy ordered the troops to retreat to safer ground and stayed alone to face the Germans. When he ran out of ammunition, Murphy climbed on top of a burning tank destroyer and used its machine gun to keep the Germans at bay, killing dozens. Although he was wounded in the leg, Murphy continued his fight for nearly one hour. At the same time, he guided the artillery bombardment of Nazi positions via field telephone. As his men began moving forward again, and aided by air support, Murphy organized a counterattack and forced the enemy to retreat. His heroic actions saved the lives of his company.

Murphy became the most decorated soldier in United States history, receiving 33 citations and awards, including the Congressional Medal of Honor. The French and Belgian governments also granted him awards for heroism.

**"I never liked being called the 'most decorated' soldier. There were so many guys who should have gotten medals and never did—guys who were killed."**

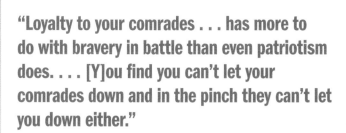

**"Loyalty to your comrades . . . has more to do with bravery in battle than even patriotism does. . . . [Y]ou find you can't let your comrades down and in the pinch they can't let you down either."**

▶ An Allied bombing raid created a firestorm in Dresden, Germany. It reduced much of the city to ashes and killed more people than any other Allied bombing raid.

# A Cultural Center Is Flattened

IN THE MOST DESTRUCTIVE BOMBING RAID OF THE WAR, THE ALLIES INCINERATED DRESDEN, KILLING NEARLY 135,000 PEOPLE.

The northern German city of Dresden, nicknamed the "Florence of the Elbe River," was filled with museums and historic buildings that dated from medieval times. Because it had not been a military target in the early years of the war, Dresden escaped the fire bombings that decimated other German cities, and it became a magnet for refugees fleeing the advancing Red Army. By February 13, 1945, Dresden was teeming with people, far more than the city's official population of 350,000. Over the next 48 hours, an estimated 135,000 would be killed, the greatest loss of civilian life of all Allied bombing raids during the war. The primary goals of the attack were to wreak havoc on the civilian population and to destroy their morale.

The campaign, conducted by 800 American and British aircraft, unleashed more than 3,400 tons of explosives on the city. Most were incendiary bombs, which ignited a firestorm that burned for days and destroyed eight square miles within the city. Charred corpses littered the streets. Some citizens were lucky enough to escape and ended up with only burned feet. A few people tried to find refuge in the city's reservoirs, only to drown.

Why was Dresden targeted so late in the war? Some have argued that any Nazi city—even if it had little military value—was fair game. Others have stated that Dresden was a major communications center, and destroying the city prevented the German army from sending messages. Dresden may have been selected because Churchill and Roosevelt had promised Stalin that they would bomb eastern Germany. Or, the city may even have been chosen as a warning to Stalin not to stray from the agreements the Allies had made earlier in the war. The United States and Britain hoped that their display of fearsome firepower would discourage the ambitions of the power- and land-hungry Russian leader.

> "We saw terrible things: . . . whole families burnt to death, . . . dead rescuers and soldiers, . . . and fire everywhere, everywhere fire . . ."
> —Lothar Metzger, a survivor of the Dresden bombing

"It seems to me that the moment has come when the question of bombing of German cities simply for the sake of increasing the terror, though under other pretexts, should be reviewed."

—Winston Churchill, March 28, 1945

> ## "I would have destroyed Dresden again. The bombers kept over a million fit Germans out of the German army."
> — British air marshal Sir Arthur "Bomber" Harris

▲ Residents of Dresden lined up for a streetcar amid the ruins of the city.

## A Different View

British air marshal Sir Arthur "Bomber" Harris assisted in carrying out the firebombing of Dresden. In an interview he gave 30 years later, Harris justified the attack by saying that it thwarted the Nazis' ability to wage war.

Others took a different view, including American prisoner of war Kurt Vonnegut, who survived the firestorm and later became a novelist. Vonnegut described the assault in his

book *Slaughterhouse-Five* and also commented about Dresden in his book *Palm Sunday: An Autobiographical Collage,* in which he wrote: "The Dresden atrocity, tremendously expensive and meticulously planned, was so meaningless."

◀ Kurt Vonnegut, author of *Slaughterhouse-Five*

▲ Elderly people lent a hand in the rebuilding of Dresden, but there was little they could do. The process would take decades.

## FACES *of* WAR

**APRIL 20, 1889–APRIL 30, 1945**

# ADOLF HITLER

*A charismatic leader, Hitler easily rallied his countrymen to follow him. He founded Germany's Nazi Party, led the country into World War II, and caused the deaths of millions of innocent civilians.*

---

Adolf Hitler was born in Austria-Hungary and as a young man dreamed of becoming an artist. He served in the Bavarian army during World War I carrying messages between German units and was awarded the Iron Cross for his bravery in action. Following the war, Hitler returned to Munich and became involved in nationalist and Socialist politics. In 1923, he took part in an attempt to overthrow the government, the "Beer Hall Putsch," and was jailed. He wrote his plan for transforming Germany, *Mein Kampf,* while serving his sentence.

Hitler returned to politics after his release and found success in Germany's 1930 election, when the Nazi Party won 107 seats. Two years later, the Nazis secured 230 seats and became the largest party in the Reichstag. Through means legal under the Weimar constitution, Hitler was named chancellor of Germany in January 1933. The next month, when a fire severely damaged the German parliament building, the Nazis claimed a Communist revolution was underway and passed the Enabling Act, effectively making Germany a dictatorship and Hitler its sole leader. He assumed the title Führer, meaning "Leader," in August 1934. Over the next few years, in violation of the Treaty of Versailles, Hitler ordered the buildup of Germany's military power. He began to annex neighboring territory in order to fulfill his dreams of Aryan *lebensraum* ("living space") and an expanded German empire, thus setting in motion the Second World War.

> **"It is not truth that matters, but victory."**

> **"Any allegiance whose purpose is not the intention to wage war is senseless and useless."**

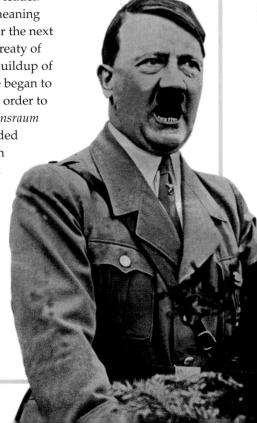

◀ This Nazi propaganda poster featured Hitler's image with the swastika-emblazoned German flag. Hitler used censorship and pervasive propaganda to promote Nazi ideas.

**Es lebe Deutschland!**

# Vengeance Weapons

GERMANY'S DEADLY ROCKETS TERRORIZED
GREAT BRITAIN AND BELGIUM.

In June 1944, Germany's army may have been retreating in Europe and its *Luftwaffe* in dire need of fuel, but the Nazis were by no means ready to surrender. It was time to unleash the Vengeance Weapon 1, or V-1.

Designed to terrorize London's civilian population, the V-1 was an outgrowth of research on space exploration rockets that

German scientists had been conducting since the start of the war. The German government believed that these rockets could be used for warfare and had begun testing them in 1941. On June 13, 1944, a week after the invasion at Normandy, the Nazis launched the first-ever V-1.

Powered by a pulse jet engine, the V-1s made a distinctive sound that gave rise to

German soldiers moved a V-1 rocket into position for launching toward London.

## Launched from the Netherlands

The first V-1 rockets had a range of just 150 miles, and the Germans launched them toward Britain from sites in northern France. Over time, the Germans enhanced the weapon's design so that the rockets could hit targets 250 miles from the launch site. This helped the German campaign tremendously, as the flying bombs could be fired off from secure bases in German-occupied Netherlands. This increased reach also meant the Germans had no trouble hitting sites in and around London and elsewhere in Great Britain.

their nickname, the "buzz bomb." As the summer of 1944 wore on, the Germans fired off thousands more of the missiles at London from sites along the French and Dutch coasts.

But by late in the year, the British had successfully installed a series of defenses and were intercepting over 80 percent of the V-1s. At the same time, the Allies reached and seized the last V-1 launch site in range of Britain, bringing the campaign to an end.

By that time, at least 8,000 V-1s had been aimed at Londoners, killing over 6,000. Germany continued to deploy the bombs against targets in both Britain and Belgium, including the port of Antwerp, until March 1945, when the advancing Allied forces overran and took those launch sites.

▲ V-1 rockets were positioned on launch ramps before being fired, as shown here at the Imperial War Museum in Britain.

### Hanna Reitsch: Test Pilot and Pioneer of Women's Aviation

Aviator Hanna Reitsch (1912–1979) broke many gender barriers: She was the first German woman to be granted a captain's license, the first female helicopter pilot, the first female test pilot in Germany, and, in 1942, the first German woman to be awarded the Iron Cross. Once the war began, Reitsch served as a test pilot for a variety of German military aircraft, including a modified V-1 plane called the Fieseler *Reichenberg*. These planes were air-launched, piloted V-1 rockets. Reitsch's task was to find out why test pilots were crashing and dying during landing. She discovered that the planes stalled out when pilots tried to land at high speeds and bailing out was impossible.

In late April 1945, Reitsch got the assignment to fly the new head of the *Luftwaffe*, General Robert von Greim, to meet Hitler in Berlin while the city was under siege by Soviet forces. Within days, the Nazi leader would commit suicide, and Reitsch would be one of the last people to see him alive. After the U.S. Army captured Reitsch, she testified about Hitler's "complete disintegration," which she witnessed in the Berlin bunker. Following her release from prison, Reitsch continued to set aviation records and eventually moved to Ghana, Africa, where she established a flight school.

▲ A British clean-up crew salvaged what they could from these buildings in north London that had been hit by V-2 rockets.

## Killed with Deadly Vengeance: The V-2s' First and Last Victims

Germany targeted both civilian neighborhoods and strategic military installations with their V-2 rockets. The first missile strike on London killed three people. The youngest victim was three-year-old Rosemary Clarke, who died on September 8, 1944, when a V-2 decimated the neighborhood where she lived, leveling more than ten homes and damaging at least 500 more. The last V-2 civilian victim in England was 34-year-old Ivy Millichamp, who died on March 27, 1945, when her house in Orpington, Kent, was hit.

## Slave Labor Construction

The Mittelbau-Dora concentration camp, an offshoot of the infamous Buchenwald concentration camp, was created to build the V-2 production facility in central Germany. More than 10,000 prisoners worked to excavate the underground factory where the rockets were constructed. Prisoners lived in the dark tunnels they were building. The air was thick with gypsum dust from the excavating operation, and food was always scarce. Thousands would die from the horrible conditions.

> "It seems likely that if the Germans had succeeded in perfecting and using these new weapons earlier than he did, our invasion of Europe would have proved exceedingly difficult, perhaps impossible."
>
> —Dwight Eisenhower

### From the V-1 to the V-2

About the same time that the Germans were developing the V-1 rocket, they had also been working on a missile that would become known as the V-2. The efforts dated to the early 1930s, when the Nazis recruited Wernher von Braun, a young scientist, to help design and develop liquid-fueled rockets. Von Braun was put in charge of a cutting-edge laboratory in northern Germany where the rockets would be created.

By early 1944, von Braun's team had developed a rocket that was powered by a liquid ethanol-water mixture and liquid oxygen—the V-2. These new liquid-fueled rockets, the first long-range ballistic missiles, traveled faster than the speed of sound. Another advantage: They were fired from mobile launchers that could be set up in just 30 minutes. These innovative weapons were extremely difficult to intercept, and they carried a massive 2,200-pound warhead.

The first V-2 attacks against London began in early September 1944. Because the weapon was nearly invisible, civilians had no advance warning. They only knew of an incoming bomb once it exploded, but by then it was too late to flee to safety. An accurately placed V-2 bomb not only killed those in its path, it left an immense crater where it hit and caused significant damage to the surrounding areas. V-2 rockets hit the Royal Hospital in Chelsea, a Woolworth's store in South London, and other heavily populated sites. The destruction in London was so severe that the British government began officially reporting that the bombs came down to the north of the actual locations where they had hit.

The deception tricked the Germans into adjusting their targeting, and as a result, many rockets hit relatively sparsely populated areas south of London and around Kent instead of in central London. In all, the Germans aimed more than 1,100 V-2 rockets at the British capital, killing approximately 9,000 Londoners over a period of seven months.

Belgium, which had been liberated by the Allies in February 1945, was the target of even more V-2 rockets than England. On December 16, 1944, a V-2 rocket hit the Rex Theater in Antwerp, Belgium, killing 567 people, including 296 Allied military personnel. It was the single deadliest rocket attack of the war. The last V-2 strike on Belgium happened on March 27, 1945. Germany also used the missiles to hit key bridges along the Rhine.

> "If we had these rockets in 1939, we should never have had this war. . . . With such weapons, humanity will be unable to endure it."
>
> —Adolf Hitler

▲ The deadly V-2 rocket, larger and faster than the V-1, was a source of pride to the German military.

▲ Wernher von Braun with a model of a proposed rocket ship

## Wernher von Braun: Mastermind of Germany's Rocket Program

Born in Wirsitz, Germany (now Wyrzysk, Poland), Wernher von Braun (1912–1977) was one of the world's most important aerospace engineers. Obsessed with rockets from a young age and an avid reader of science fiction, von Braun received a PhD in physics in 1934 and quickly became technical director of the German military rocket program. He oversaw the team that developed a new generation of rocket systems, including the V-2 model.

When it became clear that the Nazis would lose the war, von Braun arranged for the 500 rocket scientists who worked for him to surrender to the Americans. He believed it was more likely that his team would be allowed to continue its research in the United States, and he was concerned about their fate should they be captured by the Russians.

The agreement was worked out with the Office of Strategic Services (OSS), which brought more than 1,500 foreign engineers and scientists to the United States following the war in a program dubbed Operation Paperclip. Stateside, von Braun's team continued its rocket development work, first for the U.S. Army and later for NASA. In 1952, von Braun was named technical director of the U.S. Army ballistic weapons program, and, under his leadership, in 1958, the United States launched its first satellite, *Explorer I*. The Saturn rocket, a vehicle designed to launch spacecraft, was based on the work with rockets that von Braun had developed for Germany.

# Operation Lumberjack

THE BATTLE OF THE BULGE WAS OVER, BUT CROSSING INTO GERMANY WAS NOT EASY.

Following their January victory at the Battle of the Bulge, where combat had stretched from southern Belgium to Luxembourg, the Allies continued their slog toward Germany. Their goal was to capture the west bank of the Rhine River and three strategic German cities: Cologne, Bonn, and Remagen. Allied leaders agreed that while resistance would be fierce, enemy forces would not be able to stop the campaign code-named Lumberjack.

The 21st Army Group, composed of British, Canadian, and American divisions, closed in on the Rhine in the north, while the U.S. First Army headed for Cologne and Koblenz. As the First Army forged its way east, the men came across lines of desperate German civilians trying to escape to the west.

The German military, however, stood its ground. In an attempt to slow the Allied advance, Hitler ordered the bridges over the Rhine destroyed. One of the few spans left intact was the Ludendorff Bridge, 15 miles south of Bonn, which crossed the Rhine at the ancient Roman town of Remagen. Named for General Erich Ludendorff, who had led the final German offensives on the Western Front during World War I, this strong railway bridge dominated the town and provided passage to retreating German soldiers, escaping refugees, and livestock.

On March 7, the U.S. First Army began its advance to Remagen, led by Lieutenant Karl Timmermann, commander of Company A of the

▲ When the Germans failed to destroy the railroad bridge at Remagen and the first U.S. forces crossed, a sign appeared: "Cross the Rhine with dry feet. Courtesy of the 9th Armored Division."

27th Armored Infantry Battalion. Timmermann believed that the Germans, who were stationed on either side of the river, would destroy the Ludendorff before he arrived. But when the lieutenant put his field glasses to his eyes and looked toward the Rhine, he saw that the bridge was still standing. The Germans were planning to destroy the bridge as soon as their soldiers crossed. On the other side of the river, white flags and sheets of surrender hung from windowsills.

▲ After crossing the Rhine, Americans planted the U.S. flag on the towers of the Ludendorff Bridge at Remagen.

## Moving Across the Rhine
Following their victory in Belgium, the Allies' next objective was to cross the Rhine and seize Germany's heartland.

▲ U.S. Army engineers worked to repair damage done by Germans to the Ludendorff Bridge.

## A Bridge Too Far

At around 2 PM, just as the Americans were about to advance toward the bridge, a dark torrent of earth, paving stones, and iron exploded on its western ramp. The Germans had blown a 30-foot crater in the roadway leading to the bridge. Bullets then rained down on the advancing GIs from the bridge's towers. "I'll see you on the other side," one of Timmermann's men said as the troops pressed forward. Company A was then rocked by another tremendous explosion. When the smoke cleared, the soldiers expected once again to see that the Ludendorff had collapsed into the Rhine.

Instead, the bridge was still standing. Two of Timmermann's men raced up the girders to cut the wires leading to the remaining German demolition charges, while the rest of Timmermann's men fought their way to the other side. By nightfall, 120 men of Company A had crossed the Ludendorff. Before the German captain in charge of the Nazi efforts surrendered, he sent this message to his superiors: ". . . the demolition of the bridge was unsuccessful . . . the Americans have crossed."

The capture of the Ludendorff, dubbed the "Miracle of Remagen," allowed Allied armies to stream across the river. Within the first 24 hours, more than 8,000 soldiers had passed over the last natural barrier to Germany's heartland. An attempt by the Nazis to retake the bridge failed. Ten days later, the bridge had been hit by nearly one dozen German-fired V-2 rockets, and the heavily damaged span collapsed, taking 24 Americans to their death. The Ludendorff, however, had served its purpose. For the Allies, it was a one-way, eastbound street. They were now poised to push into the interior of Germany.

## FACES *of* WAR

**FEBRUARY 12, 1893–APRIL 8, 1981**

# OMAR BRADLEY

*This soldier was known as the "Honest Mechanic" for his competence on the battlefield and as the "GI's general" for his concern for ordinary troops.*

General Omar Bradley, the commander of the U.S. First Army, was one of the first to receive word that the bridge at Remagen had been taken by the Americans.

Bradley had participated in planning the invasion of France and commanded the troops who waded ashore on Omaha and Utah Beaches on D-Day, June 6, 1944. There, he was forced to watch as enemy machine guns cut down his men. Those who were not killed in the water struggled ashore. The situation was so bad that Bradley considered retreating.

Now, nine months later, as his 12th Army Group crossed the Rhine, Bradley called Eisenhower to give him the good news. "Brad, that's wonderful," the supreme Allied commander answered. "Sure, get right on across with everything you've got. It's the best break we've had."

By the end of the war, Bradley had cumulatively commanded more troops than any other general in American history. His modest style made him a favorite of the GIs. Eisenhower called him "the master tactician of our forces . . . America's foremost battle leader."

▲ Omar Bradley

**"In war there is no second prize for the runner-up."**

▶ General Bradley (far left), commander of the U.S. First Army, strategized with British major-general Ralph Royce (center) and Bradley's aide, Major Chester Hanson, at the battlefront in northern France in 1944.

**"Wars can be prevented just as surely as they can be provoked, and we who fail to prevent them must share in the guilt for the dead."**

▲ German troops who fought in the Ruhr Valley were held in a prison camp following their surrender on April 17.

# Into the Heartland

ONCE THE ALLIES HAD CROSSED THE RHINE, EISENHOWER'S
ATTENTION SHIFTED TO THE RUHR VALLEY.

Once they crossed the Rhine River, the Western Allies began a determined drive into Germany's heartland. Eisenhower set his sights on the Ruhr Valley, an area bordered roughly by the Rhine to the west, the cities of Dortmund and Hagen to the east, the Ruhr River to the south, and the Lippe River to the north. This strategic area was rich with coal and iron deposits, and it was the Third Reich's primary industrial center.

The plan called for British field marshal Bernard Montgomery to march toward the Elbe River in the north, while the Americans pushed south toward the Ruhr. The goal was to encircle and eliminate the German forces that remained in the region.

But Eisenhower's strategy surprised other Allied war planners, who presumed the commander's objective would be to continue the advance east and take Berlin, as he had said earlier. Montgomery and Churchill were unhappy. "Berlin remains of high strategic importance," Churchill wrote to Roosevelt, arguing for a shift in tactics. "The Allied armies of the north and center should now march at the highest speed towards the Elbe."

Eisenhower, unmoved, won the dispute and proceeded, dismissing Berlin as "nothing but a geographical location." On April 1, the Americans finished surrounding the Ruhr Valley and cut off about 500,000 Nazi troops.

> ## "My purpose is to destroy the enemy's forces and his powers."
> —Dwight Eisenhower

▲ Allied air attacks targeted German industries in the Ruhr Valley. Survivors of the bombings surveyed the damage to their streets and homes.

▲ Despite the danger, on March 25, 1945, Winston Churchill crossed the Rhine accompanied by several U.S. and British generals.

The Germans, led by Field Marshal Walther Model, tried unsuccessfully to counterattack, first in the north, then in the south. Model also balked at orders from Hitler to destroy the industries in the area to prevent their capture. "All fear comes from the Devil," he wrote his wife, as the Americans closed in. "We must all die at some time or other."

When Bradley ordered more troops to squeeze the Ruhr Valley from both the north and the south, Model gave his men the option of trying to go home or fighting their way out of the Ruhr. Most decided to surrender. "What is there left to a commander in defeat?" Model told his officers, "In ancient times, they took poison." And on April 21, Model, one of the Third Reich's best commanders, committed suicide.

◄ General Dwight Eisenhower (right), supreme commander of the Allied forces in Europe, conferred with British field marshal Bernard Montgomery about Allied battle plans.

### Eisenhower the Diplomat

Managing the personalities of his commanders and of the Western leaders—on top of day-to-day military problems—was often a challenge for Eisenhower. To relieve the stress, he read stories of the Wild West at night. That way, "I don't have to think," he said.

Eisenhower was especially irritated by some decisions by Montgomery. In one well-known incident recorded by photographers (see far right, above), after the Americans had captured the Ludendorff Bridge in Germany, Montgomery allowed Churchill to commandeer a river launch and cross the Rhine River. The British leader, who had been visiting Montgomery, took several members of the Allied forces with him, and spent about 30 minutes in enemy territory. No harm came to the group.

# The Capture of Hanover

WHEN AMERICAN SOLDIERS REACHED THE CITY, THEY
SAW THAT ALLIED BOMBS HAD REDUCED IT TO RUBBLE.

The road through the heart of Germany was paved with bombed-out buildings and ruined cities, the results of repeated aerial assaults. One of the hardest-hit metropolitan areas was Hanover, an important railroad junction and industrial center.

The British had begun their aerial missions over the city during the summer of 1941, attacking rail yards, oil refineries, metal works, and other strategic targets. In September 1943, the Allies dropped over 2,100 tons of bombs on Hanover, followed by another 1,600 tons in October of that year. Yet the Allies were not done. On January 5 and 6, 1945, they blanketed the city with 2,300 more tons of explosives. The raids left 90 percent of the inner city in ruins. Residential areas were nearly obliterated, and some 6,000 civilians were killed.

Yet, the Allied ground advance on Hanover was slowed by pockets of German resistance, mostly by determined SS detachments. It wasn't until the second week of April 1945 that the Americans, led by Major General Alexander Bolling and his 84th Infantry Division, reached the city's outskirts. They took two days to capture the city, and when it fell on April 10, the 84th Infantry was ready to push through to Berlin. Three days later, Bolling and his men reached the Elbe River. There, they received orders to stand their ground and halt their advance.

◀ Hanover's railway station was destroyed during the Allied assaults on the city.

# THEN AND NOW

## HANOVER, GERMANY

*Located on the picturesque Leine River, this city was once
the capital of the kingdom of Hanover and the family
seat of the Hanovarian kings of Great Britain.*

Hanover was once a principality within the Holy Roman Empire and later its own kingdom. Throughout history, the city was an important transportation junction.

By the time the 84th Infantry reached Hanover in April 1945, little remained. Carpet bombing had reduced most of the buildings to rubble and only a few historical landmarks were left standing.

Today, Hanover looks nothing like its prewar self. It has large green areas with forests and parks, and is mostly flat. The Leine River meanders through the various quarters and few remaining hills. One of the oldest structures is the Opera House, which was built between 1845 and 1852.

▲ **THEN** Allied bombing raids devastated Hanover, a key German industrial and manufacturing site.

◀ **NOW** Hanover's New Town Hall, built in 1913, survived the war with minimal damage.

# The Fall of Nuremberg

HAND-TO-HAND FIGHTING MARKED THE DEMISE OF THE SPIRITUAL CENTER OF THE NAZI PARTY.

Berlin may have been the political center of Nazism, but Nuremberg was its spiritual hub. A city with historical ties to the Holy Roman Empire, Nuremberg was chosen by Nazi officials to host the party's annual rally, a ritualized spectacle designed to energize the faithful. In the early years, the gatherings lasted four days, then later for eight days. They became so huge that Albert Speer, the Third Reich's chief architect, designed a vast complex of buildings and parade grounds, dubbed the *Zeppelinfeld*, on the edge of the city to accommodate the crowds.

The assemblies included dramatic military parades, mass callisthenic classes, music, and singing. The dramatic high point came on the evening of the "Day of the Political Leaders," an homage to the party's "martyrs" who had been killed in the failed 1923 Munich "Beer Hall Putsch," Hitler's attempted coup d'état.

In 1935, the Nazis used the rally to announce the infamous Nuremberg Laws, which stripped Jews of their citizenship and deprived them of many political rights.

## Destroying the Old City

During the war, Nuremberg became a significant site for the manufacture of aircraft, submarines, and tank engines. In January and February 1945, the old city suffered its heaviest rounds of bombing by Allied planes. These systematic raids by the British Royal Air Force and the U.S. Army Air Force destroyed most of the city's center including medieval walls, a castle, and two historic churches. In addition, manufacturing plants in outlying areas were demolished. In the raid that took place on January 2, nearly 2,000 people were killed in just one hour. The following month, in February, another bombing raid killed another 1,000. In all, about 6,000 residents of the city lost their lives in the air raids and 100,000 were left homeless.

▲ Allied bombing raids pounded Nuremberg and its factories into rubble, opening the way for U.S. troops to enter the city.

### Karl Holz: Nazi Fanatic

When American troops arrived in Nuremberg in April 1945, Karl Holz (1895–1945) was the high-ranking Nazi Party official in charge of defending the city. Holz issued orders to his troops to shoot anyone attempting to flee. He also announced that laborers who failed to appear for work would be arrested. Anyone hanging or waving a white flag would be executed. "Who does not want to live with honor must die in shame," he said.

Rather than cede any ground to the arriving Americans, Holz planned to destroy entire neighborhoods including factories, public buildings, and bridges. When the mayor of the city said he wanted to surrender, Holz shot him. Two days later, on Hitler's birthday—April 20—Holz was found dead. To this day, it is unknown whether he committed suicide or suffered a battle injury.

▶ Surviving residents of Nuremberg carried their belongings through the Egidienplatz, site of the destroyed Benedictine Abbey of Saint Giles, in the city center. The statue of Kaiser Wilhelm I and the entire church were rebuilt in the years following the war.

## Door to Door

On March 28, the U.S. Seventh Army crossed the Rhine and began its march toward Nuremberg, a distance of some 200 miles. They reached the city by April 16 and began their attack from the north and south. Hitler ordered his troops to defend Nuremberg at all costs, and the Nazis trained their antiaircraft guns on the American invaders. For the next four grueling days, U.S. troops fought hand to hand and block by block, one building, one street at a time. When the Americans breached what remained of Nuremberg's medieval walls, troops quickly over-whelmed about 2,000 enemy soldiers; on April 21, the Allies officially took the city and installed the American flag high above Adolf Hitler Platz.

As with Hanover, much of Nuremberg lay in ruins, and legions of residents had fled. Many ancient landmarks had been destroyed or were badly damaged. A handful of dead Nazi loyalists remained where they had fallen in the streets.

Soon thereafter, on the southeast edge of the city, an American Army rabbi arrived at Speer's immense *Zeppelinfeld* to offer a prayer of thanksgiving. Later, reporters watched as the Americans blew up the infamous, large statue of the swastika that had loomed over the parade grounds.

The Germans rebuilt Nuremberg after the war. While architects and workers did their best to restore the city to its former glory, many of the city's ancient buildings were beyond repair or reconstruction.

▲ Albert Speer (left) designed buildings for Adolf Hitler during the war. Here, the men examine an architectural model.

### Albert Speer: Architect of the Third Reich

Albert Speer (1905–1981) received his architectural license in 1927, and in 1930, after hearing Hitler speak, he joined the Nazi Party. Hitler quickly became a fan of Speer's work, made Speer his personal architect, and appointed him to design ever more grand structures, including the Reich Chancellery and the *Zeppelinfeld* stadium in Nuremberg. Hitler and Speer became close friends, and in 1942 Hitler named Speer the new Minister of Armaments. In this role, he oversaw a massive increase in arms production, employing prisoners and slave labor. He is estimated to have used more than seven million slave laborers and two million prisoners of war in German war production.

During the 1946 Nuremberg trials that followed the war, Speer claimed he was unaware of the genocide taking place in the concentration camps. He was nevertheless convicted of war crimes and crimes against humanity. In a letter that was not made public until 2007, Speer admitted that he attended the conference during which Heinrich Himmler, head of the SS, stated that all Jews would be killed.

◄ British troops crossed the Rhine on March 26, 1945, on their march to Nuremberg.

# The Fall of Berchtesgaden

HITLER'S FAMOUS MOUNTAIN RETREAT WAS A
PRIME TARGET AS THE ALLIES SQUEEZED GERMANY.

As early as the fall of 1943, Eisenhower had worried that Nazis would entrench themselves in heavily fortified strongholds in Bavaria in southeastern Germany. Now, as the end of the war loomed, the general began to focus on Nazi Party diehards who he thought would either withdraw to Bavaria's rugged mountains and make a desperate last stand or hole up there and wage a guerrilla-style war.

One of the region's prime strategic targets was Berchtesgaden, a remote village 80 miles southeast of Munich. It was here, on the bucolic slopes of a mountain retreat, the Obersalzberg, that Hitler had come after his failed 1923 "Beer Hall Putsch" and where he had written the second volume of *Mein Kampf*. The chalets and lodges of top Nazi leaders, including Hermann Göring, head of the *Luftwaffe*; Martin Bormann, Hitler's

◄ On May 4, U.S. Army soldiers ripped down the Nazi flag that was flying over Hitler's retreat at Berchtesgaden. British bombs had damaged the complex, and retreating SS troops had set fire to it.

private secretary; and Speer, were located on the Obersalzberg. The area also held a large consignment of troops from the SS that provided security.

### The Dash to Berchtesgaden

Allied troops, both Free French and Americans, raced to capture Berchtesgaden. At first, they targeted the enclave from the air, hoping to destroy both Hitler's home and the Eagle's Nest, the chalet where Hitler entertained dignitaries and guests. On April 25, a group of British Royal Air Force planes dropped an estimated 1,400 tons of bombs, designed to destroy underground bunkers that the Allies believed existed beneath the Obersalzberg complex. The homes of Bormann and Göring and the

Eagle's Nest all sustained heavy damage. After the raid, local Germans raced up the mountain to loot the contents of the buildings. They stole furniture as well as Bormann's collection of watercolors.

On May 4, departing SS troops set fire to Hitler's home, and it was still smoldering later that day when two Allied infantry battalions, including the U.S. Army's Third Infantry Division, marched on the village. The soldiers tore down the Nazi flag and ripped it into souvenir shreds. Finally, the Americans made their way to the Eagle's Nest. There they found wine, teacups, and spoons etched with "A.H." Göring's house yielded 18,000 bottles of wine and liquor, thousands of cigarette lighters and cameras, and two dozen suitcases stuffed with clothing.

The mountaintop Eagle's Nest was built for Hitler's 50th birthday.

In 1933, Hitler bought a house on Obersalzberg Mountain at Berchtesgaden near the Austrian border. He eventually expanded the site into a large complex of buildings.

▲ On April 14, the Allies routed the Germans from Arnhem, the first step in liberating the Netherlands. Here, they work to stabilize damaged buildings.

# Allies Free the Netherlands

THE LIBERATION OF ARNHEM, NETHERLANDS, WAS NOT EASY, AND BOTH GERMANS AND THE WESTERN ALLIES FOUGHT HARD FOR THIS STRATEGIC TOWN.

As the Western Allies crossed the Rhine and advanced slowly into Germany, they were simultaneously fighting to liberate Arnhem in the Netherlands from its Nazi occupiers. The initiative, dubbed Operation Cannonshot, was led by the Canadian First Army and launched April 11, 1945. As Canadian troops crossed the IJssel River and began to attack Arnhem, the Royal Air Force provided cover, targeting and destroying German positions within the city. A separate assault was mounted from the south, but those soldiers encountered such strong German resistance that the Allies relocated their forces and continued the battle from the east. Over the next several days, Allied progress was slowed by mines and demolished bridges, but in the end the Nazis could not hold Arnhem. By April 14, the Canadians had secured most of the city, with mop-up

operations taking another two days. It was a victory that paved the way to liberate the Netherlands. In early May, German forces surrendered the country.

### A City in Ruins

The liberated city of Arnhem was a shell of its prewar self. The occupying Nazis had taken almost everything of use, and the damage from multiple bombing runs and artillery barrages had left most buildings empty skeletons. Homes that were still standing had no furniture, no windows, and no doors. Bridges had been destroyed, and temporary, movable spans were the only means to travel from west to east. Allied casualties during the battle were relatively small; about 60 Allied soldiers lost their lives and over 130 were wounded. No exact counts exist, but the number of injured and dead Germans is estimated to be in the thousands.

▲ Allied troops faced stiff resistance from Nazis in Dutch cities. These British soldiers took cover from sniper fire during a battle.

▲ Throngs in Bologna, Italy, gave an exuberant welcome to Italian resistance movement members who freed their city on April 21.

# The Allies Move North Through Italy

HELPED BY ITALIAN RESISTANCE FIGHTERS, THE ALLIES ADVANCED FROM SOUTHERN EUROPE.

### Celebrating Freedom

April 25, Liberation Day, is a national holiday in Italy. During the 2014 celebration, Italian President Giorgio Napolitano, who had joined an anti-Fascist group in 1942, praised the partisans. ". . . The Resistance, the commitment to reconquer Italy's liberty and independence, was a great civil engine of ideals, but above all it was a people in arms, a courageous mobilization of young and very young citizens who rebelled against foreign power," he said.

In 1943, following its surrender to the Allies, Italy had officially changed sides in the war. But Germans still occupied the northern part of the country, and the region had its own puppet Fascist government led by Il Duce Benito Mussolini. As 1945 proceeded, the Nazis stationed in Italy were determined to prevent the Allies from using the country as a base for attacks against northern Europe and the Balkans to the east.

To unseat the Germans, the Allies planned a spring offensive. They started on April 6 with two diversionary attacks on the coasts, a ploy to draw the German defenders away from the main planned thrust through the country's center. By April 19, British and American troops had surrounded the northern city of Bologna. Two days later, another group of Allied fighters entered Bologna and secured the

city. American troops continued moving north and on April 23 crossed the Po River. They were roughly 250 miles south of the German border. As they proceeded to Salò, the small town where the puppet government was headquartered, they encountered less and less resistance.

### Italians Join the Battle

As the Allied forces pushed north, an Italian political group representing resistance forces opposed to the Fascist regime, the partisans, organized a general strike and armed uprising in the major cities of Genoa, Milan, Turin, and Venice. The partisans intended this "Day of Uprising," scheduled for April 25, to demonstrate that the Fascists no longer controlled the country. The strike also freed partisans from their day jobs so they could participate in the battle against the remaining Germans and Fascists. The uprising was successful, and some historians believe that it saved key industrial sites in northern Italy from destruction by retreating enemy forces.

## Total Surrender

Over the next few days as the uprisings continued, Fascist governments in northern cities began to crumble. Some were ousted even before the Allied troops arrived. On April 25, anti-Fascists forced the Nazis out of Turin and Milan. On April 27, General Reinhart Meinhold, the commander of German forces in Genoa, found himself surrounded by anti-Fascist forces and surrendered—one of the few times in history that military forces capitulated to civilians. The next day,

German troops in Venice were also forced to cede to the partisans.

In the wake of these Nazi capitulations, some confusion ensued over the surrender agreement in Italy. Secret negotiations for a settlement had been underway in Switzerland since March. But on May 1, General Albert Kesselring, commander of German forces in southern Europe, voiced his opposition to the agreement. But the next day, he consented, allowing the surrender to take effect. Approximately one million German soldiers laid down their arms.

At war's end, Allied troops in Italy had fought their way over 1,000 miles. More than 300,000 U.S. and British troops and 430,000 German troops had been killed, severely wounded, or were missing.

▼ Liberation in Italy gave rise to strong emotions in those who had suffered during the war. An elderly woman gave an American soldier a welcoming kiss.

## Nazi Occupation in Northern Italy Ends

As the partisans, supported by Allied forces, united in Italy's northern cities, Benito Mussolini's Fascist government came to an end. The dictator himself, trying to escape, was caught near the Swiss border.

# The Rise and Fall of Mussolini

THE FASCIST DICTATOR'S REACH FOR POWER AND EMPIRE ENDED IN FAILURE AND DISGRACE.

▲ An Italian postcard with Benito Mussolini's signature

Italy may have been a minor player in the war, but its leader, Benito Mussolini, had aggressive military ambitions. The Italian dictator, who called himself "Il Duce," meaning "The Leader," claimed to come from humble origins: His father was a Socialist journalist and blacksmith and his mother a schoolteacher. Mussolini became active in Socialist politics at an early age, first in Switzerland and later in Austria-Hungary. He returned to Italy and became the editor of the Italian Socialist Party's newspaper, *Avanti!* But the Socialist Party ousted him over his stance on Italy's participation in World War I, and, as a result, Mussolini founded the Italian Fascist Party.

Following the Fascist "March on Rome" in October 1922, Mussolini was appointed prime minster, the youngest in Italy's history. He seized control as dictator in 1925 and quickly took steps to outlaw all opposition political parties in the country. Under Mussolini's leadership, Italy claimed and occupied territory in North Africa, creating an Italian empire. In 1939, after the Nazis had invaded and claimed Czechoslovakia, he aligned with Germany under the Pact of Steel, linking the two countries politically and militarily. Mussolini then went on the offensive. Determined to assert Italy's presence in the Balkans and increase its territory, he ordered troops to invade and seize Greece. He also sent troops to North Africa to defend Italy's territorial holdings there.

By 1941, Italy still had not conquered Greece, and Germany felt it was necessary to send in its own troops to take the country. Mussolini also failed to fend off the Allies in North Africa, and Germany again had to send manpower and tanks to aid the Italians. The fighting continued there until May 1943, when Axis forces surrendered after a final battle in Tunisia. Two months later, the Allies invaded Sicily, a toehold for their next move, the invasion of Europe from the south, through Italy.

In light of these developments, Mussolini lost credibility in Italy, where support for the war was declining. On July 25, 1943, Italian king Victor Emmanuel removed him from office. The country's military police immediately arrested Mussolini and imprisoned him on the island of Ponza, then moved him to an island off the coast of Sardinia, and finally held him at a mountaintop hotel in

"Let us have a dagger between our teeth, a bomb in our hand, and an infinite scorn in our hearts."

—Benito Mussolini

the Apennine Mountains. But he would not remain there for long. Hitler, intent on saving his "friend and loyal comrade in arms," ordered Mussolini's rescue. In a daring maneuver, heavily armed German commandos used gliders to reach the remote peak on September 12, 1943. They overpowered the Italian military guards, freed Mussolini, and brought him to Germany to meet with Hitler. Mussolini quickly agreed to the Führer's demand to set up a puppet Fascist government in northern Italy, and until early 1945 he directed his new government from the town of Salò.

In April 1945, as German defenses in Italy collapsed and the Allies advanced, Mussolini attempted to flee in a German truck headed for Switzerland. Partisans stopped the convoy and discovered the former leader, along with his mistress Clara Petacci, in one of the vehicles. The two were taken to the village of Mezzegra, about 50 miles north of Milan, where partisans executed them on April 28, 1945. They took the bodies to Milan and hung them from the girders of a gas station along with 13 other prominent Fascists, to prove they were dead.

▲ Italian partisans captured and executed Mussolini, his mistress Clara Petacci, and other leading Fascists on April 28, as they tried to flee Italy. Their bodies were hung in a town square in Milan.

## Partisans: Civilian Resistance to the Axis

The civilian resistance to German occupation in northern Italy was organized by the Committee of National Liberation, a coalition of anti-Fascists known as partisans. There were as many as 200,000 of these men and women, and they managed to kill enemy soldiers, destroy communication lines and transportation centers, and disrupt Axis supply lines. The Allies supplied the partisans with arms and other goods, usually by parachute drop from the Royal Air Force or the American Office of Strategic Services. German and Fascist forces did their best to suppress any resistance activity and often executed partisans and made a public display of the bodies to dissuade others from joining the group. Over the course of the war, nearly 50,000 partisans lost their lives in the fight to free Italy.

▶ Partisans were finally free to walk the streets of Milan after its liberation on April 25, 1945.

▲ The debris left behind in the Führerbunker, where Hitler and Eva Braun committed suicide, included a 16th-century painting that had been looted from a Milan museum.

# The Final Days in the Führerbunker

LIVING UNDERGROUND IN BERLIN, HITLER ISSUED HIS FINAL ORDERS.

In January, Hitler relocated to Berlin and took refuge in the Führerbunker, a self-sufficient underground air-raid shelter that had 18 rooms and its own water and electrical supply. The bunker was adjacent to the Reich Chancellery in the city center, and it was to be the final home of the Nazi regime.

When Hitler first moved into the Führerbunker, his days followed a certain pattern. In the afternoon, he came to an undamaged wing of the Chancellery building, where he consulted with his top military advisers and aides. Following these meetings, he had tea with his secretaries and other officials. He then retreated underground and spent the nights in the bunker. This routine soon gave way to another. Hitler emerged to take his dog, an Alsatian named Blondi, on short walks in the Chancellery gardens and then spent the rest of his time underground. Hitler continued to confer with his top advisers, including

◀ At war's end, the Führerbunker was still intact. However, on December 5, 1947, the Soviets tried to demolish it completely. In 1959, the area was leveled and turned into a park.

▲ Following the capture of Berlin, American soldiers examined the remains of the Reich Chancellery.

Göring, Heinrich Himmler, and Joachim von Ribbentrop, in the bunker, usually meeting them at night.

In March, amidst desperate, last-ditch fighting and with the Allies closing in on Berlin, Hitler issued this order: "All military transport and communication facilities, industrial establishments and supply depots, as well as anything else of value within Reich territory, which could in any way be used by the enemy immediately or within the foreseeable future for the prosecution of the war, will be destroyed."

Hitler demanded that Albert Speer, Minister of Armaments and War Production and the primary planner of the country's war economy, oversee the destruction. Speer refused to obey what has become known as the Nero Decree, believing that the German people would need the infrastructure and supplies after the war's end. Speer was able to persuade generals to ignore the order. Soon thereafter, he traveled to Berlin and told Hitler of his actions. By that time it was too late to countermand Speer's decision, and, as a result, at least some of Germany's industrial base survived the war.

In April, Hitler's mistress, Eva Braun, and Joseph Goebbels and his family joined Hitler in the Führerbunker. Later that month, on April 20, Hitler came up to award Iron Crosses to members of the Hitler Youth. It would be his last trip to the surface, for on that day Berlin was hit by Soviet artillery fire. Just two days later, Hitler was forced to admit that the

Nazis could not win the war. He blamed his generals for the loss and stated that he would stay in Berlin until the end.

By the 27th, Berlin had lost all secure radio communications and the staff that remained in the bunker were forced to rely on telephone lines to send instructions and orders to those still in the field. Events progressed quickly, and public radio became the main source of news and information about the war.

On the 28th, Hitler learned that Himmler, head of the SS, had been trying to arrange surrender terms to end the war, and Hitler ordered Himmler's arrest. The next day, when Hitler was told of Mussolini's capture and killing, the Führer vowed he would never become a similar spectacle. On the 29th at 4:00 AM, Hitler signed his will, in which he stated that he chose suicide over capture and that he wanted his body to be burned at the Chancellery. To ensure the cyanide pills that the SS had given him were effective, he tested one on his dog.

On April 30, Hitler was informed that Berlin would fall before the end of the day. That afternoon, Hitler and Braun went into his study and killed themselves. Braun bit into one of the cyanide pills and died. Several minutes later, Hitler shot himself in the head. As per his orders, soldiers took the two bodies up to the Chancellery and burned them. Guards then concealed the charred remains in a shell crater next to the building.

▼ Allied soldiers inspected the grave site next to the Chancellery where the charred bodies of Hitler and Braun were said to be buried. Gasoline cans remained next to the site.

## FACES *of* WAR

**ADOLF HILTER & EVA BRAUN**

# A WARTIME ROMANCE AND UNDERGROUND WEDDING

*Eva Braun once described Hitler as "a gentleman of a certain age with a funny moustache." She would become his mistress and devoted companion, then the wife who would die within just a few hours of her marriage.*

Hitler met Eva Braun, his companion and mistress, in 1929 when she was working for Hitler's photographer.

Braun moved to Hitler's chalet in Berchtesgaden in 1936 and served as hostess there, but the couple were rarely seen together in public.

Braun was extremely loyal to the Führer, writing to him in 1944 that "From our first meeting I swore to follow you anywhere—even unto death—I live only for your love." After joining Hitler in the Führerbunker in Berlin in April 1945, she refused to leave his side or to attempt escape.

The two were wed in a small civil ceremony in the early hours of April 29, but their life as a married couple would be short. They both committed suicide the next day.

Hitler always carried this signed picture of Eva Braun in his wallet, which was found by American troops. ▲

▲ Only a few photographs were taken of Hitler and Braun together.

▲ Braun lived with Hitler for about six years and became his wife only one day before they both committed suicide on April 30, 1945.

# 2 | THE EASTERN FRONT

THE SOVIETS HAD MILLIONS OF TROOPS TO DEPLOY AGAINST THE GERMANS, AND THEY WERE DETERMINED NOT JUST TO WIN, BUT TO RETALIATE.

**"Not one step back!"**
—Joseph Stalin, July 1942

Soviet infantry troops attacked German positions in eastern Europe.

▲ Following the defeat of the Polish Home Army in 1944, German soldiers rounded up members of the resistance movement. Members were guaranteed prisoner-of-war status in a capitulation agreement.

# Poland: A Key State on the Eastern Front

THOUSANDS OF POLES JOINED IN THE CAMPAIGN TO LIBERATE WARSAW, BUT THE ADVANCING RED ARMY LEFT THEM ON THEIR OWN.

As August 1944 approached, Soviet troops leading the drive into Nazi-occupied Poland closed in on the Vistula River, just east of Warsaw. Encouraged by the advancing Red Army, residents in the capital revolted against the Nazis. An underground resistance group of some 40,000 ill-trained and poorly supplied Polish soldiers formed their own army and planned to take control of Warsaw before the Soviets arrived.

The Home Army, as it was called, was strongly anti-Communist and had close ties to the Polish government-in-exile in Great Britain. For Soviet premier Joseph Stalin, members of the Home Army were not heroes but traitors, and their revolt constituted a criminal act. Instead of ordering Russian general Konstantin Rokossovsky and his swiftly approaching troops to aid the resistance fighters, Stalin issued a command forbidding it. He also

rejected calls by the British to air-drop supplies to the Home Army and to the city's starving residents. Elite Nazi units began crushing the uprising, battling ferociously from street to street, and they showed no mercy to any who opposed them. An estimated 150,000 Polish partisans were killed.

On October 2, 1944, a shattered Polish Home Army surrendered to the Germans. Over the next several months, the Nazis exercised complete control over Warsaw, decimating the city's remaining population and deporting thousands of civilians to concentration camps. During these months, the Germans also destroyed what little remained of the once vibrant and beautiful capital, including residences, public buildings, schools, and scientific institutions, as well as farmland, mines, electrical power plants, and other industrial facilities.

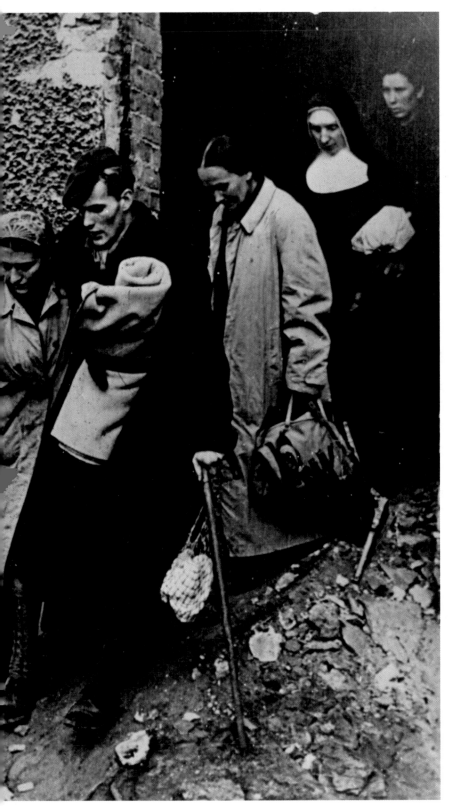

▲ Polish civilians carried what belongings they could when Germans deported them to either forced labor camps or extermination camps.

# Events on the Eastern Front

The Soviet Union battled German forces in a relentless drive through Prussia, Poland, and Hungary to capture Berlin.

**1945**
**JAN**

**JANUARY 17** Soviets captured Warsaw, Poland's capital.

**FEB**

**FEBRUARY 13** Soviet ground forces captured Budapest, Hungary, a Nazi stronghold.

**MARCH 6** The Germans launched their last major offensive to hold the oil fields in Hungary, but were defeated within a month by the USSR.

**MAR**

**MARCH 12** An Allied air raid on Vienna decimated the city. By early April, the city was in Allied hands.

**APR**

**APRIL 16** Soviet forces crossed into Germany and began a bombardment of Berlin.

**APRIL 30** Adolf Hitler committed suicide to avoid capture.

**MAY**

**MAY 2** Soviets hoisted their flag over the Reichstag in Berlin.

▲ The Red Army displayed its military might as it advanced through the cities of eastern Europe.

# The Soviets Push from the South and the East

## THE USSR PLANNED A PINCER MOVE TO SURROUND GERMAN FORCES.

By early 1945, the Allies were squeezing Adolf Hitler's Reich, poised to enter Germany from nearly every direction. The Red Army was beginning its move west through Poland and Prussia, south from the Baltic states, and north from Hungary. The Western Allies were pushing east from France's Normandy coast and north through Italy.

▶ These Red Army snipers used their rifle skills to help conquer the Germans in East Prussia.

## The Eastern and Western Fronts 1945

The Soviets pressed Germany from the east in their drive toward Berlin as the Western Allies pushed from the west.

▲ Vistula River, Warsaw

## The Vistula River

The longest river in Poland meanders from the Beskid Mountains at the nation's southern border all the way to the Baltic Sea in the north. The Vistula flows 650 miles through Krakow, the former Polish capital, Warsaw, and Gdansk.

In ancient times, when the Vistula was connected to the Dnieper River, it was part of a trade route called the Amber Road that stretched from the Baltic Sea to the Mediterranean Sea. Today, the Baltic coast near the Vistula delta contains about 90 percent of the world's amber.

In one of the many Polish legends about the river, a princess named Wanda became queen of Poland when her father died. A German prince wanted to marry her, but when she rejected him, he invaded the country. Her soldiers blocked the incursion, but Wanda leaped into the Vistula River and drowned, committing suicide so he would never again invade Poland.

As the Allied vice tightened, the Nazis were forced to fight on several fronts at once, and they did so in spite of critical shortages. Germany's manufacturing facilities had been devastated, and the country could not replace planes for its depleted *Luftwaffe*. Crude oil and fuel for its remaining panzer divisions were in short supply. Troops were running out of ammunition. So many soldiers had been lost that the military had to use young boys and old men to fill the gap.

In the east, where the Nazis had been engaged in a defensive struggle for two years, it had become increasingly difficult to keep the Soviet forces at bay. Red Army troops, with their eye on Berlin, seemed to be everywhere, advancing in one place, and at the same time, deploying thousands of fighters to battle in other locations. Much of the fighting converged in Poland and around its borders.

### A Strange Kind of Liberation

The New Year opened with the Soviets, led by Russian general Georgy Zhukov, in a strong position to capture Warsaw.

Zhukov's troops crossed the Vistula River and converged on the city from the north and the south. Then, on January 17, the Red Army finally overcame the remaining resistance from the Germans and marched into the capital to officially liberate it.

On their arrival, the Soviets discovered that there was little left to set free—much of the city had been reduced to rubble. Still they moved quickly, rounding up surviving resistance fighters to prevent them from rising up against their new occupiers. The Soviets designated dissenters "enemy agents" and treated them accordingly—deporting, imprisoning, or executing them. Once entrenched in Warsaw, the Russians would not leave the city for 45 years.

The fighting in Poland took a heavy toll: By war's end, the country would lose 30 percent of the buildings; 60 percent of its schools, scientific institutions, and public administration facilities; about 35 percent of its agricultural regions; and one-third of its mines, electrical power plants, and industries.

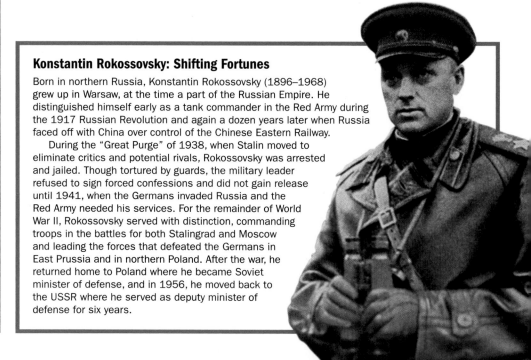

### Konstantin Rokossovsky: Shifting Fortunes

Born in northern Russia, Konstantin Rokossovsky (1896–1968) grew up in Warsaw, at the time a part of the Russian Empire. He distinguished himself early as a tank commander in the Red Army during the 1917 Russian Revolution and again a dozen years later when Russia faced off with China over control of the Chinese Eastern Railway.

During the "Great Purge" of 1938, when Stalin moved to eliminate critics and potential rivals, Rokossovsky was arrested and jailed. Though tortured by guards, the military leader refused to sign forced confessions and did not gain release until 1941, when the Germans invaded Russia and the Red Army needed his services. For the remainder of World War II, Rokossovsky served with distinction, commanding troops in the battles for both Stalingrad and Moscow and leading the forces that defeated the Germans in East Prussia and in northern Poland. After the war, he returned home to Poland where he became Soviet minister of defense, and in 1956, he moved back to the USSR where he served as deputy minister of defense for six years.

# FACES *of* WAR

## DECEMBER 1, 1896—JUNE 18, 1974

# GEORGY ZHUKOV

*The gifted military leader was said to be the only person who did not fear Stalin. He led the Red Army as it routed Nazi forces in the battles of Kursk and Berlin.*

Born a peasant, Georgy Zhukov worked his way up through the ranks of the Imperial Russian Army and later, the Red Army. He had a reputation for being both outspoken and stern, and he was often at odds with Stalin. Even so, he became the most successful Russian general of World War II and achieved recognition as "the man who did not lose a battle."

Stalin acknowledged Zhukov's military skills when he named him deputy supreme commander of the Soviet Army in 1942. With this appointment, Zhukov became the second most powerful man in the Soviet Union and soon took on the defense of Stalingrad. That brutal battle stretched on for months, but eventually Zhukov's troops outlasted and overwhelmed the Germans. The victory marked a turning point of the war.

In the summer of 1943, Zhukov led the Red Army in the Battle of Kursk, some 300 miles south of Moscow. There he routed Hitler's armies in one of the greatest tank clashes of the war. In 1945, he would triumph once again at the Battle of Berlin, when after a hard-won siege, joyous Soviet troops raised the Soviet flag over the German capital.

▲ Marshal Georgy Zhukov

**"It is a fact . . . that large-scale battles and whole wars are won by troops which have a strong will, clear goals, high moral standards, and devotion to the banner under which they go into battle."**

▲ Zhukov (left) met with British field marshal Harold Alexander (right) to celebrate the capture of Berlin.

POLAND
• Warsaw

# THEN *AND* NOW

## WARSAW, POLAND

*Once the home of Polish kings, 400-year-old Warsaw
is the country's largest city. It has a dynamic economy,
lively political scene, and vibrant cultural life.*

The Polish capital of Warsaw, which in 1939 was home to approximately 1.3 million people, suffered immensely during the course of World War II. By the time the Nazis took full control of the city on September 27, 1939, nearly a quarter of the infrastructure had been destroyed and more than 25,000 civilians had lost their lives during the month long attack.

In short succession, the Nazis set up their own government and closed all the city's universities. They imprisoned the capital's nearly 400,000 Jews in a walled ghetto, and then in 1942 sent many of them to die at Treblinka. Most of those who remained took part in the April 1943 Warsaw Ghetto Uprising, which lasted for several weeks. The Germans crushed the revolt and summarily executed most of the Jews who were still alive.

The non-Jewish Poles living in the city fought back against the Nazis as well, forming an underground Home Army. In August 1944, the resistance group staged another revolt, the short-lived Warsaw Uprising, but it too failed. When the Soviets arrived in January 1945 to liberate the capital, they discovered that the Germans had destroyed 85 percent of the city, razing most of Warsaw. Only 153,000 residents remained.

Warsaw and its Old Town were reconstructed in the years following the war. The Communist regime, which held power in the country until 1989, began the rebuilding campaign, adding prefabricated housing and a palace of culture and science and restoring the ancient streets, buildings, and churches. In 1980, the city's Old Town was added to the list of UNESCO's World Heritage sites. After the fall of the Berlin Wall in 1989, business enterprises and investments flowed in and the city began to flourish. Shopping malls opened with fast-food restaurants and fancy boutiques. Tourists from around the world flocked to the city whose landscape was marked both with restored historical buildings and modern skyscrapers.

▶ **THEN** Residents struggled to survive in a ruined postwar city.

▲ **NOW** The Palace of Culture and Science in Warsaw was built between 1952 and 1955 as a gift of the Soviet people to the Polish nation.

▲ **NOW** The Warsaw Uprising Monument portrays heroic Home Army members who gave their lives battling the German occupation forces during the Warsaw Uprising. It was unveiled in 1989 on the uprising's forty-fifth anniversary.

▲ **NOW** Warsaw's reconstruction produced a luminous modern metropolis.

▲ Fighting in the city of Königsberg was fierce, with snipers in nearly every building.

▲ Polish pilots flew with Britain's Royal Air Force.

## Polish Forces Helped the Allies Win

Soon after Germany invaded and occupied Poland, Polish leaders who had escaped formed a government in exile, first based in France and later in London. This group provided direction to the Polish Home Army and other units of the Polish resistance.

Polish escapees also included thousands of soldiers, sailors, and airmen. These men joined the Allied forces in the campaigns in North Africa, Italy, and France, and participated in the Normandy invasion. Polish pilots served in special British air force squadrons and fought the German *Luftwaffe* to help defend Britain.

During this time, Polish intelligence cryptographers discovered how to unscramble military messages created by the German coding machine, Enigma, and shared the information with the British. The Poles' work led to the Allies developing a decoding device. By 1945, the Allies had intercepted thousands of German communications, one of the keys to winning the war.

# The Königsberg Offensive

AS RUSSIA CONTINUED ITS MOVE EASTWARD, THE NAZIS WERE INCAPABLE OF STOPPING THE ONSLAUGHT.

Even as the Soviets liberated Warsaw, much of the rest of Poland was still under German control. By mid-January, East Prussia, a German province, was brimming with thousands of troops that the Nazis had brought to the front lines, hoping to slow the Russian advance. They were intent on defending the East Prussian port city of Königsberg, on the Baltic Sea.

The population around Königsberg, which was predominantly ethnic German with a small minority of Poles, had been decimated by the war. By 1945, most of those who were left were women, children, and elderly men. They had received no warning and were surprised by the approach of Soviet troops. On January 21, in an attempt to flee the advancing Russians, the people of Königsberg began a mass evacuation.

Their efforts were cut short by the Red Army, which blocked all routes out of the city, including the road to Pillau, a port that had become the main evacuation site for those hoping to escape. About 200,000 civilians remained trapped in Königsberg during what turned out to be one of the coldest winters in history. The Nazis who had arrived to defend the area, including the Third Panzer Army, also found themselves penned in by the Soviet forces.

▲ Adolf Hitler attended the 1937 launch of the *Wilhelm Gustloff*, a cruise ship that was later converted into a hospital.

## A Watery Grave: Torpedoes Sink the German Evacuation Ship

Operation Hannibal, the evacuation of Germans from East Prussia, successfully moved more than two million troops and civilians from the area by the end of January 1945. With thousands of civilians still on the run, German admiral Karl Dönitz ordered a thousand ships into operation, many of them civilian, to help relocate the refugees crowding into nearby port cities.

One of the largest vessels called into service was the *Wilhelm Gustloff*, a cruise ship that had been converted into a hospital at the start of the war. The craft had also served as a floating barracks for naval personnel stationed in Gdynia, Poland.

The *Wilhelm Gustloff* set sail from Gdynia on January 30, overloaded with some 10,000 people—more than four times its capacity. Its destination was Kiel, a northern German port about 60 miles north of Hamburg. Shortly after leaving the dock, the ship was hit by three torpedoes fired by a Russian submarine. Just 40 minutes later, the vessel sank, taking with it an estimated 9,000 passengers, including more than 4,000 children. It was the largest loss of life in history from the sinking of a single ship.

| | |
|---|---|
| **Baltic Sea** | ••••• Front on April 6, 1945 |
| Pillau ●Königsberg | --- Front on April 9, 1945 |
| **EAST PRUSSIA** | ← Soviet offensives |
| | ← German counters |
| **POLAND** | Outer defenses |
| | First defense line |
| | Middle defense line |
| | Inner defense line |

Königsberg

Frisches Haff Bay

N W E S

## The Königsberg Offensive

Soviet troops launched an air and ground attack on April 6 and quickly forced a German surrender on April 9.

### The Battle for the City

Königsberg had strong defenses: It was surrounded by three rings of fortified barriers with towers, fortresses, and moats. Realizing that it would be difficult to seize the city, the Red Army stationed troops to encircle it, while others were ordered to continue their march toward Germany. This tactic benefited the Germans who were able to reopen a safe passage from Königsberg to Pillau, where ships were waiting to help evacuate the remaining population.

By March, the Soviets had made capturing Königsberg a priority, and in early April, the Russians launched an air offensive to take the city. They bombed the town for four days, strafing it day and night. On April 6, the Soviets followed up with a ground assault. Within just a few days, the Russians had crushed German resistance. Thousands who had been unable to evacuate died during the battle.

The fate of Königsberg's defenders became clear. General Otto Lasch radioed Hitler asking for permission to surrender. The Führer refused the request and ordered Lasch to fight to the last man. A large group of civilians tried to escape to Pillau, but Russian troops mowed them down as they ran. Two days later, with over 80 percent of the city in ruins and no hope of reinforcements, Lasch disobeyed Hitler and surrendered his troops. Russian soldiers then swept into Königsberg bent on revenge for previous German atrocities in Russia.

▲ Admiral Karl Dönitz (left) inspected submarines under his command to ensure battle readiness. His interactions with crew members reinforced discipline and morale.

### Karl Dönitz: Operation Hannibal

Karl Dönitz (1891–1980) joined the German Imperial Navy in 1911 and during World War I began serving on submarines. At the outbreak of World War II, Dönitz was a senior submarine officer. He quickly rose to the rank of grand admiral, and in 1943 became commander in chief of the German navy. He was responsible for Operation Hannibal, the effort to transfer people away from the advancing Soviets. The movement turned into one of the largest emergency evacuations ever conducted at sea.

Hitler named Dönitz to succeed him as Germany's head of state, and in May 1945, following Hitler's suicide, the admiral became president of the Third Reich, a position he held for just 23 days. During the Nuremberg trials, Dönitz was charged with war crimes, including waging unrestricted submarine warfare. He served a ten-year prison term.

# The Germans Lose Their Grip on Poland

THE NAZIS TRIED TO HOLD A STRONG FRONT LINE,
BUT THEY WERE NO MATCH FOR THE SOVIETS.

▲ Bridges across the Vistula River ferried both men and equipment into Poland.

While the Red Army was battering the Nazis along the northern fronts of Poland, the German army still held a vise like grip on most of the country. Hitler's military knew, however, that the Russians were approaching from the south and from the east, and that the Soviets had millions of men to pour into the offense. German intelligence reported an immense enemy buildup along the eastern front: 225 Soviet infantry divisions and 22 armored corps, all assembled and ready to attack.

To prepare for the confrontation, the Germans established defensive lines in eastern Poland that stretched from the Narew and Vistula Rivers in the north to the Carpathian Mountains in the south. German soldiers had strict orders to hold the line and give no ground to the Russians. A loss would give the Red Army a clear path to the German homeland.

On January 9, Heinz Guderian, chief of the German general staff, made his third trip in three weeks to see Hitler. He discussed the severity of the threat, reviewed the possible consequences of losing the battle, and requested that Germany send in reinforcements to counter the Soviet assault.

> ## "The Eastern Front is like a house of cards. If the front is broken through at one point all the rest will collapse."
>
> —Heinz Guderian to Adolf Hitler, January 9, 1945

### The Eastern Front, 1945

Soviet forces battled across the Vistula River and forced a German retreat. This offensive pushed the Eastern Front closer to Berlin.

### Heinz Guderian: German Tank Mastermind

German commander Heinz Guderian (1888–1954) revolutionized the way in which armored vehicles were used on the battlefield.

Prussian by birth, Guderian served with the German army in World War I, remained in the German military, and in 1934 became chief of staff of Motorized Troops Command. In 1938, Hitler named Guderian to the new position of chief of Mobile Troops. He became a student of mechanized warfare and published a number of papers describing how tanks should be used in battle, including his famous work *Achtung-Panzer!* (*Attention, Tank!*). Guderian went on to pioneer the use of a variety of systems for tank troops to communicate with each other during battle. This tactical advantage led to much of Germany's early success in World War II.

In 1941, Hitler dismissed Guderian for criticizing his decision to withdraw and hold his tanks at the outskirts of Moscow instead of pushing forward into the Russian capital. But after the Russians humiliated the Nazis at Stalingrad in February 1943, Hitler again turned to Guderian, elevating him first to inspector-general of Armored Troops and then to chief of staff of the army in 1944. American forces captured Guderian in May 1945, and he remained a prisoner until his release in 1948.

The general's efforts were unsuccessful. Hitler had already ordered that some tanks leave the Vistula region and move to Hungary, in hopes of retaking that country's valuable oil fields. He dismissed Guderian's concerns about the massive Russian buildup and insisted that the Soviet troops and tanks were a deceptive snare designed to divide the German forces. Left with only 12 armored and 50 infantry divisions stretched over 700 miles, Guderian knew his troops were no match for the Russians.

Early on the morning of January 12, the Red Army, under the direction of Rokossovsky, the Soviet general who had led the assault on Warsaw, launched an attack along the Vistula River in southern Poland. Ignoring Guderian's recommendation to allow the Fourth Panzer Army to retreat to more defensible positions, Hitler instructed that the tanks advance into battle, putting them within range of the Russian artillery. In only a few hours, the Soviets destroyed most of the division and continued their deadly barrage north of Warsaw. The well-armed Russian forces easily broke through the German lines, creating a huge breach nearly 200 miles wide.

▲ Polish people welcomed Soviet forces that had crushed German defenses in January 1945.

# Fighting in the Baltics

HITLER IGNORED A WARNING ABOUT THE
DANGEROUS SOVIET MOVE IN THE NORTH.

---

The Soviets embarked on their Baltic offensive to retake the strategically important states of Lithuania, Latvia, and Estonia in September 1944. Their goal was to conquer the region, bounded on the west and north by the Baltic Sea, on the southwest by Poland, and on the southeast by Russia, in order to open another corridor south into Poland and to deny the Nazis an important route to port cities.

The assault should not have been a surprise to the German occupiers. Hitler's generals had repeatedly warned that the Soviets would strike in the east and all recognized the strategic

**The Baltic Offensive**
A victory in the Baltic region offered the Soviets an avenue into Poland and a means to block German access to ports.

importance of the Baltic states. What they had not planned on was the vengeance that the Russian troops would wreak on the civilian population.

Russia had suffered horribly from German aggression—some 20 million Soviets would lay dead by the end of the war—and in the waning days of the

conflict, Red Army soldiers behaved as if the time had come for retribution. As they moved through the Baltics, Soviet troops raped and murdered women and girls and looted shops and homes. They often targeted noncombatants of German ethnicity and those whose allegiance had changed, usually by force, to support their German occupiers. Russian soldiers dragged Nazi officials into the streets and executed them. Soviet airplanes gunned down refugees who were trying to escape. Panic-stricken civilians and Nazi soldiers alike rushed to the Baltic ports in an effort to flee the rampaging forces of the Red Army.

▲ Armed German ferryboats on the Baltic Sea transported troops and equipment.

▲ Civilians in Danzig hurried to leave the city as the battle loomed.

# The Siege of Danzig

THE RUSSIANS PUSHED ALONG A 165-MILE FRONT, CAPTURING THE
PORT CITY WHERE THE FIRST SHOTS OF THE WAR HAD BEEN FIRED.

Danzig, now known as Gdańsk, is one of the oldest cities in Poland, and it holds an important location directly on the Baltic coast. Under German occupation, Danzig suffered the same disastrous fate as Warsaw. Civilians who did not conform to the so-called purity of the Aryan race were shipped to extermination camps.

As the Red Army approached in January, Danzig's German occupiers began evacuating their people, just as they had from Königsberg. They were determined not to give up this

key port without a fight and set out to inflict as much damage on the advancing Soviets as they could. The Nazis scuttled ships in the harbor and blew up buildings and equipment. Members of the SS, the elite German military corps, roamed the streets, killing those whom they believed had failed in their duty to protect the city. They hung the corpses from trees, often with a sign dangling around the neck: "I was too cowardly to fight."

By March 13, Red Army soldiers were stationed on the outskirts

of Danzig, ready for battle. Three Soviet armored columns, followed by motorized infantry, converged on the city from the west, east, and south. Two days later, on March 15, the siege began. Ferocious battles raged in all areas of the city as the remaining residents tried to escape to safety.

The Germans held out for two weeks, but they could no longer fend off the well-armed Soviet troops. On the night of March 27, German soldiers received orders to complete an evacuation. When the remnants of the Nazi forces withdrew on March 28, the city fell. The Soviets had killed some 39,000 Germans during the battle and captured roughly 10,000 more.

▶ Red Army troops entered Danzig after defeating German forces.

## Poland's Changing Borders

By the fall of 1939, Poland was occupied on the west by Germany and on the east by the Soviet Union, and the country's borders shifted. Poland would not regain its lost territory until May 1945.

▲ The battle left much of Danzig in ruins.

▲ Austrian children explored the ruins that were left in Vienna after the Allied assaults.

# Continuous Bombardment

EVEN HISTORIC CITIES LIKE VIENNA WERE
VULNERABLE TO ALLIED ASSAULTS.

Known for its rich history and culture, Vienna, Austria, was a vital cog in the Nazi war machine. The city had been occupied by the Germans since March 1938 and was home to the Floridsdorf oil refinery, which was essential to the Nazis. Moreover, the Danube River, just east of the city center, served as a major transportation artery used by German ships to move supplies and essential equipment.

Due to its position in central eastern Europe, just outside the range of American bombers that struck many Nazi targets, Vienna initially escaped destruction. But in late 1944, the Allies established an air base at Foggia in southern Italy, and Vienna became a prime target. In February and March 1945, American and British aircraft executed an intensive aerial campaign to bring the German-occupied city to its

◄ After the bombing raids ended, residents of Vienna tried to return to their normal, daily activities.

### Allied Access to Vienna

The Allied victories in Italy enabled them to establish an air base in Foggia. From there, Allied bombers were in range of Vienna and its oil refinery that supplied German forces.

knees, and working together, they soon set Vienna ablaze.

The British preferred to fly at night under the cover of darkness. This was safer for the men, but night flights made for less accurate targeting. American crews, who were escorted by fighter planes, chose to attack during daylight hours. This made for more precise targeting, but cost a higher percentage of American aircraft and airmen. As a result, Vienna endured the threat of raids around the clock. The only defense left to the city was its antiaircraft guns.

The most extensive air raid on Vienna was conducted on March 12, when 747 bombers, escorted by 229 fighter planes, blasted the city for nearly 90 minutes. While the main target, the Floridsdorf oil refinery, survived, the air raid severely damaged or destroyed such renowned sites as the Albertina Museum, the Messelpalast Fair Palace, and the Vienna State Opera.

When the two-month assault was over, the Allies had dropped 80,000 tons of bombs and nearly 30,000 people had been killed. Much of Vienna's infrastructure and many of its homes had been demolished. Bridges were unusable, and the shelling left more than 3,000 craters in the once beautiful city.

▲ Red Army soldiers overpowered the weak German defenses in Vienna.

# Vienna Falls to the Russians

SOFTENED BY AN AERIAL BOMBARDMENT, THE AUSTRIAN CITY WAS UNABLE TO FIGHT OFF A GROUND ATTACK.

Vienna, now weakened by the Allies' spring bombing campaign, was high on Stalin's list of European targets to seize or "liberate" as part of his plan to maximize his postwar influence. On April 2, he dispatched Red Army ground troops to surround the crippled city, which was defended by severely depleted Nazis forces. Scrambling to make due with the manpower available, the German forces focused their resistance on the most strategic locations, leaving other sections undefended. But the effort failed. Within a week, the Nazis had surrendered the western section of Vienna—an important goal because that part of the city housed the main railway station. Then, on April 13, 1945, they handed Vienna over to the Red Army. Just as at Königsberg and Danzig, Soviet forces exploded in a wave of violence and looting.

# THEN AND NOW

Vienna•
**AUSTRIA**

## VIENNA, AUSTRIA

*The Allied air assaults on Vienna severely damaged much of the city. When the war ended, a new provisional government and relief efforts helped it recover and rebuild. Today, Vienna exhibits much of its prewar grandeur.*

▲ **THEN** Amidst the ruins and severe shortages, people in Vienna had to scavenge for food and firewood. They flocked to black markets that materialized in public squares to sell any goods they still owned.

By the end of the war, nearly one-fourth of Vienna's buildings were either partially or completely destroyed. The city's population had fallen from about 2.2 million to 1.3 million. Food, water, and shelter had to be provided, and the transportation system was in rubble.

Today, Vienna is the largest city in Austria and, following the 1955 treaty that granted the country its postwar independence, it is the nation's capital. The city and its surrounding metropolitan region are home to over two million people, more than 20 percent of the country's population. Vienna has undergone a major rebuilding, and some say that life in the city is much as it was before either world war: The same music can be heard in rebuilt concert halls; one can eat the same food in rebuilt restaurants and stroll through the city's many parks. The home of OPEC and a number of UN agencies, in 2001, Vienna was designated a World Heritage site by UNESCO.

▲ **NOW** Austrian emperor Franz Joseph commissioned the building of the Vienna State Opera House, begun in 1861 and completed in 1869. Annually, 50 operas and 15 ballets are staged to entertain audiences.

▲ Soviet troops fought for control of Budapest.

# The Siege of Budapest

THE BATTLE FOR THE HUNGARIAN CAPITAL TURNED
INTO A HARD-FOUGHT, BLOODY CAMPAIGN.

Hungary was Germany's last ally in Europe, as well as a gateway to southern Bavaria and the location of the Nazis' last remaining crude oil plant. Hitler did not want to see Budapest fall, especially to the Russians. He hoped that a muscular defense of Poland, punctuated by strong counteroffensives in Hungary, would keep the Soviets at bay.

It was not to be. In October 1944, Russian and Romanian forces launched a major offensive against Budapest, hoping to capture the Hungarian capital, isolate and eliminate German troops in southern Europe, and carve a corridor north to Germany. By late December, the Russians controlled large areas of southwest Hungary and had cut the last link between Budapest and Austria. The offensive left 67,000 Axis soldiers and 800,000 civilians surrounded.

Still, the Germans were not willing to go down without a fight. On December 29, Nazi forces fired on two groups of Russian diplomats who had been negotiating the surrender of Budapest. Although the emissaries were all traveling under white flags, some of them were killed. The Soviets' response was rapid, ferocious, and relentless, and they redoubled their efforts to take the city.

Germans fought tenaciously and reinforcements poured into Budapest, helping the troops already there launch a series of counteroffensives. The soldiers attempted several times to fight their way out of the city but failed, and nearly 190,000 German and Hungarian troops were trapped. After four months of brutal combat, Budapest finally surrendered on February 13. In a now well-established pattern, Soviet troops began a period of looting, mass rape, and random executions.

▲ An American soldier in Budapest photographed the famous Budapest suspension bridge, which was destroyed during the fighting for the city. The royal palace in the background was practically gutted.

▲ Hungarian Nazis shot Jews beside the Danube so their bodies fell into the river. This memorial includes 60 pairs of cast-iron shoes made in a 1940s style.

## The Siege of Budapest

The cost of the Soviet capture of Budapest was extreme on both sides: 80,000 Soviet troops, 38,000 German and Hungarian soldiers, and 38,000 Hungarian civilians died.

▲ German soldiers fired antiaircraft guns on Soviet troops during the Hungarian offensive.

# One Final Push

RUNNING SHORT ON FUEL, GERMANY ATTEMPTED TO RECAPTURE HUNGARY'S OIL FIELDS.

Germany by this point was running short of fuel to power its tanks, trucks, and airplanes. In order to continue fighting, the country needed to capture dependable fields that held this valuable asset and establish secure supply lines. The most logical targets were the oil-producing fields in Hungary's Lake Balaton region, about 50 miles southwest of Budapest. In March, German forces launched Operation Spring Awakening to seize the area. They also had a backup plan: If the initiative failed, they would destroy the fields to keep them out of

**Germany's Eastern and Western Fronts**
The Allies squeezed Germany from the east and the west. Soviet forces made quick work of driving German troops further west.

▲ One of the resorts near Lake Balaton

Soviet hands. The offensive turned out to be Germany's last major initiative of the war.

Neither side in Operation Spring Awakening had a huge numerical advantage. Strategy and tactics would rule the day. The Germans and Hungarians sent 465,000 men into battle against the Soviets' 431,000. Hitler also ordered the Sixth Panzer Army to the area. The German battle plan called for a surge around the north end of Lake Balaton through to the Danube River. The Nazis planned a second thrust around the southern end of the lake, hoping to encircle and trap the Russian defenders. Anticipating Nazi moves, the Soviets created a series of traps and antitank ambush points.

As the German panzers began their strike on March 6, they made very little progress and sustained serious losses. Ten days later, the Russians struck back, forcing the Nazis to retreat. In just 24 hours, the Germans gave up ten days of gains. The Nazis failed to capture the prized oil fields, and by the end of the month, Russian forces had chased the remains of the Sixth Panzer Army back into Austria. Germany and Hungary had lost over 12,000 men and more than 30 of their prized tanks. The Russians suffered losses as well: nearly 8,500 killed and another 24,000 wounded.

**Lake Balaton**
Hungarians call Lake Balaton the "Hungarian Sea," possibly because it is the largest lake in central Europe. It measures 48 miles long and 9 miles across at its widest point and reaches a maximum depth of 37 feet. Lake Balaton was formed when erosion crumbled the ridges that divided a cluster of five smaller lakes.

Agriculture plays an important part in the area around the lake, especially vineyards on the north shore that were first established by the Romans. Nearby spas feature medical baths that attract Hungarian and foreign tourists.

▲ Until 1933, the German Reichstag was the home of the nation's parliament. Allied bombings, street fighting, and the Battle of Berlin left the building in ruins.

# On to Berlin

STALIN HAD ONE GOAL—TO REACH THE GERMAN CAPITAL BEFORE HIS WESTERN ALLIES.

American and British forces were pressing toward Berlin from the west and the south, but Stalin's armies were closest to the German capital, and they were moving in from the southeast, the east, and the north. For the Soviet leader, this was a race against his allies, and he was determined to win. He ordered generals Zhukov and Ivan Konev to reach the city by April 22, ahead of the Western Allied troops.

The Russians committed overwhelming troops and firepower to the effort, their first foray into Germany. They sent in

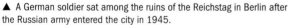

▲ A German soldier sat among the ruins of the Reichstag in Berlin after the Russian army entered the city in 1945.

1.5 million soldiers, about 3,300 tanks, and 28,000 artillery, dwarfing Nazi forces. Konev's men were the first to arrive, crossing the Oder River into Germany on April 16. Zhukov was not far behind, and the two armies unleashed a terrifying artillery blitz against the Nazi fortifications. As the Soviet troops advanced, they were pushed by their generals, who wanted the glory of capturing the German capital. The Russians found the Germans in full retreat, even as they tried to repel wave after wave of Russian attacks.

▲ In 1945, survivors of the Berlin bombing traveled past the ruins of the Reichstag, which first opened in 1894.

▲ On May 2, Soviet soldiers triumphantly raised their flag onto the Reichstag in Berlin, signaling that the city was in their hands.

Still, for Zhukov, the pace of the Russian advance was too slow. On April 22, the day the Soviets were supposed to enter Berlin, he complained that the Red Army had only reached the outskirts of the city. The soldiers picked up their pace and within three days broke through the German defensive lines protecting the capital. The Soviets moved in with tanks and blanketed Berlin with rocket fire, paving the way for more than 500,000 Russian troops to begin attacking the center of the city on April 26.

During the next three weeks, the Soviets moved through the city's rubble-strewn neighborhoods. Fighting was fierce and progressed street by street. When a German sniper inside a building aimed at a Soviet soldier, the Russians simply destroyed the entire building. The strategy proved successful, but as the battle dragged on, Russian casualties mounted quickly: 80,000 men were killed and 275,000 were injured or declared missing. On the German side, 150,000 men lost their lives and thousands more were taken prisoner. The fighting came to an end on May 2 when Red Army infantry soldiers triumphantly raised the Soviet flag on top of the Reichstag.

## FACES *of* WAR

### DECEMBER 18, 1878–MARCH 5, 1953

# JOSEPH STALIN

*He marshaled his people to defeat the Nazis and helped modernize Russia. He also conducted a reign of terror against his own people.*

Joseph Stalin, born Iosif Dzhugashvili, ruled the Soviet Union for 25 years and led the country in its transformation into a major world power. While in his 30s, he took the name Stalin, meaning "man of steel," from the Russian word *stal*, and during his years as general secretary, he earned a reputation as one of the most ruthless and brutal dictators in history. His regime would be remembered for the arrests of millions of Soviet citizens, many of whom died in custody.

The son of a cobbler, Stalin studied at a theological seminary before reading the works of revolutionary Socialist Karl Marx. Inspired by those writings, Stalin became one of the key players during the 1917 Bolshevik Revolution and quickly rose through the ranks of the Communist Party, building support that would be useful after the death of Soviet leader Vladimir Lenin in 1924.

Stalin was, at least initially, Lenin's protégé and outmaneuvered his rivals upon Lenin's death. By the late 1920s, he had consolidated his power and become the country's virtual dictator. When Germany invaded Russia in June 1941, the Russians were initially overwhelmed. Under Stalin's leadership, the Soviets regrouped and launched major counterattacks. After the war, Stalin retained an iron-fisted grip on the country, overseeing the reconstruction of the Soviet Union and the buildup of its military forces and armaments. He died in 1953.

> **"In the Soviet army, it takes more courage to retreat than advance."**
>
> —1941

▼ Joseph Stalin posed for a formal photograph at Potsdam, Germany, in July 1945.

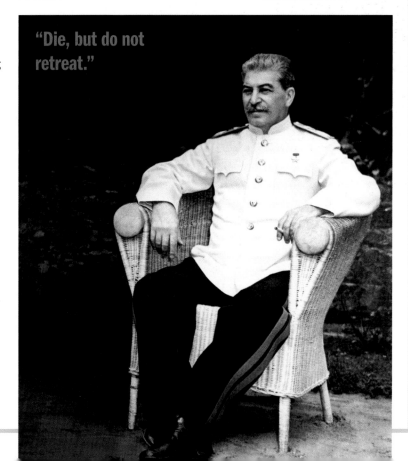

"Die, but do not retreat."

> **"Ideas are far more powerful than guns. We don't let our people have guns. Why should we let them have ideas?"**

▲ German civilians in Berlin tried to flee the Soviet onslaught, but there was no place to find safety.

▲ A Polish mother who had sought refuge in Berlin found the city under siege and in ruins.

### End Game

The battle for Berlin forced civilians out of their homes, and during the final clashes for the nation's capital, some sought shelter in the Anhalter Bahnhof, Berlin's most important train station.

With its underground bunker and walls that were nearly five yards thick, the station seemed to provide the ideal refuge. It was stocked with canned food and also had emergency supplies, but the conditions inside were appalling. Up to 12,000 people crammed themselves into 11,811 square feet. One woman spent six days standing on the same step. Berliners knew it was suicide to leave the bunker, but many did, hoping to find fresh water or food. Those trying to escape the city fared no better. Nazi soldiers set up antitank barricades along major intersections and summarily executed deserters, no questions asked.

Stalin and his Red Army had won the race to Berlin, but his Western Allies were not far away. With the capital in the hands of the Allies, the war would soon be over.

# THEN AND NOW

## BERLIN, GERMANY

GERMANY

Berlin

*Germany's capital today is home to the famed mural- and graffiti-covered remains of the Berlin Wall as well as historic sites, museums, theaters, and universities. Forests, parks, gardens, and lakes adorn one-third of the metropolis.*

Berlin, the capital of Germany, has long been the center of the country's cultural life and home to many great musicians, scientists, and philosophers. It has also played an important role in the country's political affairs. Berlin was a key player in the two world wars, in the Cold War, and, ultimately, in Germany's reunification.

Following World War II, Berlin lay in ruins, with most of its buildings shattered and its streets torn apart. And when the Allies divided Germany into zones of occupation, the city was divided as well. East Germany, controlled by the Soviet Union, made East Berlin its capital. West Berlin was linked to West Germany, but it was surrounded by East German land, leading to one of the most challenging periods in Berlin's history. West Berlin became prosperous and democratic. East Berlin experienced far slower economic growth and was Communist. So many East Berliners flooded to the West that, in 1961, the Communists erected the Berlin Wall.

The eventual collapse of communism in 1989 gave Berlin another chance to rebuild itself. The wall came down. The city and country were finally unified. Today, Berlin is prosperous and diverse, and its war-torn yet rich history can be seen in the architecture, a mix of remnants of old world and new, communism and social democracy.

▲ **THEN** Built in the eighteenth century, the Brandenburg Gate was, and is still, one of the most famous landmarks in Germany. Commissioned by King Frederick William II of Prussia in the 1800s, it was to have served as a sign of peace. Instead, the Nazis used the gate, which is topped by a chariot pulled by four horses, as a party symbol. On May 2, Russian soldiers raised the Soviet flag next to the heavily damaged sculptures of the horses in a symbolic gesture signifying the Allies' triumph over the Nazi Party.

▶ **NOW** The Brandenburg Gate was located in what became East Berlin, and until 1961, when the Berlin Wall was built, people and cars could pass through the historic, but still damaged, structure. In 2000, the gate was restored to its prewar grandeur.

> "We meet in true and victorious comradeship and with inflexible resolve to fulfil our purpose and our duty. Let all march forward upon the foe."
>
> –Winston Churchill, April 27, 1945

▲ American and Soviet troops met on a damaged railroad bridge at Torgau, Germany, on April 27 and exchanged congratulatory handshakes.

# Meeting at the Elbe

SOVIETS AND ALLIES CONVERGED IN GERMANY, SPLITTING THE GERMAN ARMY.

On April 25, the Germans suffered another terrible defeat when Soviet and American soldiers converged at the Elbe River near Torgau, some 70 miles south of Berlin, effectively splitting the German army. For the Germans, it was another death knell.

For the Allied troops, it was an occasion for exuberance. For the first time, Western and Eastern Allied soldiers were able to join hands. They exchanged vodka and chocolate and posed for photographers who recorded the formal handshakes.

American general Omar Bradley commented on the occasion, praising Soviet troops for their determined efforts on German soil, and lauding his American forces, saying, "In ten months you have advanced 1,120 kilometers (696 miles) from the invasion beaches. All this has been attained thanks to your courage, your spirit and initiative and thanks to your comrades who died in order to achieve this."

◀ American general Emil Reinhardt shook hands with his Russian counterpart, General Vladimir Rusakov, as they celebrated the meeting of their troops.

"This is not the hour of final victory in Europe, but the hour draws near, the hour for which . . . people have toiled and prayed so long."
—Harry Truman, April 27, 1945

◀ On April 25, a smiling American Lieutenant William Robertson exchanged greetings with Russian Lieutenant Alexander Sylvashko.

"Our task and our duty are to complete the destruction of the enemy. . . . The Red Army will fulfill to the end this task and this duty to our people and to all freedom-loving peoples." —Joseph Stalin, April 27, 1945

# GERMANY'S TIGER TANKS

**These armored vehicles were the pride of the nation and the backbone of the Nazi military.**

In less than a decade, German engineers and plant workers designed and turned out over 25,000 tanks, each version larger, more sophisticated, and more deadly than its predecessor.

**SERIES I** The Nazis developed the first Panzer tank, the Pz. 1, for training in 1934. The German army used over 1,400 Pz. 1s, small but mighty tanks no taller than a man, in the battle for France.

**SERIES II** By the start of the war, German factories were turning out the Pz. 2 for combat duty.

**SERIES III** When the Soviets began manufacturing tanks that outgunned the 10-ton Pz. 2, the Germans created the more heavily armed Pz. 3. This tank, covered in 2- to 3-inch armor, was armed with a 50 mm gun, weighed 20 tons, carried a crew of five, and was used both in the Soviet Union and southern Europe.

**SERIES IV** The Pz. 4 weighed 25 tons and came with two 75 mm guns and two machine guns. It was designed to match improving enemy designs and was produced between 1936 and 1945.

**SERIES V** Many historians believe that the Panther, the Pz. 5, was the best tank any country built during the war. Though it weighed 45 tons, this vehicle was still highly mobile in rugged terrain. And, with its 75 mm gun and over three inches of armor at the front and nearly two inches on the back and sides, it was an effective weapon on the battlefield.

**SERIES VI** The Pz. 6 Tiger was much bigger but slower and less agile than the Panther, and the Germans used the Tiger most often in defensive operations. At 70 tons, it was the heaviest tank produced by any country during the war. And armed with an 88 mm gun, it decimated its lighter foe, the U.S. Sherman tank.

▲ The huge, fearsome German Panzer tanks provided excellent protection for infantry troops as they advanced on the battlefield.

**SERIES I** Panzer 1 or Pz. 1

Introduced in 1934
*Number built: 830

**SERIES II** Panzer 2 or Pz. 2

Introduced in 1935
*Number built: 1,850

**SERIES III** Panzer 3 or Pz. 3

Introduced in 1936
*Number built: 5,775

**SERIES IV** Panzer 4 or Pz. 4

Introduced in 1936
*Number built: 8,800

SERIES V  Panther or Pz. 5

Introduced in 1942
*Number built: 5,000

SERIES VI  Tiger I or Pz. 6

Introduced in 1942
*Number built: 1,350

*All numbers
are estimates.

# 3 | MOVING TOWARD PEACE

WITH THE ALLIES IN FIRM CONTROL OF EUROPE, NAZI LEADERS
BEGAN SEARCHING FOR WAYS TO END THE WAR.

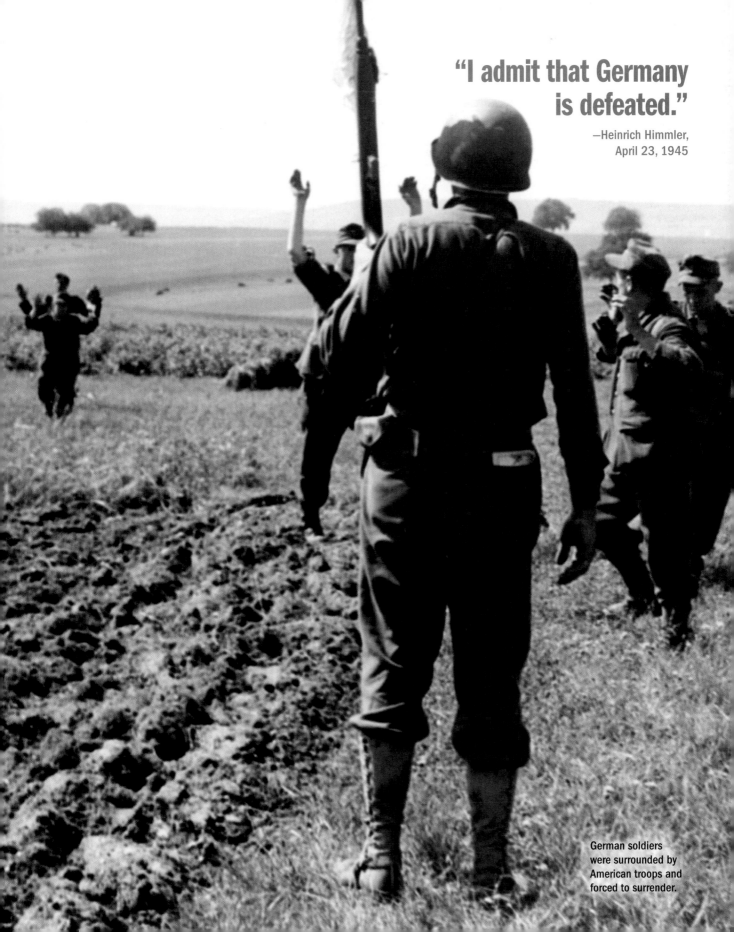

"I admit that Germany is defeated."

—Heinrich Himmler,
April 23, 1945

German soldiers were surrounded by American troops and forced to surrender.

▲ Nazi leader Heinrich Himmler was responsible for the huge Nazi bureaucracy; his duties included implementing plans to murder Europe's Jewish population.

# Peace Overtures

WITH THE ALLIES BATTERING GERMANY ON TWO FRONTS, NAZI GENERAL HEINZ GUDERIAN HOPED A FAVORABLE ACCORD COULD BE ACHIEVED.

In the summer of 1944, Nazi military commander Heinrich Himmler attempted to initiate peace talks with the United States, but President Franklin Roosevelt, who wanted to end the war unconditionally, refused the offer. Just six months later, as the Allies began their advance toward Berlin, the Germans once again raised the prospect of establishing peace talks with both the Americans and the British.

It started on January 25, when General Heinz Guderian, the German army's chief of staff, asked his country's foreign minister, Joachim von Ribbentrop, to approach the Western Allies and ask for a negotiated settlement. Instead, von Ribbentrop reported the conversation to Adolf Hitler, who then accused Guderian of treason. The Third Reich leader did not discipline Guderian, but warned that anyone saying the war was lost would be punished as a traitor.

The general did not give up. Hoping that a peace settlement would save the German army from being completely destroyed, Guderian spoke to Himmler on March 21, telling him that they should "put an end to the senseless slaughter." Over the next week, Guderian continued to argue with Himmler and Hitler over military strategy. On March 28, Hitler dismissed Guderian from office.

◄ Germany suffered devastating losses throughout 1945, which would also affect its postwar development.

▲ General Heinz Guderian, a frequent critic of Hitler's military plans, was dismissed for urging a peace settlement with the Allies.

## Joachim von Ribbentrop: Ambition and Zeal

▲ Joachim von Ribbentrop

Joachim von Ribbentrop (1893–1946) was Hitler's minister of foreign affairs from 1938 until the end of the war.

The son of an army officer, von Ribbentrop attended schools in Germany, Switzerland, France, and England, and then served with the German army during World War I. He married the daughter of a wealthy champagne maker, a match that made him financially independent. He met Hitler in 1932 and became one of the first members of the Nazi Party.

Ambitious and zealous, von Ribbentrop quickly rose through the ranks of the Nazi hierarchy. As minister of foreign affairs, he negotiated Germany's nonaggression pact with the Soviets, which allowed for the division of Poland. Von Ribbentrop was captured by the Allies in June 1945, tried at Nuremberg, and sentenced to death. Von Ribbentrop was executed on October 16, 1946.

### From Ribbentrop to von Ribbentrop

In German, the word *von* means "of" or "from," and when it is part of a family name it usually denotes nobility. In 1925, 32-year-old Joachim Ribbentrop was adopted by a distant relative, Gertrud von Ribbentrop. At that time, the young man was able to add the aristocratic title *von* to his name.

► At Yalta, President Franklin Roosevelt and Prime Minister Winston Churchill talked privately about the future of Europe and also about how to bring the Soviet Union into the war with Japan.

▲ Roosevelt was in failing health and brought his daughter Anna to help care for him during the conference.

▲ Yalta, a resort city on the northern coast of the Black Sea, was a holiday destination for Russians and gained worldwide fame when it was selected as the site for a "Big Three" meeting.

# The Yalta Conference

THE BIG THREE MET AT THE CRIMEAN RESORT TO DISCUSS
THE UNCONDITIONAL SURRENDER OF GERMANY.

With the war in Europe winding down, the time had come for Roosevelt, British prime minister Winston Churchill, and Soviet premier Joseph Stalin to decide the continent's postwar fate, and they agreed to meet at the Black Sea port of Yalta to discuss the plan. It was the second wartime meeting of the three Allied leaders.

Each man arrived on February 4, along with an entourage of diplomats, military officers, soldiers, and aides. Among those attending for Great Britain were Alexander Cadogan, under-secretary for foreign affairs, and Anthony Eden, Britain's foreign secretary. Stalin was accompanied by his minister of foreign affairs, Vyacheslav Molotov, and the Soviet ambassador to the United States, Andrei Gromyko. Roosevelt brought his secretary of state, Edward Stettinius, and Averill Harriman, U.S. ambassador to the Soviet Union. The president, who had been recently elected to a fourth term,

also brought along his daughter Anna who served as his personal assistant, instead of his wife Eleanor.

### Three Different Agendas

Aside from agreeing to demand the unconditional surrender of Germany, the agendas of the three men could not have been more different. While Stalin wanted to expand the USSR, Roosevelt and Churchill were focused on the war in the Pacific. They hoped to get Stalin to declare war on Japan once Germany surrendered, but they knew this would be a difficult task. Unbeknownst to Churchill, Roosevelt secretly secured the Soviet dictator's cooperation by agreeing to grant the Soviets a sphere of influence in Manchuria once Japan had capitulated.

The Allied leaders also discussed dividing Germany into zones of occupation. Each of the three nations, as well as France, would control one zone. Churchill and Roosevelt also agreed that all future governments in eastern Europe should be "friendly" to the Soviet Union. In exchange, Stalin agreed to allow free elections in each of the liberated eastern European countries.

## The Future of Poland

The status of Poland had been a contentious issue among the Allies throughout the war. Churchill, a stalwart anti-Communist, met with Stalin in October 1944 to discuss the Russians' treatment of the Polish Home Army during the Warsaw Uprising. By early 1945, the Soviets were well positioned within Poland's borders, and Churchill feared that within just a few months, Communist forces would occupy all of eastern Europe.

Now, at Yalta, Churchill was determined to try to keep the Soviets out of Poland's internal affairs. Stalin disagreed: "For the Russian people, the question of Poland is not only a question of honor but also a question of security. [It] is a question of life and death. . . ."

Despite their different viewpoints, the Allied leaders agreed that the Soviets could keep eastern Poland and make it part of the USSR. The Allies would compensate Poland with German territory in the west. The three leaders also agreed that the Communists would have a role in Poland's future national government; that free elections should be held as quickly as possible; and that anti-Communist Poles living in exile in Great Britain should have a place in a new Polish government.

With the Poland question settled, Stalin then consented to help with the establishment of the United Nations, which Roosevelt desperately wanted to create. The president believed this new organization would be able to step in when conflicts arose and help countries settle their disputes peacefully.

## The Impact of Yalta

The initial reaction to the Yalta agreements was one of celebration, especially in the United States. It seemed as though the Western Allies and the Soviets would continue their wartime cooperation into the postwar period.

Historians continue to debate the impact of the conference, but one thing remains clear: By the spring of 1945, any hope of continued American and Soviet cooperation had been dashed. After Yalta, Stalin reneged on his promises concerning eastern Europe, especially the agreement to allow free elections in all territories that were liberated from Nazi control. As the USSR installed governments that were dominated by the Soviet Union in these countries, the one time allies found themselves on the path to another, more ideologically driven conflict—the Cold War.

▲ Soviet premier Joseph Stalin consulted with his minister of foreign affairs, Vyacheslav Molotov.

▼ The Big Three—Churchill, Roosevelt, and Stalin—took time to pose for official photographs.

▶ Newspapers around the world announced that Roosevelt had died. These young sailors and a soldier read the details in New York City papers.

# The Death of FDR

THE PASSING OF THE AMERICAN PRESIDENT SHOCKED THE WORLD.

At 1:00 PM on April 12, Roosevelt was sitting in a chair at his cottage in Warm Springs, Georgia, signing documents at the same time an artist stood in front of an easel completing the president's portrait. Roosevelt turned to the painter to remind her that there were only 15 minutes left in the session; he then grabbed his head and complained of a sharp pain. Roosevelt slumped silently in his chair and within minutes died from a cerebral hemorrhage. America's war president was 63 years old.

Radio broadcasts and newspapers across the country conveyed the news. "President Roosevelt is Dead, Truman to Continue Policies," read the headline of the *New York Times*.

▶ Grief-stricken and stunned, Americans crowded along streets in Washington, D.C., watching the funeral procession.

"I felt like the moon, the stars, and all the planets had fallen on me."

—Harry Truman, April 13, 1945

▲ Former First Lady Eleanor Roosevelt and President Harry Truman shared a private moment as they paid their respects to the former president.

The death was an unexpected and overwhelming development. For many people, Roosevelt was the only president they had ever known. Even Vice President Harry Truman, who received word while visiting Sam Rayburn, the Speaker of the House, for an end-of-day libation, was surprised. Truman still had a drink in his hand when an aide asked him to call the White House.

"Holy General Jackson!" Truman said as he put down the phone. He rushed to the president's private quarters and met First Lady Eleanor Roosevelt in the hall. Placing her hand on Truman's shoulder, Mrs. Roosevelt broke the news again, going on to say the oft-quoted words: "Is there anything we can do for you? For you are the one in trouble now." Around 7:00 PM that evening, Truman, who had served just 82 days as vice president, was sworn in as president.

▲ Churchill and his wife, Clementine (far left), traveled to Roosevelt's home in Hyde Park, New York, to pay tribute to their friend and wartime colleague. Following her death in 1962, Eleanor Roosevelt (left of Churchill) was also buried at the family estate in New York.

# Himmler's Proposal

THE POWERFUL GENERAL WANTED TO SURRENDER AND DIVIDE THE ALLIES.

▲ Himmler inspected a prisoner-of-war camp that held captured Russian soldiers. Under Himmler's policies, the men were kept in deplorable conditions and under strict guard, so there was little chance of escape or of repatriation.

At around midday on April 24, Truman went to the Pentagon for a private transatlantic phone call to London to speak with Churchill. The prime minister had important news: The Germans were willing to surrender.

According to Churchill, Himmler had spoken with the head of the Swedish Red Cross and asked him to arrange an immediate meeting with American general Dwight Eisenhower. Germany was prepared to surrender all its troops in the west. The German military leader acknowledged to the Red Cross leader, Count Folke Bernadotte, that the Nazis had lost. Now Himmler wanted to try to drive a wedge between the Western Allies and the Soviets. "I have always been, and I shall always remain, a sworn enemy of Boshevism," he told Bernadotte.

## Facing Facts

Bernadotte, who had held many conversations with Eisenhower, suspected the general would balk at the idea, because Eisenhower had made it clear he would accept nothing less than the unconditional surrender of Germany to all of the Allies. Still, Bernadotte agreed to forward Himmler's proposal to the Swedish government on the condition that the surrender of Nazi troops in Denmark and Norway was part of the package. Himmler agreed.

▲ Count Folke Bernadotte

## Folke Bernadotte: Pedigreed Diplomat

Count Folke Bernadotte (1895–1948) was not only a diplomat and the head of the Swedish Red Cross, he was a member of Swedish royalty, related to both Sweden's King Gustav V and Jean-Baptiste Bernadotte, the crown prince of Sweden in the early nineteenth century.

Bernadotte is noted for many accomplishments during World War II, including the negotiated exchanges of injured German, British, and American prisoners of war. He also met with Himmler several times to arrange for the transfer of 4,500 Norwegian and Danish prisoners in Nazi concentration camps to Neuengamme, a slave-labor concentration camp outside Hamburg.

When Bernadotte observed the horrendous conditions at Neuengamme, he extracted other humanitarian concessions from Himmler, including the evacuation of all prisoners to Denmark who were ill, as well as women, students, and Danish policemen.

Bernadotte survived the war, only to be gunned down in 1948 in Jerusalem by a radical Zionist group.

Truman rejected the suggestion out of hand, and the British reply to the Swedish government was equally blunt: Surrender would have to occur on all fronts. Moreover, if any Nazi resistance persisted after a final agreement had been reached, the Allies would continue fighting until they had won a total, decisive victory.

Bernadotte relayed the information to one of Himmler's aides on April 27, and the next day, reports about Himmler's efforts appeared in the press. Upon hearing the news, Hitler, sheltered deep inside his Berlin bunker, stripped his good friend and loyal soldier of all his titles and ordered his arrest.

▲ Himmler (left) and Hitler worked together to establish most of the Third Reich policies. Here, they met to observe parading Nazi storm-troopers.

## FACES *of* WAR

### OCTOBER 7, 1900–MAY 23, 1945

# HEINRICH HIMMLER

*A man with a humble beginning rose to one of the most powerful positions in Germany during World War II.*

Born in 1900 to a middle-class Catholic family, Heinrich Himmler grew up a fervent German patriot. He left high school during World War I to join the military, then returned to school after his training as an officer candidate was cut short when the war came to an end.

Like many German youth of the era, Himmler joined one of the right-wing soldier organizations that formed after World War I. He took part in the failed 1923 Beer Hall Putsch, when Hitler tried to seize power, and in 1925, Himmler joined the Nazi Party.

After a brief, unsuccessful stint as a poultry farmer, Himmler worked as an assistant to the Nazi Party propaganda leader and earned a reputation for his strong nationalism and for his anti-Semitic views. In 1929, Hitler appointed him as *Reichsführer SS*, responsible for all internal security within the Third Reich. Within one year, the organization grew from about 300 to 3,000 and continued a meteoric increase in recruits.

Once the Nazis came to power in January 1933, Himmler was given control of the Munich police forces, and he rose to oversee all German police units; at the same time, he expanded the power and dominance of the SS. Himmler became the chief architect of the Holocaust and developed the Nazi concentration camp system, which resulted in the ruthless massacre of millions of people.

As the war progressed, Himmler created a powerful state within a state that citizens and many in the military dared not oppose. His influence with Hitler increased after a group of German officers tried to assassinate the Führer in the summer of 1944. But after Himmler attempted to negotiate a surrender with the Allies in the spring of 1945, Hitler stripped him of all of his leadership positions and had him arrested.

▲ Heinrich Himmler

Following Germany's surrender to the Allies, Himmler tried to escape, but was captured by the British. Less than a month after his Führer committed suicide, Himmler followed suit on May 23 by biting down on a cyanide pill that he had hidden in one of his teeth.

"One principle must be absolute for the SS man: we must be honest, decent, loyal and friendly to members of our blood and to no one else. What happens to the Russians, what happens to the Czechs, is a matter of utter indifference to me."

—October 4, 1943

# 4 LIBERATING THE CAMPS

THE ALLIES DISCOVERED THE INCONCEIVABLE ATROCITIES
AND MASS MURDER SPAWNED BY NAZI RACIAL IDEOLOGY.

The entrance gate to the concentration camp in Auschwitz,
Poland, proclaimed "Work Makes You Free."

"The world must know what happened, and never forget."

—General Dwight Eisenhower, 1945

▲ Starving, sick, and emaciated, survivors of the concentration camp at Buchenwald, Germany, struggled to the infirmary following the camp's liberation in April 1945. General Louis Audibert, a member of the French Resistance, is at the front. His wife died at Ravensbrück, a women's camp in northern Germany.

# The "Final Solution"

PUTTING HIS ANTI-SEMITIC IDEAS INTO ACTION, HITLER LAID PLANS TO ERADICATE EUROPE'S JEWISH POPULATION.

Adolf Hitler, who had begun expressing ultra-nationalistic and anti-Semitic ideas as early as 1919, believed strongly in the superiority of the German, or "Aryan," race. Elected chancellor of Germany in 1933, he began the government-sponsored persecution of Jews. He warned like-minded people of the supposed danger that Jewish people would take over the world.

Initially, official racism was limited to the passage of anti-Jewish laws and economic boycotts of Jewish businesses. German shops and restaurants posted signs barring Jews from entering. The government also spread its anti-Semitic ideology in newspapers, speeches, posters, and in schools. Then in November 1938, the Nazi Party instigated two days of violent attacks against Jewish homes, businesses, and synagogues throughout Germany and Austria. Eventually, those attacks would escalate into mass murder.

## Nazi Concentration Camps

During World War II, the term *concentration camp* referred to a compound where ethnic minorities, political opponents, and other noncombatants were confined under harsh conditions.

### The Concentration Camp System

Almost as soon as the Nazis seized power in 1933, they began building camps of varying sizes and purposes to hold their enemies prisoner. There were 23 main facilities, each of which could have dozens of satellites, for a total of nearly 20,000 camps by the end of the war. Some locations were primarily used for mass executions, while others served as forced-labor centers or temporary stops on the way to the death camps. Only a small percentage of the millions of prisoners sent to the camps survived the ordeal.

▶ About a month after the April 11 liberation of Buchenwald, American soldiers, accompanied by a German guide, read this sign painted on a barracks wall. U.S. troops liberated 21,000 people in the camp.

▲ Americans, including this colonel from the Third Army, took time to visit those who had been moved to hospitals. The road to physical recovery was a very long one; the journey to mental recovery would be even longer.

After Germany invaded Poland in September 1939, the Nazis began forcing Jews to live in ghettos, separated from other civilians. These areas were often in the poorest, run-down neighborhoods, and many more people were crowded into them than there was room for. The first ghetto was established in Poland, in Piotrków Trybunalski, followed by many others in towns across the country. Soon, the Germans built walls or barbed-wire fences around the ghettos to ensure that Jews were isolated.

In many cases, Jews and other "undesirables" such as Roma (Gypsies), Jehovah's Witnesses, dissenting priests and pastors, the disabled, and homosexuals were transferred to the system of concentration camps established around Germany and in the occupied territories. There, prisoners were either forced into relentless labor or exterminated, usually by poison gas. Bodies were burned in large crematoriums. This system was the centerpiece of the Third Reich's "Final Solution," which resulted in the deaths of 11 million people.

◀ Soldiers from the Sixth Armored Division spoke with some of the survivors about the conditions in the camps. Buchenwald, shown here, was one of the largest.

▲ Prisoners at Dachau, like this Hungarian surgeon, were liberated on April 29, 1945. At the time the Allies entered the camp, a typhus epidemic was raging; an estimated 2,500 former prisoners died from the disease in the weeks between May 29 and June 16.

HIER FÜHRTE IN DEN LETZTEN KRIEGSTAGEN IM APRIL 1945 DER LEIDENSWEG DER HÄFTLINGE AUS DEM KONZENTRATIONSLAGER DACHAU VORBEI INS UNGEWISSE

▲ This statue commemorates the 7,000 prisoners who were forced to walk 70 miles from Dachau to Tegernsee, both in Germany. Those who could not keep up on the six-day march, which began on April 26, were shot. Many died of hunger, illness, or exhaustion. After the first monument was erected at Dachau, 22 identical statues were placed along the route that stretched south to Tegernsee.

# The Death Marches

MORE THAN 250,000 PRISONERS PERISHED IN FORCED EVACUATIONS OF CONCENTRATION CAMPS.

In July 1944, Soviet forces arrived at the Majdanek camp in eastern Poland and liberated its survivors. The stories of the prisoners' suffering and Nazi atrocities quickly spread, and at other camps, SS officers began to destroy evidence of Nazi barbarity. In late 1944 and early 1945, as the Allies squeezed Germany from the east and west, the Nazis began to relocate prisoners from concentration camps located near the front, forcing them to travel on foot to camps farther inside Germany. These one-way trips became known as death marches.

# FACES *of* WAR

## MARCH 19, 1906–MAY 31, 1962

# ADOLF EICHMANN

*A traveling salesman became Hitler's chief executioner.*

Adolf Eichmann, who would become one of the major organizers of the Holocaust, was born in Solingen, Germany, in 1906, then later moved with his family to Austria. As a young man, Eichmann hoped to be an engineer, but he left school early for the workplace and took a series of positions, including a post as a traveling salesman for an American oil company.

Eichmann joined the Nazi Party in 1932 and became a member of Heinrich Himmler's SS. He steadily rose through the ranks, and in 1938 was put in charge of removing Jews from Vienna and overseeing the main office that handled "voluntary" emigration. When the war started, Austria's policy of "allowing" Jews to emigrate shifted to a policy of forced deportation.

As chief of the Jewish office of the Gestapo, the Nazi secret police, Eichmann implemented Hitler's "Final Solution" to exterminate Europe's Jews. He not only organized the convoys that brought Jews to the death camps, he also designed the camps themselves and developed many of the execution techniques the Nazis used.

Eichmann brought a sustained zeal and commitment to his job and thought of himself as an efficient bureaucrat who did not harbor any particular hatred of the Jewish people. Yet, like other Nazis, Eichmann was a devoted follower of the party's racial ideology.

The Americans captured and imprisoned Eichmann in 1945. A year later, he escaped and moved around the Middle East until he finally fled to Argentina in 1958. On May 11, 1960, Israeli agents abducted Eichmann near Buenos Aires and brought him to Israel to stand trial. During his court hearing, which brought international attention to the Holocaust, Eichmann was defiant, claiming he was just following the orders of his superiors. He was found guilty of crimes against humanity and hanged in Israel on May 31, 1962.

▲ Adolf Eichmann

**"I will leap laughing into my grave because the feeling that I have five million people on my conscience is for me a source of extraordinary satisfaction."**

▲ An unapologetic Nazi, Eichmann eventually stood trial for his war crimes.

► These men survived a death march and were freed from the camp at Neuengamme, Germany.

▲ The Nazis confiscated all prisoners' belongings, especially those that might have some value. Allied troops liberating Buchenwald concentration camp in Germany found these wedding rings along with watches, precious stones, and gold fillings.

The evacuation marches were brutal. Prisoners, clad in nothing more than rags or threadbare blankets, were often roused with little notice and forced to move at a ferocious pace to keep ahead of the approaching Allied forces. They marched in bitterly cold weather. With very little food and few places to take shelter, many captives died from starvation, exposure, or exhaustion. Those too ill or frail to keep up were shot by guards.

One by one, the camps at Auschwitz in Poland, Buchenwald, Dachau, and others in Germany were emptied of many of the prisoners as the Allies drew closer. The death marches, during which an estimated 250,000 prisoners died, lasted until Germany's surrender in May.

In January 1945, with the Soviets closing in on Auschwitz, almost 60,000 prisoners were forced to walk 35 miles west to rail lines. Nearly all perished along the way. Those prisoners who did survive were put into boxcars and transported to other concentration camps.

In another death march that occurred in late January, 7,000 prisoners were forced to walk from the East Prussian city of Königsberg to Palmnicken, some 31 miles away. Nearly half of the prisoners died during the journey. Most of the survivors were slaughtered by Nazi officers on a frozen Baltic Sea beach.

To this day, no one is sure who gave the order to evacuate the camps. No evidence exists that Hitler or Himmler, the leader of the SS, wanted the camps liquidated or even gave the order to do so. Most historians suspect that as the end of the war approached, there was a gradual administrative breakdown, which led to the massive slaughter.

## FACES *of* WAR

SEPTEMBER 30, 1928–

# ELIEZER "ELIE" WIESEL

*A victim of Nazi atrocities became an advocate for human rights and justice.*

▲ Elie Wiesel, a "messenger to makind," won the Nobel Peace Prize in 1986.

**"There may be times when we are powerless to prevent injustice, but there must never be a time when we fail to protest."**

Eliezer "Elie" Wiesel, who would achieve global renown for his memoir *Night*, about surviving the Holocaust, was born in 1928 in Sighet, Transylvania (present-day Romania). Following a series of territorial disputes in 1940, Transylvania joined the Axis powers, and the new government soon began persecuting Jews. In June 1944, when Wiesel was 15, his family was deported to the Auschwitz concentration camp in a cattle car. Later he would write, "Life in the cattle cars was the death of my adolescence."

Wiesel's mother and younger sister were sent to the gas chamber at Auschwitz, and Elie and his father, Shlomo, were assigned to work as slave laborers. Like all prisoners, the Wiesels were regularly starved, were beaten, and witnessed the brutal abuses and murders of other captives. In January 1945, the Wiesels were among 20,000 prisoners of the Auschwitz system forced on a ten-day death march to meet a train for Buchenwald. Shlomo Wiesel survived the trip but died on arrival. Elie lived and was liberated along with other prisoners on April 11, 1945, by American army troops. Of Wiesel's five immediate family members, only his two older sisters survived the war.

Wiesel's book *Night* was published in 1958 and was the first of over 60 works of nonfiction and fiction about human suffering and man's relationship with God. Among the many awards and honors he has received are the Nobel Peace Prize, the Presidential Medal of Freedom, the U.S. Congressional Gold Medal, the Dayton Literary Peace Prize Lifetime Achievement Award, and a knighthood in the United Kingdom.

Wiesel and his wife founded the Elie Wiesel Foundation for Humanity. Its mission is to combat indifference, intolerance, and injustice through international dialogue and youth-focused programs that promote acceptance, understanding, and equality. Wiesel summed up his life's message when he spoke at the dedication of the U.S. Holocaust Memorial Museum in Washington, D.C.: "For the dead and the living, we must bear witness."

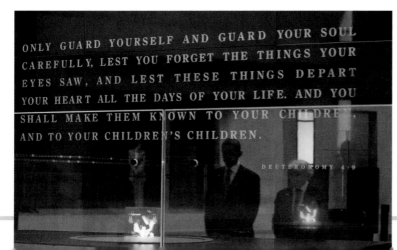

ONLY GUARD YOURSELF AND GUARD YOUR SOUL CAREFULLY, LEST YOU FORGET THE THINGS YOUR EYES SAW, AND LEST THESE THINGS DEPART YOUR HEART ALL THE DAYS OF YOUR LIFE. AND YOU SHALL MAKE THEM KNOWN TO YOUR CHILDREN, AND TO YOUR CHILDREN'S CHILDREN.

DEUTERONOMY 4:9

◀ On April 23, 2012, President Barack Obama (left) and Wiesel (right) joined together for a moment of silent reflection in Remembrance Hall at the U.S. Holocaust Museum in Washington, D.C.

▲ On April 12, General George Patton, General Omar Bradley, and Major General Troy Middleton visited a concentration camp at Ohrdruf, Germany, and witnessed the evidence of Nazi atrocities.

# The Catastrophe Revealed

IN THE WANING DAYS OF THE WAR, THE WORLD BEGAN TO UNDERSTAND THE REAL MEANING OF THE HOLOCAUST.

*H*olocaust is a word derived from Greek, meaning "sacrifice by fire." The Holocaust is also called *Shoah*, a Hebrew word meaning "the catastrophe." Soldiers liberating the camps discovered unimaginable atrocities: gas chambers for mass executions and humans who had been tortured, starved to death, and used as subjects in "medical" experiments.

Soviet troops, who were pushing westward toward Berlin through Poland, were the first to uncover the horrors when they entered the Majdanek camp in Lublin, Poland, on July 23, 1944. The Germans had already evacuated most of the prisoners to other camps farther west, so fewer than 500 weak and emaciated inmates remained. In their haste, the Nazis only destroyed part of the camp, leaving nearly intact the horrifying evidence. The Russians discovered the gas chambers, crematorium ovens, and human skeletons.

▲ Red Army troops found skeletal human remains outside the crematorium ovens at the Majdanek camp where Nazis burned dead prisoners' bodies.

Corpses, burned remains, and bones were found buried in pits at various locations in the camp and nearby woods. The Soviet troops uncovered stacks of passports and a death register listing those who had been killed—more than 100,000 total. Records showed that prisoners' money and other valuables had been confiscated and sent to Berlin.

In April 1945, as American troops began liberating Buchenwald and Dachau, they encountered scenes as disturbing as those the Soviets had found. Bill Barrett, a journalist with the U.S. Army, described what he witnessed:

"There were about a dozen bodies in the dirty boxcar, men and women alike. They had gone without food so long that their dead wrists were broomsticks tipped with claws. These were the victims of a deliberate starvation diet. . . ."

Allied troops tried to provide comfort to the survivors. They gave their rations to the starving, only to find that many were too weak to eat or digest the food. Doctors and relief workers tried, mostly in vain, to save the incarcerated. Half of all prisoners the Allies discovered in Auschwitz in January 1945 died within a few days after liberation.

▲ These shoes were all that remained of the men, women, and children annihilated in Poland at the Majdanek concentration camp. Nazis stored the shoes for sorting and salvage, but there were so many that they spilled out of the windows and doors of the building.

## FACES *of* WAR

AUGUST 4, 1912–1947

# RAOUL WALLENBERG

*A Swedish diplomat stared down evil and helped rescue thousands.*

▲ Raoul Wallenberg, diplomat and businessman

▶ In 1944, Wallenberg gave a protective pass to a 14-year-old Jewish girl, Judith Kopstein, who later emigrated to Canada. When Judith was 83 years old, in 2013, the Canadian postal service issued a commemorative stamp honoring Wallenberg that featured Judith's Swedish identity document. She said it was an honor to be pictured with the man who saved her life.

Although Hungary joined the Axis powers in 1940, by 1944, the country's leaders realized that Germany was on the path to defeat and decided to seek a separate armistice with the Allies.

Hitler discovered the plan and moved quickly to prevent it. In March, he dispatched German troops to occupy Hungary and installed a puppet regime. He also put Adolf Eichmann in charge of rounding up Jews and other so-called subversives. The Nazis seized Jewish homes around the country and sequestered Jews in ghettos. By May,

Eichmann was sending thousands of Jews to the death camps.

As the deportations progressed, alarmed Jewish citizens in Budapest reached out to the embassies of neutral countries for help. Sweden responded quickly, issuing protective passes that identified Jews as Swedes. The move encouraged the U.S. War Refugee Board, an organization created to protect Jews from Nazi persecution, and it began to search for a Swedish national who would undertake a massive rescue operation in Budapest.

The group found their deliverer in Raoul Wallenberg, a 32-year-old businessman and member of one of the wealthiest families in Sweden. After Wallenberg indicated he was willing to take on the mission, he was appointed to the Swedish diplomatic staff and sent to Budapest. When he arrived in July, 200,000 Jews remained in the city.

Wallenberg went to work. He found some powerful Hungarians who helped him, and he was able to bribe others to support his work. He negotiated approval from the Hungarian government to issue 4,500 Swedish passes to the Jews, then proceeded to grant more than 15,000 of these identity cards. He also rented buildings that flew the flag of Sweden and served as hiding places for Jews.

Wallenberg's assignment became more complicated in October 1944,

▲ These Hungarian Jews arrived in Auschwitz-Birkenau in June 1944, some of the more than 430,000 Hungarian Jews who were deported to Auschwitz.

when German troops forced another change in Hungary's government. The newly installed Arrow Cross Party redoubled its anti-Semitic attacks, and Eichmann accelerated the deportation of Jews by train and forced death marches. Wallenberg was undeterred and continued his work, carrying food and medical supplies to those on the marches and saving the residents of the Budapest ghetto before the city fell to the Russians.

### A Mysterious End

In January 1945, the Soviets reached Budapest, where they discovered that about 100,000 Jews had survived. In mid-January, Wallenberg was en route to a meeting with Russian military officials when he disappeared. The diplomat was never seen again.

Swedish authorities, fearful that the Soviets were holding Wallenberg under suspicion of espionage, made inquiries about his condition and whereabouts. The Soviet replies were vague. In 1956, after another request by Sweden, Soviet authorities agreed to investigate. The following year, they announced that Wallenberg had died in a Soviet prison in 1947, although no hard evidence was presented. His disappearance remains a mystery.

> "The road was straight, when Jews were deported to death. The road was winding, dangerous and full of obstacles, when Jews were trying to escape from the murderers."

▲ Women at Ravensbrück concentration camp in northern Germany awaited their release, which had been ordered by Heinrich Himmler in late April.

# An Unlikely Meeting

A LAST-MINUTE SUBSTITUTE NEGOTIATED WITH HIMMLER FOR THE RELEASE OF PRISONERS.

As the war was ending, Swedish businessman Gilel Storch was one of many people who desperately sought to rescue Jews who remained in German concentration camps. But Storch, who was Jewish, had an unusual contact in the Nazi hierarchy: Felix Kersten, personal doctor to Himmler. Through Kersten, Storch arranged to meet Himmler in Germany in April 1945 to discuss freeing some of the captives.

It is unknown why Himmler agreed to the encounter. Had Hitler been informed of it, he surely would have vetoed the plan, and by consenting, Himmler put his own life at risk. Some have speculated

the motive was self-interest and that he was trying to position himself as someone willing to negotiate with the Western Allies as the war drew to a close.

At the last minute, Storch was unable to attend the meeting and Norbert Masur, a Swedish representative of the World Jewish Congress, went in his place. On April 19, after being promised safe passage, Masur and Kersten boarded a plane from Stockholm to Berlin. They were the only passengers on the flight, which carried Red Cross packages.

"For me as a Jew, it was a deeply moving thought, that, in a few hours, I would be face to face with the man who was primarily responsible for the destruction of several million Jewish people," Masur wrote in his report to the Jewish organization. "But my agitation was dampened by the thought that I finally would have the important opportunity to be of help to many of my tormented fellow Jews."

For two and a half hours on April 20, Himmler and Masur talked at Kersten's estate near Berlin. Masur asked Himmler to free the Jews in camps near the Swedish and Swiss borders and requested that the Jews in the other camps be properly cared for and surrendered to the Allies without resistance.

Himmler was quick to agree with the proposal and ordered the transfer of Jewish women from the Ravensbrück concentration camp, the largest camp for women in Hitler's Reich, to a location in Sweden. It is estimated that between 1,000 and 15,000 prisoners were liberated in the operation.

▲ In 2010, survivors of Ravensbrück concentration camp gathered to commemorate the sixty-fifth anniversary of the camp's liberation and to remember the thousands of prisoners who died there. The banner reads, "Ravensbrück camp community and circle of friends."

▲ Several trains arrived at Auschwitz every day, each carrying more than 1,000 prisoners.

# Chronology of Liberation

ALLIED SOLDIERS FOUND THE SAME HORRID CONDITONS AT EACH CAMP.

Soviet forces liberated the Majdanek concentration camp in Poland in July 1944. Beginning in January 1945, as the Allies advanced into Germany from the east and the west, American, British, and Soviet troops were able to free thousands of prisoners in other camps.

### January 27: Auschwitz

The largest camp complex in the Nazi system, Auschwitz, had three main locations near the town of Oswiecim in Germany and more than 40 subcamps. At the height of its operation, Auschwitz held up to 150,000 prisoners and operated as a prison, extermination, and labor camp.

The location called Auschwitz I housed prisoners and forced laborers, provided facilities for the camp's chief doctor, Josef Mengele, to conduct "medical" experiments, and had a gas chamber and a crematorium for killing small groups. The second main location, Auschwitz-Birkenau, was primarily an extermination center, with eight gas chambers, 46 ovens, and four crematoria. Auschwitz-Monowitz served as housing for forced laborers who worked at a nearby factory.

By the time the Soviet troops arrived at the Auschwitz complex, the Nazis had already evacuated more than 60,000 prisoners. Seven thousand others considered too sick or already close to death were left behind.

"When I saw the people, it was skin and bones. They had no shoes, and it was freezing. They couldn't even turn their heads, they stood like dead people," said one Soviet soldier. Troops found prisoners who were still alive between the bodies of prisoners who had already died. The stench they encountered from the decay was horrendous. It is unknown exactly how many people died in the Auschwitz camp system, but conservative estimates range from 1.1 million to 1.3 million.

# Liberation of the Concentration Camps

As the Allies moved across Europe, they encountered thousands of ill, emaciated, and dying prisoners who had been left behind.

▲ JANUARY 27  Auschwitz
An estimated 1.1 million prisoners died in this network of Polish camps, which was liberated by Soviet forces.

▲ FEBRUARY 13  Gross-Rosen
Nearly 40,000 prisoners died at this camp located in present-day Poland. Those who remained were freed by Soviet troops.

*Estimated deaths

1945  JANUARY  •  •  •  FEBRUARY  •

▲ Liberated Auschwitz inmates told Soviet soldiers what they had experienced at the hands of the Nazis.

▲ Josef Mengele in his SS uniform

## Josef Mengele: Medical Horrors

Josef Mengele (1911–1979), the son of a wealthy German manufacturer, became known as the "Angel of Death" for the notorious experiments he performed on prisoners at Auschwitz.

After completing doctorates in medicine and anthropology, Mengele began working for a scientist known for his research on twins, a job that led to Mengele's own interest in the subject. In 1943, he was named chief doctor at Auschwitz, and along with the other medical staff, he met incoming prisoners to select test subjects, while sending others to their deaths in the gas chambers.

Mengele performed thousands of unimaginable experiments on inmates, including injecting prisoners with chemicals to see what effect they would have on living tissue or removing the eyes from corpses to study pigmentation. He was particularly fascinated with twins; most were children and many died during the experiments. Often the surviving twin was slaughtered in order for Mengele to compare the condition of the bodies postmortem.

As Allies approached Auschwitz, Mengele fled and went into hiding, eventually making his way to South America. He died by drowning on February 7, 1979, in Brazil, after suffering a stroke while swimming. He was buried under the pseudonym "Wolfgang Gerhard." His death was confirmed in 1985 by Brazilian forensic scientists, and in 1992 DNA evidence proved conclusively that it was Mengele.

◀ **APRIL 11  Buchenwald**
When American troops reached this large camp in central Germany, they found a trailer piled high with corpses. The death count here totaled about 56,000.

**APRIL 15  Bergen-Belsen**
The British liberated this camp in northern Germany where approximately 35,000 were killed.

**APRIL 29  Dachau**
American forces liberated this camp in southern Germany, not far from Munich. Approximately 32,000 lost their lives here.

**APRIL 29–30  Ravensbrück**
The Soviets liberated this camp north of Berlin. The death toll is unknown.

**MAY 4  Neuengamme**  The British opened this camp in northern Germany where 56,000 died.

▲ **MAY 5  Mauthausen**  Around 120,000 died at this camp in Austria, but prisoners who were strong enough gave a rousing welcome to the American soldiers who arrived to free them.

**MAY 8  Theresienstadt**  Nearly 33,000 lost their lives here in Czechoslovakia before the Soviets liberated the camp.

**MAY 9  Stutthof**  Soviet forces liberated this camp where the death count reached 65,000.

● **MARCH** ● ● **APRIL** ● ● **MAY**

▶ Five days after the liberation of Buchenwald, Germany, Jewish survivors still slept in their barracks. American troops did their best to provide food and medical care for the former inmates.

### April 11: Buchenwald

When Buchenwald opened its doors in 1937, it was used primarily to house political prisoners. Within the year, the SS began sending Jews to the site, and by the end of the war, Buchenwald was one of the largest death camps in the Reich. It contained more than 80 subcamps and was designed to accommodate up to 11,200 prisoners, many of whom were used as slave laborers.

In April 1945, as American forces closed in on Buchenwald, the Germans evacuated some 28,000 prisoners; those who remained seized control of the camp and waited. They would gain their freedom on April 11 when the U.S. Army arrived. The Americans were shocked at what they found. Soldiers remembered how the camp reeked of excrement and of burning human flesh and hair.

"More than 3,200 naked, emaciated bodies had been flung into shallow graves," remembered General Omar Bradley. Starving prisoners, Bradley said, "had torn out the entrails of the dead for food."

It is believed some 250,000 Europeans were imprisoned at Buchenwald during the war. Bradley's troops found more than 21,000 survivors. One soldier reported that some found the strength to express their joy by picking him up, tossing him upward, and catching him, over and over again.

▼ The phrase on the main gate at Buchenwald, *Jedem das Seine*, translated as "to each his own" or as "everyone gets what he deserves."

◀ Typhus, a disease spread by insects, was an ever-present hazard in the camps. One common precaution after liberation was to spray prisoners with the insecticide DDT, as British soldiers did at Bergen-Belsen.

### April 15: Bergen-Belsen

Built in 1940 in northern Germany, Bergen-Belsen was designed as a prisoner-of-war camp that could hold up to 10,000 people, but three years later the SS converted part of the facility into a holding camp. Over the course of its operation, Bergen-Belsen housed Jews, political prisoners, Roma, homosexuals, and others.

As with all such camps, conditions were deplorable. There were few latrines, a grossly inadequate fresh water supply, and overcrowded barracks. Prisoners could go several days at a time without food and were ravaged by dysentery, typhus, tuberculosis, typhoid fever, and other diseases.

By April 1945, Bergen-Belsen was teeming with 60,000 inmates. On April 15,

three days after the Allies opened negotiations with the Germans for the camp's peaceful surrender, British forces liberated Bergen-Belsen. Most of the inmates were very ill.

The British soldiers were shocked to encounter prisoners who were still alive but so emaciated that they looked like living skeletons. They also discovered thousands of corpses scattered around the camp. The stench in the camp from disease, excrement, and death was overwhelming. Having survived the horrible conditions in the camp, more than 10,000 of those who had been liberated still died because of their illnesses.

When the British left, they burned Bergen-Belsen in order to stop the spread of disease. The last building was ceremonially burned on May 21, 1945.

▲ British soldiers made German civilians from the nearby towns of Bergen and Belsen carry the bodies of concentration camp victims to municipal cemeteries for burial. The British also forced the civilians to tour the camp, where a British officer told them, "What you see here is such a disgrace to the German people that their names must be erased from the list of civilized nations . . ."

▲ American troops passed candy and cigarettes through the fence to prisoners when Dachau was first liberated.

### April 29: Dachau

Dachau was the first camp that the Nazis opened, in March 1933, just five weeks after Hitler was elected chancellor of Germany, and it became the model for others that followed.

Located near Munich, Dachau had a main camp that contained 32 barracks; one of them was most often used for gruesome medical experiments. In addition, there were approximately 30 subcamps where prisoners were forced to work on armaments.

When the Americans entered Dachau on April 29, they found 30 railroad cars crammed with corpses that had arrived from other death camps and thousands more dead inside the facility. There were 30,000 survivors, most of whom were malnourished and riddled with disease. Some GIs were so aghast that they machine-gunned 30 SS guards who had been captured.

It is unknown exactly how many people were interned in the Dachau system, but it is estimated that between 160,000 and 190,000 people were imprisoned in the main camp. An additional 90,000 prisoners passed through the subcamps, many through a series of relocations from camp to camp. The estimated number of deaths associated with Dachau is 32,000.

▲ The survivors at Dachau who were strong enough to walk eagerly greeted American forces.

▲ Exuberant cheering broke out among captives as they welcomed the American liberators.

▶ Two Dachau prisoners secretly wrote "Dachau Song" about the motto *"Arbeit Macht Frei"* ("work makes you free"). It began with these words: "Barbed wire, loaded with death, is drawn around our world. . . . But we have learned the motto of Dachau and it made us as hard as steel: Be a man . . . for work, work makes you free!"

▲ Survivors of a subcamp of Neuengamme helped one another into a transport truck after the camp was liberated.

## May 4: Neuengamme

The Neuengamme camp, located at an abandoned brickworks factory outside Hamburg, Germany, was known for working prisoners to death. Among other jobs, inmates produced bricks, mined clay, made armaments, and removed rubble from cities bombed by the Allies. They were starved, beaten, kept in filthy conditions, and made to work regardless of weather conditions.

Nazi medical researchers used the inmates at Neuengamme, including children, to test drugs intended to combat a variety of diseases including malaria, typhus, and tuberculosis. As the British approached Neuengamme in early May 1945, the Nazis evacuated nearly 10,000 prisoners from the main camp and subcamps, placing them on three ships in the Baltic Sea. The British arrived a few days later—on May 4—but tragedy followed the liberation.

Pursing the Nazis, the British accidentally attacked two of the ships holding the prisoners during an air raid, killing some 7,000 people aboard. Only about 500 were rescued.

▲ While the sign over the entrance to Theresienstadt declared "Work Makes You Free," Nazi propaganda described the camp as a "spa" where elderly German Jews could "retire."

## May 8: Theresienstadt

Theresienstadt was a walled ghetto located in what is today the Czech Republic. The Nazis planned to use the ghetto to house European Jews who were privileged and famous, but it ended up serving many purposes. Czech Jews in transit to forced-labor camps in Poland, Belorussia, and the Baltic countries were interned in Theresienstadt; the ghetto also became a labor camp and a holding area for thousands in poor health.

In the last weeks of the war, the Nazis forced between 13,500 and 15,000 additional prisoners from other camps into Theresienstadt. Most, although not all, were Jewish, and Himmler and Security Police Chief Ernst Kaltenbrunner planned to use the inmates as a way of opening peace negotiations with the Western Allies. On February 5, they released 1,210 prisoners from Theresienstadt as a token of good faith. All reached Switzerland safely, and the Swedish Red Cross was soon able to truck another 423 out of the camp.

On May 3, as the commandant and SS guards fled, the International Red Cross took over Theresienstadt. On May 8, Soviet troops entered the camp and liberated the 19,000 prisoners who had been left behind.

▲ Imprisoned artists stole paper and other items to record their experiences, and they shared the paper with children in the camp. Liberating forces discovered hidden artwork and poems by thousands of children, most of whom did not survive.

▲ The text on the memorial wall at Dachau reads, "May the example of those who were exterminated here between 1933–1945 because they resisted Nazism help to unite the living for the defense of peace and freedom and in respect for their fellow men."

# Dachau Transformed

THE SITE OF INFAMOUS NAZI ATROCITIES
HAS BECOME A SOMBER MEMORIAL.

When American GIs liberated Dachau on April 29, 1945, they found, in the words of Colonel William Quinn, ". . . sights, sounds, and stenches horrible beyond belief, cruelties so enormous as to be incomprehensible to the normal mind." They were shocked by thousands of decomposing corpses and the pale, skeletal survivors staring at the liberators in disbelief. Some hardened battle veterans cried at what they saw; others raged as the magnitude of the death and suffering began to sink in.

To commemorate those who were imprisoned or died at Dachau, a group of survivors began planning a memorial in 1955. They received financing from Germany's Bavarian state government and began construction in 1962, opening the site three years later.

Today, visitors to the memorial can inspect some of the original structures, including guard towers, inmate barracks, the camp prison, and the crematorium. There is also a museum with exhibits that focus on the prisoners' biographies, their eyewitness accounts, and the camp's history. A two-mile "Path of Remembrance," the road that captives had to walk from the railroad station to the camp, features information displays set up at various points along the route.

▲ Hungarian Jew Nandor Glid survived the war, and in 1958 created this piece, International Monument. It was selected to serve as a memorial for the victims of Dachau, and in 1968, the sculpture took its place at the museum entrance.

▲ When coal ran out for fueling the crematoriums, Dachau victims were buried in mass graves. This plaque marks one of several such sites at the Dachau Memorial.

▲ Angela Merkel and Holocaust survivor Max Mannheimer at Dachau, August 2013

## Paying Tribute

In August 2013, Angela Merkel became the first German chancellor to visit the former concentration camp. She laid a wreath at the site and said she wanted her visit to Dachau to be "a bridge from history to the present and into the future." Max Mannheimer, a 93-year-old survivor of the camp, accompanied the chancellor and said of her visit, "It is a great honor and an historic event for us survivors."

# 5 | V-E DAY

AFTER SIX YEARS OF WAR AND INCALCULABLE SUFFERING, THE ALLIES DEFEATED HITLER'S FORCES AND RESTORED EUROPE'S FREEDOM.

"This is a solemn but glorious hour. General Eisenhower informs me that the forces of Germany have surrendered. . . . The flags of freedom fly all over Europe."

—President Harry Truman, May 8, 1945

Allied soldiers and French civilians in Paris celebrated victory in Europe, May 8, 1945.

"With this signature the German people and the German armed forces are for better or worse delivered into the victor's hands. . . . In this hour I can only express the hope that the victor will treat them with generosity."

—German general Alfred Jodl, May 7, 1945

▲ Numerous German soldiers captured near the war's end were kept in rural camps in Allied-occupied Germany.

# Surrender to the Big Three

EISENHOWER FORCED GERMANY TO CAPITULATE
TO BOTH THE WESTERN ALLIES AND RUSSIA.

By April, both German civilians and the country's military knew that they would be forced to admit defeat. The Soviets had captured Berlin, and Nazi soldiers still stationed along the Eastern and Western Fronts were surrendering daily. Axis forces in Italy and southern Austria capitulated on May 2, and just two days later German troops in Denmark and the Netherlands gave up the fight. The following day, the remaining German armies in Austria followed suit. For all these men, the fighting was finally over.

▲ General Alfred Jodl, Chief of the Operations Staff of the German High Command

## General Alfred Jodl: Violating Rules of War

Alfred Jodl (1890–1946) was a German artillery officer during World War I and remained in the service after the armistice. At the outbreak of World War II, Jodl joined the German army command staff, which was responsible for the overall actions of the army.

As a member of the general staff, Jodl signed off on two of Hitler's orders that were clear violations of the rules of war. The "Commando Order" directed German forces to immediately kill all captured Allies without trial. The "Commissar Order" directed that German troops immediately execute, again without trial, any Soviet political officer they captured.

At the war's conclusion, Jodl was authorized by Chancellor Karl Dönitz to sign the surrender documents with the Allies and to agree to the unconditional surrender of German forces. Jodl was convicted of war crimes at the Nuremberg Trials and then hanged in 1946.

▲ On May 2, British field marshal Bernard Montgomery explained partial surrender terms for German forces in the Netherlands, Denmark, and northwest Germany. The next day, Nazi officers returned to Montgomery's field headquarters near Hamburg and agreed to the surrender terms.

◄ An American soldier guarded German prisoners during the Allied advance into Germany.

"By command of Admiral Dönitz the Armed Forces have given up the hopeless struggle. A heroic fight that has lasted for nearly six years thus comes to an end . . . the German Armed Forces have succumbed to overwhelming superior strength. . . . To show obedience, discipline and absolute loyalty to our Fatherland, bleeding from innumerable wounds, is the sacred duty our dead impose upon us all."

—Final order of the German Armed Forces, issued on May 9, 1945

### Germany Admits Defeat

Before Adolf Hitler committed suicide on April 30, he named German naval commander Karl Dönitz to succeed him as chancellor.

Dönitz immediately began acting on his belief that the Americans and British would treat German troops better than Soviet premier Joseph Stalin. On May 7, he dispatched General Alfred Jodl, a trusted commander who held a lead position in the German Armed Forces High Command, to meet with General Dwight Eisenhower in Reims, France.

Negotiations for Jodl were difficult. Eisenhower rejected his offer that the Germans would surrender only to the Western Allies and insisted that the Germans concede to the Russians as well as to the Western Allies. The Nazis were out of options. Jodl radioed Dönitz, requesting permission to sign surrender documents. Four versions were needed: English, French, German, and Russian. Government officials in London, Paris, and Moscow quickly approved the transcripts. By the end of the day, Dönitz made German defeat official.

## The War in Europe Ends

Axis forces in Europe finally surrendered. As the news spread, joyful celebrations erupted around the world. Soon, American troops began their long-awaited trip home to reunite with loved ones.

**MAY 2** The remaining Axis forces in Italy and southern Austria surrendered.

**MAY 4** Nazi forces in Denmark and the Netherlands ceded to the Allies.

**MAY 5** All Nazi forces still fighting in Austria surrendered.

MAY

Shortly before midnight on May 8, a second, slightly different declaration was executed with Russian officials, at Stalin's insistence. Meeting in Karlshort, just outside Berlin, German field marshal Wilhelm Keitel formally conceded his country to Soviet general Georgy Zhukov. The final documents were signed on what was actually May 9 in Moscow, and this became the official surrender date for the Russians.

The war that began in September 1939 had come to an end in Europe. American forces received a message from Eisenhower after the surrender, in which he said, "The route you have traveled . . . is marked by the graves of former comrades. . . . Our common problems of the immediate and distant future can be best solved in the same conceptions of co-operation and devotion to the cause of human freedom as have made this Expeditionary Force such a mighty engine of righteous destruction."

## Karl Dönitz: Germany's new leader

Following Hitler's death on April 30, and in accordance with the Führer's will, Grand Admiral Karl Dönitz (1891–1980) became Germany's new head of state, president of the Reich. A loyal, obedient, and zealous Nazi, Dönitz was known for his ruthless cunning and lack of respect for human life on the battlefield. In his memoirs, Dönitz recounted: *. . . I did not for a moment doubt that it was my duty to accept the task . . . it had been my constant fear that the absence*

*of any central authority would lead to chaos and the senseless and purposeless sacrifice of hundreds of thousands of lives . . . I realized . . . that the darkest moment in any fighting man's life, the moment when he must surrender unconditionally, was at hand. I realized, too, that my name would remain forever associated with the act and that hatred and distortion of facts would continue to try and besmirch my honor. But duty demanded that I pay no attention to any such considerations. My policy was simple—to try and save as many lives as I could.* At his 1946 war criminal trial at Nuremberg, Dönitz was sentenced to ten years in prison and was released in 1956.

◀ Karl Dönitz, shown here, was wearing the Iron Cross, which was awarded for exceptional bravery and leadership on the battlefield.

**MAY 7** Alfred Jodl traveled to Reims, France, and acting on behalf of the German government, signed an unconditional surrender with the Western Allies.

**MAY 8** German officials met with Soviet military leaders in Berlin and signed similar surrender papers.

▲ **MAY 8** V-E Day was announced, and celebrations began around the world.

**MAY 9** Russians joined the celebrations marking the end of the war.

**JUNE** Soldiers stationed in Europe began coming home to the United States.

▲ Thousands of civilians and military, including these members of the Women's Royal Army Corps, filled London's Trafalgar Square to celebrate V-E Day.

# V-E Day in the British Commonwealth

THE EMPIRE SAVORED A SWEET MOMENT OF TRIUMPH.

The announcement that Germany had officially and unconditionally surrendered was broadcast in Britain late at night on May 7, and on the following day, a sense of euphoria reigned throughout the country. People flocked to city streets to sing, dance, and celebrate. Others spent the day quietly at home and in church, reflecting on the events they had endured. For those who had fought, a commonly heard phrase was simply "I survived."

In London, bands played, flags flew, and crowds gathered outside Buckingham Palace to cheer for King George, who came out on the balcony eight times. Princess Elizabeth and her sister, Princess Margaret, joined the thousands of citizens in the streets. Prime Minister Winston Churchill, who spoke from the balcony of the Ministry of Health, drew the loudest cheer of all when he reminded the elated throngs assembled below, "This is your victory."

In Toronto and throughout Canada, people gathered in the streets to celebrate, and in many cities, May 7 was commemorated with thanksgiving services. *The Globe and Mail*, Toronto's newspaper, called the festivities a "carnival of joy," marked with laughter and tears, blaring car horns, and open churches where people gathered to pray and give thanks. It was a day filled with exhilaration, flags, and official speeches, as well as with hymns and calls to remember those who had lost their lives.

In comparison, the celebration in New Zealand was subdued. When V-E Day was announced, the country's prime minister insisted that no celebrations be held until May 9, when Churchill officially announced that peace had come.

For New Zealanders, the day began with bells and sirens and gave way to speeches by government officials, parades, and thanksgiving services. Citizens won compliments for their "commendable restraint."

The declaration of victory, however, was not shared throughout the British Commonwealth. In Australia, the *Sydney Morning Herald* led with the question, "Since when has it been customary to celebrate victory halfway through a contest?" For as servicemen and women recalled comrades lost and hardships endured, they may have also been wondering if they would be sent to fight the Japanese. Like their New Zealand neighbors, the Australians knew that the war was still to be won.

▲ Winston Churchill spoke to the cheering masses, which burst into a round of "For he's a jolly good fellow."

► Soldiers and civilians filled the streets of Paris to celebrate V-E Day and remember the 217,000 soldiers and 567,000 civilians who had made victory possible but not lived to celebrate it.

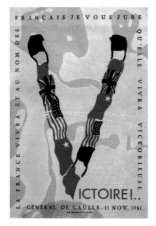

▲ A French victory leaflet featured Charles de Gaulle's wartime promise, "France will live, and in the name of the French people, I swear to you that she will live victorious."

# Victory Day in France

THE BELLS RANG OUT ANNOUNCING THE GOOD NEWS.

On May 8, Charles de Gaulle, leader of the Free French Forces, announced Germany's surrender in a radio broadcast to his fellow citizens. Church bells pealed in the villages, towns, and cities throughout France, signaling the end of Nazi oppression and announcing that it was time to celebrate. An American airman stationed in France at the time wrote: "The people went mad. Mad with laughter and mad with happiness, mad with anything and everything. All up and down the streets the cheering populace let it be known that Hitler was KAPUT. . . ."

De Gaulle's address to the French people began simply: "The war has been won." He continued, ". . . [T]he country turns its thoughts and affection first of all toward those who died for her and then toward those who in her service struggled and suffered so much. Not one single act of courage or self-sacrifice of her sons and daughters, not one single hardship of her captive men and women, not one single

▲ Jubilant Parisians paraded through the Arc de Triomphe and along the Champs-Elysées to celebrate Germany's defeat.

bereavement and sacrifice, not one single tear will have been wasted in vain. . . . Honor, eternal honor, to our armies and their leaders. Honor to our nation, which never faltered, even under terrible trials, nor gave in to them."

In Paris, parading crowds took to the streets and filled the city's center, kissing one another and singing the national anthem. One journalist reported that there was ". . . hardly any place to breathe and no place at all to move." The sounds of bells and car horns joined the blast of air-raid sirens. It was a day of glory, knowing that many of those who had collaborated with the Vichy government and the Nazis would be brought to trial for treason and other crimes.

▲ Overjoyed V-E Day crowds jammed Times Square in New York City so tightly that neither streets nor sidewalks were visible.

# V-E Day in the United States

"OUR VICTORY IS ONLY HALF OVER." —HARRY TRUMAN

In the United States, victory celebrations marking the end of the war in Europe were joyous and, as elsewhere around the world, filled with a tremendous sense of relief. The night sky of the East Coast and particularly New York City radiated with light as evening blackout conditions were no longer required. Jubilant crowds filled Times Square, flags flew high, church bells rang, car horns blared, and people danced in the streets.

But the festivities lacked a sense of finality. The United States was still at war in the Pacific, and everyone knew the nation faced a deadly enemy.

In a radio broadcast on May 8, President Harry Truman added a somber reminder to the celebratory atmosphere: "For this victory, we join in offering our thanks to the Providence which has guided and sustained us through the dark days of adversity. Our rejoicing is sobered

and subdued by a supreme consciousness of the terrible price we have paid to rid the world of Hitler and his evil band. Let us not forget, my fellow Americans, the sorrow and the heartache which today abide in the homes of so many of our neighbors—neighbors whose most priceless possession has been rendered as a sacrifice to redeem our liberty."

He continued, "We can repay the debt which we owe to our God, to our dead, and to our children, only by work, by ceaseless devotion to the responsibilities which lie ahead of us. If I could give you a single watchword for the coming months, that word is work, work, and more work. We must work to finish the war. Our victory is only half over."

▲ Americans filling Times Square and surrounding streets were so elated that the celebration extended far into the night, with city lights at full brilliance. During the war, businesses in New York had dimmed their lights to conserve electricity and coal.

Happy crowds in Moscow packed Red Square edge to edge during celebrations of Victory Day, May 9. For a brief period, the war was over for the USSR, as it had not yet declared war on Japan.

# Victory Day in Moscow

STALIN AND THE USSR CELEBRATED WITH GUNFIRE AND GUSTO.

The official notice that Germany had surrendered to Russia was made in the early morning hours of May 9. The chief announcer of Radio Moscow broke the news to the Russian people: "Attention, this is Moscow. Germany has capitulated. This day, in honor of the victorious Great Patriotic War, is to be a national holiday, a festival of victory."

Even though it was the middle of the night, celebrations erupted. People rushed outside to dance, pray, cry, and laugh, and impromptu celebrations lasted throughout the day. The newspaper *Pravda* led with the headline "Triumph in the Capital" and followed with a glowing tribute to Stalin. That night, fireworks lit up the sky near Red Square, and thousands came to share their joy.

The celebrations in Russia continued into June. A major parade to mark the victory was held in Red Square in Moscow on June 24, a date chosen because many war veterans had returned home and could participate in the military honors. Surviving Russian soldiers had much to memorialize, for millions of their comrades had been killed during the fighting, and several million more had been murdered by the Nazis after being captured during battle, amounting to a total loss of somewhere between 9 million and 13 million men.

The Soviets put on a massive fireworks display in Moscow to mark the victory.

"Eternal glory to the heroes who fell in the struggle against the enemy and gave their lives for the freedom and happiness of our people!"

—Joseph Stalin, May 9

▼ Russian victory ceremonies included Red Army soldiers lowering captured Nazi banners toward the ground, signifying Germany's defeat and surrender.

▲ Ecstatic crowds on the docks of New York City welcomed returning American troops on the British ship *Queen Mary*.

# Operation Magic Carpet Begins

SHIPS BEGAN FERRYING TROOPS HOME FROM EUROPE.

American soldiers in Europe had finished their job, and the U.S. military could now focus on another Herculean task: bringing their men and women home. The job was not an easy one. Many of the navy's ships were still deployed in the Pacific and unavailable to transport some three million men and women. Also, there was the question of who got to come home first.

The government addressed the first issue by converting 300 cargo ships into

◀ After the end of the war in Europe, U.S. soldiers boarded transport ships for the trip home.

▼ Families felt both relief and elation as they embraced loved ones who returned.

troop transports. For the second, the army developed a complex system of points based on seniority and time overseas to determine the order of return.

Starting in late June, the first transports began their journey, and over the next 14 months, more than 400,000 GIs a month traveled the Atlantic in an operation dubbed Magic Carpet.

The fleet also included hospital ships, which brought back more than half a million wounded soldiers. On return trips to Europe, the ships carried 500,000 German and Italian POWs to their homes.

# 6 | WAR IN THE PACIFIC

BY MAY THE WAR IN EUROPE WAS OVER, BUT FIGHTING BETWEEN
THE ALLIES AND THE JAPANESE RAGED IN THE PACIFIC.

"To die for the Emperor is to live forever."
—Japanese army slogan

A group of kamikaze pilots, each wearing a ribbon honoring his mission, posed for a final photo before beginning their suicide flights.

# The Pacific Theatre

THE ALLIES HAD TO CONFRONT AND DEFEAT A
RESOLUTE, TENACIOUS FOE AT SEA AND ON LAND.

Japan was determined to hold on to its territories in the Pacific, including the Philippine Islands, even if it meant fighting to the last man. The equally strong-willed American general Douglas MacArthur had resolved to keep his 1942 promise to return to the Philippines and retake these strategic islands. As American military forces moved to achieve this goal and progressed through the Pacific, they captured important airfields. These airstrips became essential as the Americans moved toward their final goal—striking the Japanese homeland.

Iwo Jima and Okinawa, key islands on the route, were securely held by the Japanese. Taking them resulted in brutal battles in land and sea and in the loss of thousands of military and civilian lives.

▶ Filipino resistance fighters provided vital intelligence about the Japanese and also battled alongside American soldiers during the campaign to regain the Philippines.

## Destination: Japan

By the end of 1944, Japan had suffered a stunning defeat at Leyte Gulf and was running short on vital raw materials needed for manufacturing ships, planes, war matériel, and fuel. At home, civilians struggled with dwindling food supplies and other daily necessities.

**JANUARY 9** U.S. forces invaded the island of Luzon, where Manila is located.

▲ **JANUARY 20** Japanese emperor Hirohito approved the plan for all Japanese military and civilians to fight until death in defense of the home islands.

▲ **FEBRUARY 3** The battle for Manila began, considered essential to retaking the Philippines.

**FEBRUARY 19** U.S. forces landed in Iwo Jima, beginning a five-week-long assault.

**FEBRUARY 23** Americans hoisted a U.S. flag atop Mount Suribachi, Iwo Jima; capturing the peak was a key step in controlling the island.

**APRIL 1** American troops, accompanied by the largest invasion fleet ever used, invaded Okinawa.

▲ **APRIL 7** U.S. bombers sank the Japanese battleship *Yamato*, Japan's last hope for destroying the Allied fleet.

JANUARY • • • • • FEBRUARY • • • • • MARCH • • • •

## The Pacific Battleground

Fighting took place from island to island as Allied forces moved toward their ultimate target, Japan's homeland.

▲ **MAY 12** U.S. Marines began their assault of Sugar Loaf Hill on Okinawa, to surround the main Japanese position.

**MAY 25** The U.S. Joint Chiefs of Staff authorized the invasion of the Japanese home islands, selecting November 1 as the D-day.

**JUNE 22** Allied forces captured Okinawa and declared the island securely in American hands on July 2.

**JULY 4** U.S. forces proclaimed that the Philippines were free from Japanese occupiers.

APRIL • • • • • • • MAY • • • • • • • • JUNE • • • • • • • • JULY

"People of the Philippines, I have returned."

—General Douglas MacArthur, October 20, 1944

▲ General Douglas MacArthur waded ashore at Luzon as troops under his command began the invasion on January 9.

# The Philippines Campaign

THE AMERICANS LOST HERE IN 1942, BUT IN 1945, GENERAL MACARTHUR RETURNED, DETERMINED TO RETAKE THESE KEY ISLANDS.

MacArthur's return to the Philippines began on October 20, 1944, when more than 100,000 American soldiers landed along an 18-mile stretch of Leyte's coast. It took more than 60 days, but by early December the Americans, supported by Filipino guerrilla forces, wrested Leyte from the Japanese. The battle was costly in terms of human life—about 3,500 Americans and 80,000 enemy soldiers were killed. What's more, the victory did not provide the strategic location MacArthur had counted on. Leyte's existing airfields were small and heavily damaged, and the island was too marshy to support the construction of large, new landing strips.

Undeterred, MacArthur moved northward, and later in December, U.S. landing crafts launched a rocket assault on the island of Mindoro before transporting troops to the beaches. Ten thousand American soldiers faced 1,200 Japanese and quickly captured the island. Within two weeks, U.S. Army engineers completed the construction of two airfields, making bombing assaults on Luzon possible.

## The Assault on Luzon

MacArthur wanted the Japanese to believe the assault on Luzon would come from the south. To foster the deception, he had U.S. planes conduct bombing runs along the southern shore of the island, while Filipino resistance fighters attacked Japanese forces inland. General Tomoyuki Yamashita, the Japanese commander of the island, was not fooled. He prepared for an assault on a more likely location, the northwest side of the island, the actual landing site the Americans had selected.

When the U.S. Sixth Army stormed Luzon on January 9, the Japanese were at a disadvantage. They had lost a significant number of planes in the battle for Leyte, and their remaining aircraft were unable to hold the Americans back. Although the Japanese sank 20 U.S. ships and damaged others, they could not prevent 175,000 Americans from coming ashore over the next few days. The diminished Japanese air fleet was also powerless to provide cover for their troops on the ground.

With the beaches secured, MacArthur triumphantly waded ashore as hundreds of Filipinos applauded and cheered.

## FACES *of* WAR

**JANUARY 26, 1880–APRIL 5, 1964**

# DOUGLAS MACARTHUR

*The U.S. general's determination shaped his distinguished military career and contributed to one of his greatest successes— helping Japan achieve democracy and economic strength.*

---

Widely known for his promise to the Philippines, "I shall return," General Douglas MacArthur made good on the vow on January 9, 1945.

The triumph was one of many in a long military career that ended in controversy. MacArthur graduated with honors from West Point in 1903 and rose quickly in the army, achieving the rank of brigadier general after World War I. From 1935 to 1941, he served as a military adviser to the Philippine government. On the eve of World War II, President Franklin Roosevelt recalled MacArthur to active duty. Following the Japanese invasion of the Philippines, the president ordered the general to evacuate to Australia and gave him command of all the Allied forces in the Southwest Pacific.

MacArthur was a master of military strategy; he was also a frequent critic of the decisions to expend more resources on the war in Europe rather than in the Pacific. From 1945 to 1951, he oversaw the occupation and postwar reconstruction of Japan.

In 1950, when North Korea invaded South Korea, MacArthur was also given command of UN forces and stopped

"In war, you win or lose, live or die—and the difference is just an eyelash."

◄ Douglas MacArthur

▼ The corncob pipe was one of MacArthur's trademarks. The company that produced it from MacArthur's own design still makes the pipe today.

the initial Communist advance. But he was unhappy with the way President Harry Truman handled the conflict and criticized Truman publicly. The argument cost MacArthur his job. The president removed MacArthur from his military command, a decision that was controversial with the American public. He returned to the United States a hero. In his 1951 farewell speech to Congress, MacArthur repeated his oft-quoted statement: "Old soldiers never die, they just fade away."

"The soldier above all others prays for peace, for it is the soldier who must suffer and bear the deepest wounds and scars of war."

▲ American and Filipino soldiers worked together to provide medical care for injured civilians and to move them to safer locations.

Newsreel cameras caught the moment on film, while photographers took dozens of still photos that found their way into newspapers around the globe.

Soon after landing, U.S. troops began the slow march toward their prized objective—the capital, Manila. Some of MacArthur's subordinates urged the general to bypass the city, advising their commander to let it "wither on the vine." Manila, MacArthur countered, was the key to Luzon, and Luzon the key to the Philippines. The general also expressed his belief that the Manila area would be firmly in the hands of the Allies by February.

The fairly easy landing for the Americans masked the bloody hardships that lay ahead. Yamashita had scattered 250,000 soldiers throughout the island and had built an intricate defensive network of well-fortified and well-supplied tunnels and caves. The Japanese had no intention of giving up the island without a long, brutal fight.

## FACES *of* WAR

NOVEMBER 30, 1874–JANUARY 24, 1965

# JOHN MCKINNEY

*Recognized for his spirit, fighting ability, and courage, this American soldier received the Medal of Honor for leaping into action and saving the lives of his American comrades.*

The battle for Luzon made a hero of an unlikely American soldier, Private John McKinney, known for being shy, polite, and dutiful.

Just before daybreak on May 11, about 100 Japanese troops quietly approached McKinney's outpost near Dingalan Bay on Luzon. Caught off guard by the attack, McKinney and three other GIs manning a machine-gun emplacement were overwhelmed. McKinney was struck in the head, and both of his comrades were carried away by the enemy.

Left alone to defend the emplacement, McKinney leapt into action. He used his rifle to bludgeon one attacker to death and then to shoot another. As the Japanese prepared to turn the machine gun on the American line, McKinney dove into the emplacement and shot seven of the ten enemy soldiers dead. He killed the remaining three with his rifle butt.

Though grenades and mortars were exploding around McKinney, he detected another group of soldiers advancing toward him. The private shifted position and using his rifle, cut down wave after wave of charging Japanese. Some he gunned down. Others he clubbed to death. When the fighting was finally over, 38 Japanese lay dead around the machine gun, and two more were dead 45 yards away—all killed by McKinney. For his heroic actions, McKinney received the Congressional Medal of Honor, the highest award for valor in action against an enemy force.

**"I moved about. Maybe that's what helped save me."**

**"Sometimes, I still hear the screams. . . . They were a-coming at me!"**

▲ President Harry Truman joined hands with four servicemen he had just decorated with the Congressional Medal of Honor. Standing from left to right were Sergeant John McKinney, First Lieutenant Daniel Lee, the president, Lieutenant Donald Gary, and chaplain Commander Joseph O'Callahan.

# The Road to Manila

AMERICANS SEIZED THE BATAAN PENINSULA
AND CORREGIDOR, DOORWAYS TO MANILA.

A successful attack on Manila depended on the Americans' ability to replace lengthy overland supply lines on Luzon with safe, secure access to the harbor at Manila Bay and on recapturing the Bataan Peninsula.

The route to Bataan was treacherous. American troops had to march along a long, twisting mountain path nicknamed "Zig-Zag Pass," where more than 25,000 Japanese were prepared to make a do-or-die stand from a series of well-supplied defensive positions.

Yet the enemy lines were stretched thin and vulnerable to flanking maneuvers by U.S. troops. As the Americans gained control of the pass between January 31 and February 8, Japanese troops were decimated. Only about 300 escaped inland, and another 25 were taken prisoner by the Americans. The rest of the defenders died during the fighting. The peninsula's capture provided the Americans access to their objective—a deepwater port for the impending attack on Manila.

**Luzan**

Capturing the Bataan Peninsula and Corregidor opened the way to Manila.

American soldiers followed the railroad tracks leading into Manila, passing by fallen Japanese soldiers.

## Richard Sakakida: A Mole in Japanese Headquarters

Born in Hawaii to Japanese parents, U.S. soldier Richard Sakakida (1920–1996) was already serving in the U.S. Army when the Japanese bombed Pearl Harbor in 1941. Following the attack, the army's counterintelligence arm tapped Sakakida as a spy and sent him to the Philippines to pose as a civilian. There he gathered military information from the local Japanese community.

When the Japanese captured the Philippines in 1942, they took Sakakida prisoner and interrogated and tortured him for almost a year. Sakakida eventually convinced the Japanese that he was a civilian and was released. He was then hired by the Japanese as a translator at Japanese army headquarters. From there, Sakakida managed to pass sensitive information to Philippine resistance fighters and to arrange the escape of nearly 500 Filipino prisoners.

In June 1945, as Japanese forces retreated into the mountains, Sakakida escaped. He spent months in the jungle evading enemy troops and fighting malaria and dysentery. When Sakakida finally heard a group of American soldiers talking nearby, he walked out of the undergrowth and was rescued.

Sakakida later served on the War Crimes Investigation team in Manila and testified at General Yamashita's trial. In 1999, he was posthumously awarded the Distinguished Service Medal, the country's third-highest military award.

▲ The U.S. Army's Distinguished Service Medal

▲ Paratroopers were key to taking Corregidor. Members of the 503rd Regiment dropped behind enemy lines, cleared out the island's defensive barriers, and helped open the harbor to the Allied fleet.

## Corregidor Island

The entrance to Manila Bay was guarded by the heavily defended island fortress of Corregidor, and the Americans needed to capture it in order to launch the assault on Manila.

MacArthur decided on a two-pronged strategy: to couple air strikes with a risky amphibious landing that required the airborne divisions to parachute directly into the midst of the Japanese lines. In an effort to protect his troops, MacArthur ordered ships to shell Corregidor, pounding it for three weeks before the ground invasion began.

On February 16, parachutes filled the sky while troops stormed the beach. The Japanese, 6,700 strong, had entrenched themselves in a network of caves and tunnels and were well insulated from their American attackers. As the U.S. troops sought to track down and destroy the buried positions, the Japanese retaliated with intermittent fire. Most of the Japanese died in the fierce combat.

Those who survived, however, killed themselves to avoid surrender. The 1,400-foot Malinta Tunnel, a hideout for hundreds of Japanese, became a mass grave when the soldiers committed suicide by purposely igniting a nearby ammunition dump. The resulting explosion also killed 52 Americans.

On February 19, when the Americans took possession of Corregidor, fewer than 100 Japanese soldiers remained. With the island firmly in Allied hands, the sea route to Manila was open.

◄ Although the Allies would eventually win, fighting on Corregidor was man-to-man and inch by inch.

▲ Japanese general Masaharu Homma gained fame as the conqueror of the Philippines.

## Masaharu Homma: The Bataan Death March

General Masaharu Homma (1887–1946) graduated from the Japanese Army Academy in 1907 and spent eight years in Britain as a military attaché. When Homma took command of the Japanese 14th Army in 1941, his first assignment was to invade the Philippines—a mission he executed successfully. Homma accepted the Americans' surrender at Bataan and ordered their evacuation, which became the Bataan Death March.

Among his men, Homma was known for encouraging his troops to respect the civilian population and for sometimes disagreeing with his official orders. He was forced to retire in 1943 when Japanese military authorities concluded he was not aggressive enough. After the war, Homma was tried and convicted by an American military tribunal for being responsible for the Bataan Death March. He was executed by firing squad in 1946.

▲ During the 1942 siege of Corregidor, the Malinta Tunnel was used by the Americans. It would not survive when the Allies returned in 1945.

▲ The main gate to Fort Santiago, part of the Intramuros district in the Philippines, was destroyed during the bombing campaigns. The fort's dungeons were used to hold prisoners, hundreds of whom died of suffocation or hunger, or were simply executed.

▲ A Filipino boy stood next to a sign posted by the Philippine-Japanese Volunteer Corps during the fight to retake the city.

# The Manila Massacre

THE MURDERS OF INNOCENT CIVILIANS BECAME ONE OF THE WORST INSTANCES OF WORLD WAR II BRUTALITY.

As the Americans approached Manila in February, the Japanese chose to leave little to residents or to Allied forces. Enemy troops razed buildings indiscriminately and destroyed most of the city's infrastructure. As soldiers rampaged through the capital's historic district, they dynamited or burned its famous churches, universities, and hospitals.

Even worse, the Japanese occupiers rounded up groups of Filipino civilians and summarily executed them. At De La Salle College, which was sheltering women, children, Catholic brothers, and a priest, Japanese soldiers shot or bayoneted everyone inside and threw the bodies into a pile. Of the 70 gathered there, only ten survived to tell of the

▲ Japanese soldiers were ordered to execute civilians who did not support the occupation or who provided assistance to Allied forces.

◀ The retreating Japanese bound and then killed countless Filipinos, both those who had been fighting with the Allies and innocent civilians.

horror. At Concordia College, where more than 2,000 women, children, and hospital patients had taken refuge, the Japanese chained the doors of the school and burned it to the ground. No one survived. Even people in the city's Red Cross Building were not safe. On February 10, Japanese soldiers entered the building and gunned down nurses, doctors, patients, and mothers with their newborns.

As American forces entered the city, they found piles of dead and mutilated bodies, many with hands tied behind their backs, in city streets and in buildings. In one of the city's plazas, soldiers came across dozens of bodies, mostly women and children, and in another location they found scores of people who had been shot or bayoneted and pushed into ditches. Entering a pockmarked building, U.S. troops found emaciated corpses stacked face-down in layers in a single room. From the bullet holes in their backs, it

appeared that enemy troops had shot them in successive groups as they faced the wall. On February 24, Americans opened steel doors to find a mass of 250 to 300 skeletal remains in a small, sealed room. The bodies showed signs of starvation. Estimates put the total number killed in the capital at more than 100,000.

The carnage was not limited to Manila. Those living in surrounding provinces experienced similar atrocities. In Calamba, about 35 miles south of the capital, Japanese troops killed 5,000 men, women, and children, and incinerated the town. Soldiers often blockaded civilians in rooms or buildings so they could not escape and either set fire to the structures or tossed in hand grenades.

Shortly after the war, an American military commission tried Yamashita and found him guilty of war crimes for the atrocities his troops committed. He was hanged at a prison camp in the Philippines on February 23, 1946.

### The Way of the Warrior

Like other marauding armies, the soldiers of the Imperial Japanese Army were brutal in their treatment of civilians, whom they raped, tortured, and murdered.

Historians have debated the roots of the violence. Some say that Japanese troops underwent harsh, cruel training. The average soldiers in turn may have treated non-Japanese with the same brutality with which their superiors treated them. In addition, a Japanese soldier was expected to fight to his death in the tradition of *bushido*, "the way of the warrior." The Japanese considered surrender and capture disgraceful and a shame on one's family, which is why many soldiers committed suicide rather than fall into Allied hands.

▲ Americans and Filipinos joined together to celebrate their liberation from the prison camp at Santo Tomas University where they had been held.

## Liberation

It took several more months, but on July 4, MacArthur declared that the Allies had liberated the Philippines. Not only did the announcement boost morale at home and throughout the Allied ranks in the Pacific, it also put the Japanese on notice that the war was coming to their shores. For many Japanese, it signaled that defeat was imminent.

The victory did not come without a cost: In this battle for the Philippines, the U.S. military lost nearly 14,000 men, and another 48,500 were wounded. Estimates of Japanese military and civilian deaths numbered around 250,000. Much of Manila had been leveled and its infrastructure destroyed.

For Filipinos, a major change was in the works. MacArthur made sure that responsibility for governing the islands was restored to local civilian leaders, and he promised that free elections would be held the following year.

▲ Philippine refugees and rescue workers walked the streets of Manila during the liberation, some trying to find safety and shelter, others trying to help the wounded.

◄ During the battle for Manila, the Japanese military was accused of mistreating prisoners of war, such as these two Americans.

# Moving On Toward Japan

THE ARMY AND NAVY DEBATED
THEIR NEXT MOVE IN THE PACIFIC.

As American military leaders considered the best way to continue across the Pacific toward Japan, rivalries between the U.S. Army and Navy resulted in two very different proposals.

Army tacticians pressed for an invasion of Formosa (present-day Taiwan) to be led by MacArthur. Navy planners preferred an invasion of Okinawa that would be directed by Admiral Chester Nimitz, commander of the U.S. naval forces. Ultimately, the navy won out, and orders were given to begin the assault at Iwo Jima.

Located about 700 miles south of Tokyo and some 4,000 miles from Pearl Harbor, Iwo Jima was a dot in the ocean, only eight square miles in area. In spite of its size, the island was strategically important to the Japanese, who relied on it as an early warning station for any movement against the homeland. It was also a prime site for Americans, whose long-range bombers could use the island to reach Japan easily. Should Iwo Jima's airfields fall into American hands, it would spell disaster for the Japanese.

The Japanese expected a full-scale assault because American bombers had been targeting Iwo Jima, and enemy troops had spent considerable resources fortifying their defenses. U.S. planners anticipated that the campaign would last no more than one week. Regardless of the outcome, both sides knew the confrontation would be costly.

▲ Marines readied their Corsair fighters for assaults on Japanese positions.

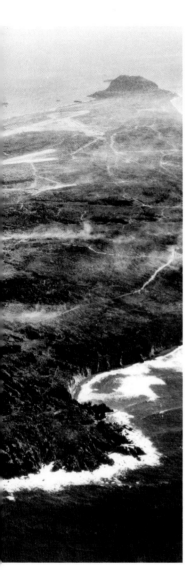

▲ This aerial view of Iwo Jima revealed a flotilla of American warships stationed just offshore.

◄ MacArthur and Admiral Chester Nimitz worked together to map out their joint strategy for the battles in the Pacific Theatre.

▲ American soldiers lived under battle conditions in camouflaged tents.

## Island Hopping

The vastness of the Pacific Ocean presented a challenge to the Allies. Hundreds of tiny islands that most people had never heard of dotted the region between Pearl Harbor and Japan, and it was impossible to capture all of them. Some were heavily fortified and defended; others had only small military forces and few defenses.

Beginning in the spring of 1942, and lasting until the end of the war, the Allied tactic in the Pacific was to attack only the islands that were of strategic importance—those they could use as supply bases and airfields. This approach, known as "island hopping," was simple and effective. It preserved men, ammunition, and equipment for more important battles.

# Digging In

THE JAPANESE EXCAVATED TUNNELS, BUILT ARTILLERY POSITIONS, AND MINED APPROACH ROUTES TO DEFEND IWO JIMA.

The Japanese had anticipated an attack on Iwo Jima as early as 1944, when the American island-hopping strategy had shrunk Japan's defensive perimeter considerably. They began increasing the number of military units on the island in March, and in May, Prime Minister Hideki Tojo assigned General Tadamichi Kuribayashi to defend Iwo Jima at all costs.

Kuribayashi arrived on Iwo Jima in June. The following month, he evacuated all civilians. Then, believing that the Americans could easily breach and destroy the Japanese beach emplacements, he pulled defensive positions away from the coast and moved them to the island's interior.

His strategy was to take advantage of the island's natural caves and rough, rocky terrain and battle the marines from underground positions. Beneath the soil of this volcanic island was porous rock that could be worked using hand tools. Kuribayashi ordered his 21,000 troops to build an extensive tunnel system connecting natural caves and bunkers. The laborious effort continued for several months. When completed, this complex maze measured about 11 miles long.

At the same time, Kuribayashi's forces also organized weaponry and equipment. The island's pumice-like rock, when crushed and mixed with

▲ There were 1,000 entrances to caves on Mount Suribachi alone, with an estimated 21,000 soldiers inside them. In addition to being stocked with ample supplies, the caves were well ventilated.

cement, made excellent material for constructing pillboxes, from which the island's defenders could rake incoming Americans with machine-gun fire and antitank rounds. The Japanese, fighting in a guerrilla-style war, camouflaged tanks and artillery,

and they planted mines on all the approach routes. They also stockpiled enough food to last several months and outfitted some caves as hospitals with medical supplies. The Japanese were well prepared for the long siege they expected.

▲ Japanese gun emplacements such as this one at the foot of Mount Suribachi were extremely difficult to capture, since many were connected to the network of caves.

▲ General Tadamichi Kuribayashi refused to allow his soldiers to conduct banzai charges, where concentrated waves of soldiers, facing certain death, rushed toward the enemy.

▶ Marines carefully surveyed the entry to one of Iwo Jima's heavily reinforced caves that harbored enemy soldiers. U.S. forces later demolished this dugout by aerial bombardment.

▲ Carrier-based Curtiss Helldiver aircraft bombed Iwo Jima in advance of the troop landings and continued bombing Japanese positions as the battle raged below. Each single-engine, two-seat plane carried 1,000 pounds of bombs. Over 7,000 Curtiss Hellcats were manufactured during the war, and these dive-bombers played a major combat role in the Pacific.

# The Assault Plan Took Shape

A COORDINATED PLAN CALLED FOR A FEROCIOUS BOMBARDMENT AND AN AGGRESSIVE INVASION.

In early February, to prepare for the ground assault, American forces increased the number and intensity of aerial bombardments and naval artillery attacks directed at Iwo Jima. They dropped volleys of napalm bombs, which incinerated the area where they fell but appeared not to faze the Japanese forces. According to Nimitz, no other island got as much "preliminary pounding."

By mid-February, more than 450 U.S. Navy ships were gathered off the island's coast. Military commanders launched the carefully planned assault with an amphibious landing on the eastern shore, where sea conditions were more favorable. From there, they directed marines to push across the island, move to isolate Mount Suribachi in the south, and capture the airfields in the north.

## FACES *of* WAR

### FEBRUARY 24, 1885–FEBRUARY 20, 1966

# CHESTER NIMITZ

*A master tactician and gifted leader, Nimitz guided navy forces to victory in the Pacific and represented the United States in accepting Japan's formal surrender.*

Fleet Admiral Chester Nimitz, who graduated from the United States Naval Academy in 1905, became a champion of underwater warfare during the early part of his career when he worked in the U.S. submarine fleet. He was a master of strategy, but he also was known as a soft-spoken team player and a man who led by example.

After the attack on Pearl Harbor, Nimitz was named commander in chief of the Pacific Fleet, and he immediately pressed his view that American forces should be on the offensive, taking the war to Japan.

At the Battle of the Coral Sea in May 1942 and the Battle of Midway in June 1942, Nimitz claimed early, important victories. Two years later, Nimitz was given the newly created rank of fleet admiral and put in charge of American naval forces as they moved through the Pacific, achieving one hard-fought victory after another. He worked well with his outspoken colleague, Douglas MacArthur. Together the two men had devised a plan to execute the "island-hopping" strategy.

On September 2, 1945, Nimitz participated in the official signing of Japan's surrender documents, which took place on his own flagship, the USS *Missouri*. In October 1945, he was honored with two parades attended by thousands, one along the national mall in Washington, D.C. and the other a ticker-tape parade in New York City. After the war, he continued to serve as chief of naval operations and argued for the development of nuclear-powered submarines as a key element of America's strategic defense.

> "Offensively, it is the function of the Navy to carry the war to the enemy so that it is not fought on U.S. soil."

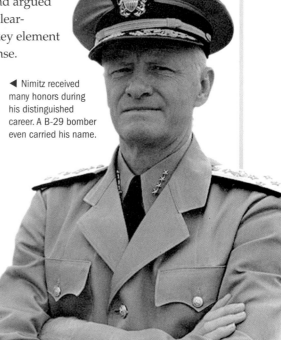

◄ Nimitz received many honors during his distinguished career. A B-29 bomber even carried his name.

▲ Just a few hours after the initial landing on Iwo Jima, troops began to unload the equipment they would need, including rations and medical supplies.

▲ A hospital ship waited offshore at Iwo Jima to treat injured soldiers. More than 7,000 Americans died in the fighting and 20,000 were wounded.

# Troops Come Ashore

THE MARINES STORMED THE BEACHES AND BATTLED THROUGH FIERCE RESISTANCE.

On the morning of February 19, the first wave of marines came ashore on Iwo Jima's eastern shores, where they met minimal sniper fire. Nevertheless, progress was slow. The coarse volcanic sand on the beaches made it difficult for the men to secure their footing. Once the marines marched into the open, they were accosted on the ground by Japanese shooting from their hidden bunkers and from above by artillery fire raining down from Mount Suribachi. The troops were only able to move inland when American tanks came ashore to provide cover.

The Japanese defensive plan was working as planned. When the marines attacked a bunker with a grenade or a flamethrower, the Japanese were able to slip away through their underground network of tunnels to another bunker or fortified position. As a result, marines were often hit by fire from bunkers they thought they had already destroyed. "You'd take a hill to find then the same enemy suddenly on your flank or rear. The Japanese were not on Iwo Jima. They were in it!" Colonel Thomas Fields remembered years later.

By the end of the first day of the invasion, 30,000 marines had come ashore and had progressed inland, but, with

◀ Fighting at Iwo Jima lasted more than a month, but five days into the struggle, U.S. servicemen triumphantly raised the American flag on Mount Suribachi. Of the men pictured here, only three survived the battle.

some units pinned down and taking heavy fire, over 2,000 men lost their lives in this initial battle.

### Old Glory Waves

On February 23, five days after the battle began, the Americans hoped that they had finally silenced the large artillery guns on Mount Suribachi. But they also suspected that Japanese forces were still hiding in the caves at the base and lower slopes of the mountain.

As morning dawned, ships, aircraft, and tanks provided covering fire for the marines, who fought their way through heavy enemy attacks to finally reach the top of Suribachi. Lieutenant Harold Schrier, the leader of one patrol, raised an American flag on a length of pipe he found at the summit. Later that day, five other marines and a naval corpsman raised a second, much larger flag, and an Associated Press photographer snapped the iconic image of the scene.

### The War-Bond Drive

Perhaps the most famous image of World War II is the photo taken by Joe Rosenthal of the Associated Press showing the marines raising the American flag over Mount Suribachi. Contrary to popular opinion, the flag raising was not staged. Rosenthal recorded the moment as it happened.

The photo was quickly transmitted around the world and reproduced in many U.S. newspapers. Pictured in the photo were Corporal Harlon Block; Navy Pharmacist's Mate John Bradley; Corporal Rene Gagnon; Private First Class Franklin Sousley; Sergeant Michael Strank; and Corporal Ira Hayes.

Roosevelt saw Rosenthal's photo and had an idea. At the time, the U.S. government was selling its seventh round of war bonds to help defray the cost of the war. The president believed the photo would help boost sales. He asked that the men in the photo come home to help publicize the campaign.

Three of the six in the photo were killed before the battle ended. The other three, who became national heroes, did not want to leave their units but returned to the United States to tour the nation as part of the war-bond campaign. As many as 3.5 million posters featuring the image were printed, according to some estimates, and the six-week drive raised approximately $26 billion, more than any other previous sale.

▶ Posters for the seventh war-bond drive featured a likeness of the photo of the flag raising on Mount Suribachi.

"Among the men who fought on Iwo Jima, uncommon valor was a common virtue."

—Chester Nimitz

▲ The heroism of marines and sailors at Iwo Jima was honored by the awarding of 27 Medals of Honor, more than for any other battle in the war.

# Iwo Jima Captured

AMERICAN FORCES FINALLY OVERCAME JAPANESE DEFENSES TO SEIZE THE ISLAND.

Although Mount Suribachi was in the hands of the United States, fighting continued on the north end of the island where Japanese fortifications slowed American movement to a deadly crawl. It seemed that everywhere the marines turned, they were exposed to mines and snipers. What's more, the Japanese had begun to accurately predict where American infantry attacks would occur, enabling them to launch artillery fire before U.S. soldiers could take cover. The marines started to call the lethal path north "the meatgrinder."

The Americans had to change tactics. Instead of bombarding enemy positions to pave the way for assaults by the infantry, U.S. troops began to attack under cover of

◄ Only rubble remained of the Japanese artillery emplacements atop the 554-foot summit of Mount Suribachi, a cinder cone formed by volcanic activity.

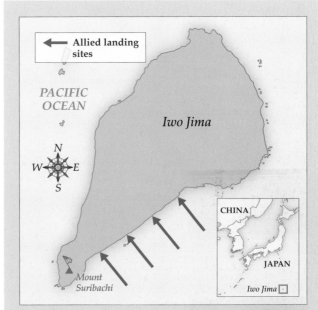

Allied landing sites

PACIFIC OCEAN

Iwo Jima

N
W · E
S

Mount Suribachi

CHINA

JAPAN

Iwo Jima ▢

**Iwo Jima**
This tiny volcanic island was the site of one of the deadliest Pacific battles, where marines fought their way onto southeast beaches against fierce enemy resistance.

▼ Medical staff such as this U.S. Navy flight nurse arrived on Iwo Jima's airstrip to help evacuate seriously wounded marines to hospitals.

darkness. The switch enabled the marines to turn the tide. By March 26, five weeks after first hitting the volcanic beaches, Allied forces declared Iwo Jima secure.

The battle became one of the bloodiest of Marine Corps history. It took nearly 7,000 American lives, and more than 20,000 were wounded. Of the roughly 20,000 Japanese soldiers defending Iwo Jima, only 216 were captured; the rest perished. When the battle was finally over, hospital ships filled with seriously wounded Americans sailed from Iwo Jima back to Guam and Saipan, while others were treated at hospitals that had been set up on the island.

▲ A marine dashed through enemy fire as he crossed "Death Valley" on Okinawa. The United States lost more than 125 men in this desolate ravine.

# Operation Iceberg

WITH MORE BATTLES TO FIGHT IN THE PACIFIC, THE ALLIES SET THEIR SIGHTS ON OKINAWA.

The Allied drive toward Japan continued with Operation Iceberg, an offensive to capture Okinawa, some 350 miles south of the Japanese home island of Kyushu. With its four airfields, Okinawa would serve as a perfect staging area for U.S. bombing runs against Japan's industrial heartland.

But the Japanese troops on Okinawa had prepared well, and their defensive tactics mirrored those they had used on Iwo Jima. Soldiers left the coastlines unprotected and instead hunkered down in concrete guardhouses, caves, and ancient castles.

The Japanese used psychological tactics as well. They conscripted the island's civilian population as reinforcements to convince the Allies that the assault would not be worth the loss of life. They also used propaganda to convince residents to fear the American "ogre-beasts," who, they were told, would surely abuse anyone taken prisoner.

The Japanese preparations, however, did them little good. On April 1, some 60,000 U.S. marines and soldiers stormed Okinawa. Within three weeks, the marines had captured the northern part of the island. In the south, it took a week for American ground forces to breach the first major line of defense. Then, on

April 19, the U.S. Navy launched its largest artillery bombardment in the Pacific Theatre.

## Attack and Counterattack

In May, the Japanese began a vicious counterattack, but they were overwhelmed by Allied firepower. U.S. Army troops captured a significant position in the east, and the marines captured Sugar Loaf Hill, a key position in the west. The battle for this small hill took the lives of 1,600 marines.

Late in the month, torrential monsoon rains turned much of the island into a swampy morass. Tanks, trucks, and troops became mired in the mud. Still, the marines persevered, and on May 22 they seized the capital city of Naha on the island's southwestern coast.

General Mitsuru Ushijima, the commander of Japanese forces in southern Okinawa, retreated to the Kiyan Peninsula on the island's southern tip, where the Japanese had stockpiled huge amounts of supplies and ammunition. By this time, Ushijima was losing 1,000 men a day, and he knew that he could not defend the position indefinitely, but he wanted the Americans to pay dearly to capture it.

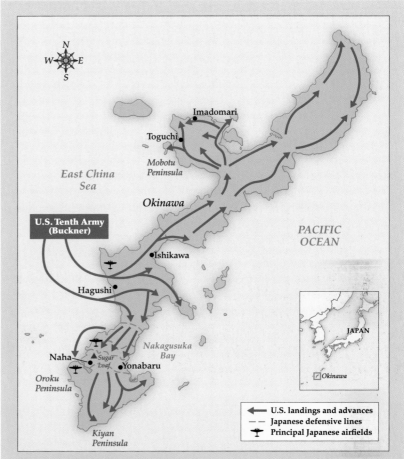

### Okinawa: 350 Miles to Japan

American troops overran the Japanese defenses in northern Okinawa by April 18. Resistance in the south was stronger, but U.S. soldiers finally overcame the retreating Japanese.

### Ice Cream, Anyone?

Americans love their ice cream, and the troops stationed in the hot, sticky climate of the Pacific yearned for it. One of the largest U.S. supply ships in the Pacific was the BRL—Barge, Refrigerated, Large—which served "fresh" frozen foods to troops weary of dry rations. The barge could keep 64 carloads of frozen meat and 500 tons of fresh produce almost indefinitely. But for the troops, one of the best features was the machine that could turn out about 1,500 gallons of ice cream an hour.

◀ Sailors aboard a U.S. Navy cruiser lined up at the ice cream counter.

# Okinawa Captured at Last

U.S. FORCES CRUSHED REMAINING JAPANESE
RESISTANCE AND SECURED THE ISLAND.

On June 4, the Sixth Marine Division launched an amphibious assault on the Oroku Peninsula, on the southern end of Okinawa, which housed a major enemy naval base. Of the 10,000 Japanese soldiers and sailors stationed at the base, roughly 4,000 retreated to the installation's subterranean headquarters. It would be their last stand. With the battle for Okinawa nearly over, all of the underground troops committed suicide.

American troops then advanced in a pincer movement to destroy the remaining Japanese defenses on the island. U.S. Army troops closed in from the east, and the marines pushed from the west. On June 18, as the Americans converged on the final Japanese position, shrapnel from an explosion struck Lieutenant General Simon Buckner, who had led the invasion, in the chest, killing him. Two days later, the U.S. Army Seventh Infantry Division reached the summit of Hill 89, where Ushijima had set up his headquarters in a cave.

The first attempt to reach Ushijima was unsuccessful because he had blocked the entrance to his underground chamber.

> "With a burning desire to destroy the arrogant enemy, the men in my command have fought the invaders for almost three months. We have failed to crush the enemy, despite our death-defying resistance, and now we are doomed."
>
> —Mitsuru Ushijima,
> June 16, 1945

▲ Very few Japanese chose surrender over death, but these three men were forced from their hiding place behind huge boulders and rubble.

▲ Japanese planes met a lacework of antiaircraft fire as they tried to attack marine forces stationed at the Yontan airfield on Okinawa. Several Corsair fighter airplanes were on the ground, waiting orders to join the night battle.

▲ U.S. Marines took cover and watched as their shells hit enemy targets on Okinawa.

▲ Iva Toguri, photographed in July 1945

## Iva Toguri: A Voice of Tokyo Rose

Most American GIs stationed in the Pacific knew "Tokyo Rose" as the sultry voice speaking American English on a Japanese radio show. That nickname, created by soldiers, applied to several women announcers who worked on the propaganda-driven program, but after the war, the U.S. government charged only one American woman, Iva Toguri (1916–2006), with treason for her role in the popular radio broadcast.

In July 1941, Toguri traveled from her home in Los Angeles, California, to Japan. When Japan attacked Pearl Harbor, it is unclear whether she was stranded or decided to stay in Japan.

In November 1943, Toguri became an announcer for Radio Tokyo broadcasts to U.S. troops. The English-language shows were supposed to undermine morale, though the programming, which included popular American music, may have actually raised spirits. It lasted until the end of the war.

The Federal Bureau of Investigation launched an inquiry into Toguri, and in September 1948 a grand jury indicted her for treason. She was brought to the United States, tried, found guilty, and sentenced to ten years in prison. Toguri was released after serving just over six years. President Gerald Ford, who believed that she had been wrongly accused and convicted, pardoned her in January 1977. Toguri died of natural causes at the age of 90.

▲ The conquest of Okinawa, only 350 miles from Japan, gave the Allies harbors, staging areas, and airfields essential to the planned invasion of Japan.

### The Final Clashes

Although a few pockets of resistance remained, the Americans claimed victory on June 22. As U.S. forces entered Ushijima's cave, the general and his chief of staff, General Isamu Chō, committed suicide. Just before he died, Chō wrote the following: "Our strategy, tactics, and techniques were all used to the utmost. We fought valiantly, but it was as nothing before the material strength of the enemy."

The Americans declared Okinawa secured on July 2, three months after the initial assault began. The Japanese lost more than 100,000, and more than 100,000 civilians—men, women, and children—who lived on Okinawa perished. Many of the civilians died when they served as human shields; others had been directed to commit suicide rather than fall into American hands. About 50,000 U.S. troops were killed, wounded, or missing.

## FACES *of* WAR

### AUGUST 3, 1900–APRIL 18, 1945

# ERNIE PYLE

*A buddy to the GIs he traveled and lived with, Ernie Pyle gained a reputation as one of the nation's most popular war correspondents for his reports about conditions on the battlefield and the lives of sailors and infantrymen. He also urged Congress to authorize extra pay to soldiers in combat, which they did in legislation that became known as "the Ernie Pyle bill."*

*"Ernie Pyle died today on Ie [Ie Shima] Island, just west of Okinawa, like so many of the doughboys he had written about. The nationally known war correspondent was killed . . . by Japanese machine-gun fire."*

So read the *New York Times* obituary announcing the death of one of the most famous newspaper correspondents of the war. Ernie Pyle told the stories of the average American soldiers, penning articles that not only described the battles the GIs fought but also chronicled their daily lives. Pyle,

who wrote for the Scripps Howard newspaper chain, won a Pulitzer Prize for his work.

Pyle operated from the front lines and followed American troops ashore during the invasion of Okinawa. On April 18, he had just moved to a front line to join troops who were advancing. Enemy machine-gun fire opened up, hitting him. The famed reporter was buried wearing his helmet alongside the soldiers he wrote about. Pyle was one of the few civilians killed during the war who received a Purple Heart.

▲ Ernie Pyle was buried wearing his helmet.

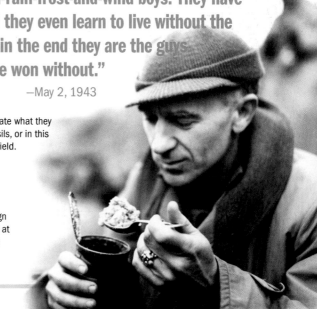

**"I love the infantry because they are the underdogs. They are the mud-rain-frost-and-wind boys. They have no comforts, and they even learn to live without the necessities. And in the end they are the guys that wars can't be won without."**

—May 2, 1943

▶ Pyle lived with the troops, ate what they ate, and used the same utensils, or in this case, cans, as the GIs in the field.

◀ Members of the 77th Infantry Division erected a sign honoring Pyle. The sign stood at the site where Pyle was killed while covering the division's actions on Ie Island.

"I firmly believe that the only way to swing the war in our favor is to resort to crash-dive attacks with our planes, there will be more than enough volunteers for this chance to save our country."

—Japanese Naval Captain Motoharu Okamura, June 1944

▲ In May, a Japanese kamikaze barely missed its target, the USS *Essex*, and crashed in the water alongside the ship.

# Divine Wind

WITH NOTHING LEFT TO LOSE, JAPANESE KAMIKAZE PILOTS TOOK AIM AT ALLIED SHIPS.

In the thirteenth century, a *kamikaze*, meaning "divine wind," saved Japan when hurricane force winds destroyed Kublai Khan's Mongol invasion fleet, preventing them from reaching Japan's shores. As the Japanese got deeper into the war, they hoped that another divine wind would save their nation. This time, suicidal pilots flying their airplanes directly into Allied warships would unleash the kamikaze.

The strategy emerged in the summer of 1944, at a time when the Imperial Japanese Naval Air Service had lost many, if not most, of its planes. The military division could not build replacement aircraft fast enough, and war planners had to devise a solution to make the most effective use of each remaining and new aircraft. The plan was to use kamikaze pilots in planes loaded with extra fuel and explosives.

The first successful kamikaze attack took place on October 25, 1944, when a Japanese aircraft crashed into the USS *St. Lo* during the Battle of Leyte

Gulf near the Philippines. The plane's bomb penetrated the ship's flight deck and exploded, causing a gasoline fire that rapidly engulfed the vessel. Thirty minutes later, in a billowing cloud of dark smoke, the *St. Lo* sank. The destruction of this American warship spawned a rapid increase in the use of these suicidal flights.

## Flying Bombs

By 1945, the Japanese had ramped up production of aircraft specifically designed for kamikaze missions. These planes were less complex, so they were easier and less expensive to build. Aviator safety was not a concern because these pilot-guided bombs would fly just one mission. Pilot training also became much simpler—pilots needed very little skill to fly directly into a target.

The Nakajima Ki-115 was one of the most popular kamikaze planes. Its undercarriage, made of wood and steel,

▲ Designed to fly one mission, Japanese kamikaze planes had only one flight to make, and pilots had just one goal: inflict as much damage as possible on their enemy.

came off after takeoff and could be used on another plane, since none would ever make a normal landing. The Nakajima carried one large bomb that the pilot could drop shortly before the aircraft hit its target. The resulting explosion was strong enough to split a warship in two.

▼ The wood used on Nakajima Ki-115 kamikaze planes made them hard to spot on radar, so antiaircraft gunners had only moments to fire after sighting them.

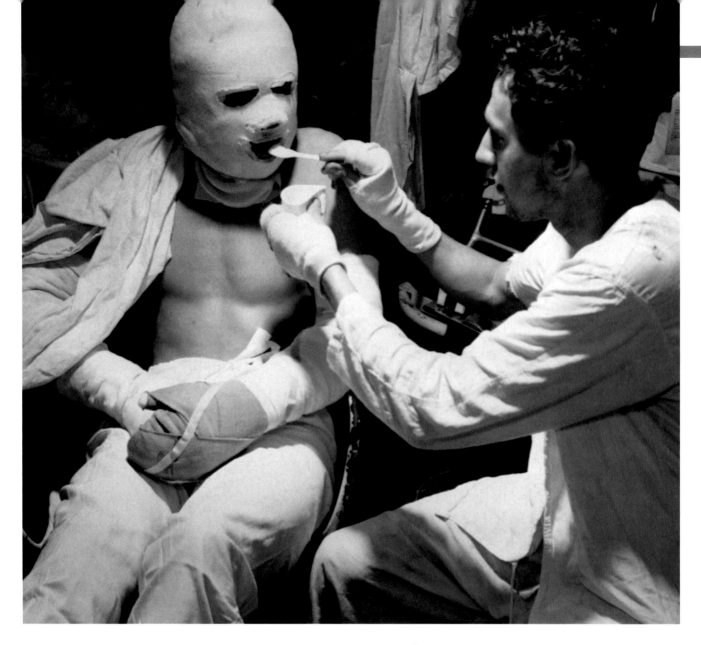

▲ Sailors aboard ships hit by kamikazes suffered horrendous burns, and survivors were sometimes transferred to hospital ships like the USS *Solace*, which provided medical care.

## Waves of Floating Chrysanthemums

On April 6, five days after the Americans invaded Okinawa, 230 Japanese kamikaze aircraft accompanied by more than 300 bombers targeted Allied ships surrounding the island. The planes sank six vessels and severely damaged several others. This was the beginning of the *kikusui*, or "floating chrysanthemum" attacks, where wave after wave of kamikaze planes nosedived toward American ships.

The next *kikusui* attack came on April 12, when several kamikaze pilots hit the USS *Mannert L. Abele*. Just one minute after this attack, a rocket-powered "Cherry Blossom" aircraft carrying a 2,600-pound warhead hit the *Abele* and exploded. The ship broke in two and quickly sank. Survivors gathered in the water and were strafed by enemy planes.

British carriers, with their armored flight decks, were more resistant to the *kikusui* attacks than their American counterparts, which had unreinforced decks. Almost all the Japanese planes and pilots perished during these attacks, and only 45 enemy aircraft took part in the tenth and final *kikusui* run on June 2 to 22. By this time, few kamikaze planes remained in the Japanese arsenal.

◄ The USS *Lindsey* was used as a minelayer and to provide support during the invasion of Iwo Jima and Okinawa. The ship was hit by two kamikaze planes at Okinawa; 60 sailors were killed and the *Lindsey*'s bow was destroyed.

## The Exploding Cherry Blossom

The Yokosuka MXY7, or Cherry Blossom, as the Japanese called it, was a single-seated, rocket-powered missile that doubled as a kamikaze aircraft. Most Yokosuka were carried and discharged by large bombers, though some were designed to be fired from submarines or shore installations.

When the pilot and the Cherry Blossom were released from the bomber, the pilot pointed his aircraft at the target ship and shifted to a deep dive. That way, he hoped to hit the boat even if he was raked by the enemy. During the dive, the aircraft could reach speeds of up to 600 mph. American sailors referred to the aircraft by the insulting term "*baka* bombs," *baka* being the Japanese word for "idiot."

◄ This "baka" bomb was captured on Okinawa. The explosive charge in the front weighed nearly one ton.

▲ A Curtiss Helldiver, an American dive-bomber aircraft, surveyed the *Yamato* as it burned.

# Operation Ten'ichigo

JAPAN ADDED ITS NAVAL FLEET
TO THE KAMIKAZE ATTACKS.

Earlier in the war, Japan had realized that it could not keep pace with shipbuilding in the United States and had ordered several vessels that could engage more than one enemy ship at a time. The result was the *Yamato* and its sister ship, the *Musashi*, among the most powerfully armed battleships ever constructed.

As 1945 unfolded, Japan's military knew that an American-led invasion of the home islands was imminent. With little left in their war arsenal, the Japanese commanders came up with a new strategy: They would mimic kamikaze missions, using naval ships instead of planes to attack the enemy fleet at Okinawa.

The undertaking was dubbed Operation Ten'ichigo. The *Yamato*, the larger of the two battleships, was chosen to execute the suicide mission and instructed to inflict as much damage as possible to the American ships with its massive guns. The commanders of the battleship and any surviving craft would then run aground and use their large guns as shore artillery.

On April 6, the *Yamato* and its escort of nine ships set sail from Japan. It carried just enough fuel for a one-way trip and

had no planes to provide protective air cover. Two U.S. submarines tracked the convoy almost as soon as it left port, and the U.S. Fifth Fleet prepared to intercept the Japanese armada.

The following day, some 270 miles north of Okinawa, U.S. carrier-based planes attacked the convoy. As waves of American dive-bombers and fighters pounded the Japanese fleet, they sank some of *Yamato*'s escort ships and damaged others. Within 15 minutes, they had also inflicted heavy damage on the *Yamato*. Repeated, coordinated strikes on the giant battleship caused it

to take on water, prompting it to list and capsize. According to most reports, ten torpedoes and five bombs hit the ship during the two-hour-long battle.

As the *Yamato* went under, its munitions supplies exploded. The sound of the enormous blast was heard more than 100 miles away. The ship's four remaining escorts, also badly damaged, rescued survivors and then withdrew from the area. Fewer than 300 of the crew of 3,300 aboard the *Yamato* survived. The Americans lost ten aircraft and 12 men in the short, fierce encounter.

▲ The *Yamato* weighed over 70,000 tons, had nine main battery guns that fired 3,200-pound shells, and the ship itself had heavy armor protection. Still, the Allies managed to sink her. Today, the ship still lies about 1,000 feet underwater in two main parts—the bow is separated from the midship and stern sections.

▲ The USS *Bunker Hill* played a major role in battles throughout the Pacific, but two kamikaze planes hit the aircraft carrier on May 11, killing 346 sailors. The ship did not sink and managed to limp back to Bremerton, Washington, for repairs.

# The USS *Bunker Hill*: Pacific Fleet Workhorse

A U.S. AIRCRAFT CARRIER SUFFERED ONE OF THE MOST SEVERE KAMIKAZE ATTACKS OF THE WAR.

The USS *Bunker Hill* was a mammoth ship "that carried the Pacific war to the Japanese," as one historian put it. It measured about 870 feet long, could move at a top speed of 33 knots, and carried a crew of 2,600 and nearly 100 aircraft. After seeing considerable action in the Pacific Theatre, the battleship sailed on for duty in Okinawa.

On May 11, as U.S. marines stormed the island's beaches, two Japanese suicide planes targeted the *Bunker Hill*. One aircraft dropped a 550-pound bomb on the flight deck and then crashed into several planes that were topside. The device sliced through the ship's deck and ended up in the ocean. The Japanese plane, which was loaded with fuel, ignited a raging fire, then skidded and somersaulted into the ocean. As U.S. sailors worked to douse the spreading flames, a second aircraft, piloted by 22-year-old ensign Kiyoshi Ogawa, dropped its bomb on the flight deck and then crashed into the vessel's superstructure where the plane exploded.

Sailor Albert Perdeck, who was on deck, completely lost his bearings. "When I finally made my way up the ladder toward the fantail, I stepped on someone. I said, 'What the hell are you doing? Get

▲ The fires on the *Bunker Hill* nearly destroyed it; the ship was out of comission for the rest of the war.

"**That smoke scared us to death. I thought I was going to die.**"

—Sailor Albert Perdeck, who survived the May 11 attack on the USS *Bunker Hill*

▲ Admiral William "Bull" Halsey, known for his calm demeanor, on the USS *Missouri*

up!' I couldn't think that he was dead . . . This is what's in my head."

It was the worst kamikaze attack of the war. It lasted just 30 seconds, but the damage was extensive. The ship managed to stay afloat, but almost 400 crew members lost their lives. Another 260 were injured.

Before his suicide mission, Ogawa wrote a last letter to his parents, telling them how proud he was to be a kamikaze pilot. "I truly believe that no one else has lived a happier life than me, and I am resolved to repay the Emperor and my father for your kindness. . . . I will go smiling, both on the day of my sortie and forever."

### Admiral William Halsey Jr.: Helming the USS *Missouri*

William Halsey Jr. (1882–1959), an intelligent and aggressive sailor, was one of the United States' most valuable assets in the Pacific Theatre.

After graduating from the U.S. Naval Academy in 1904, he served in various capacities in the navy, climbing to the rank of vice admiral in 1940, and in 1942, admiral. Halsey was en route to Hawaii aboard the aircraft carrier USS *Enterprise* when the Japanese attacked Pearl Harbor. In 1942, he became commander of the South Pacific Area.

Halsey's Seventh Fleet participated in the battles for the Philippines and Okinawa, inflicting major damage on the Japanese naval forces. He then led the U.S. Third Fleet through the final days of the war, destroying over 4,000 enemy aircraft and sinking more than 82 ships. The signing of Japan's surrender took place on his flagship, the USS *Missouri*.

# Japanese Soldiers and Sailors

JAPANESE RECRUITS TRAINED HARD AND FOUGHT WITH VALOR.

Japanese conscription during World War II applied to all able-bodied men between the ages of 17 and 40. When a man was drafted for military service, he was assigned a term pegged to the outcome of a physical exam. Training of the new recruits was harsh and included beatings and inadequate food rations. Salaries were low, with officers' earnings in 1941 dollars ranging from $200 a year (about $3,300 today) for second lieutenants to $1,500 a year (about $25,000 today) for generals. In contrast, a private in the U.S. Army earned $600 a year (about $9,900 today), and a master sergeant earned $1,600 a year (about $26,500 today). Soldiers might serve in the infantry, in tank divisions, with field artillery or engineer regiments, or as pilots giving air support to ground troops.

During the war, the Imperial Japanese Army quadrupled its divisions, with a quarter of the recruits assigned to national defense. Young men could choose to attend the Imperial Japanese Naval Academy, attaining commission as a midshipman after three or four years of study, or train as naval pilots in special aviation schools.

Regardless of their branch, every service member had to memorize

▲ A Japanese soldier's physical training included jogging, swimming, long-distance marches, and field exercises.

▲ When he finally came out of hiding to surrender, Onoda wore his 30-year-old army uniform and carried his sword.

### Hiroo Onoda: The War That Never Ended

Lieutenant Hiroo Onoda, an intelligence officer for the Imperial Japanese Army, was sent to Lubang Island in December 1944 to destroy the port and the airstrip on the small island. He was given one other order: "Never surrender."

When Allied soldiers arrived on the island in February 1945, Onoda and three other soldiers escaped into the jungle.

Seven months later, on September 2, 1945, Japan capitulated and World War II officially ended. But Onoda, hiding in the jungle, didn't hear the news. While the rest of the world, including the civilians on Lubang, celebrated the end of the war, Onoda continued to obey orders—for 30 more years.

Onoda finally emerged from the jungle in 1974, and when he did, he was feted in Japan as the ultimate warrior—the soldier who never surrendered. "I was fortunate that I could devote myself to my duty in my young and vigorous years," Onoda said. He lived in both Brazil, where he had a cattle ranch, and Japan, where he established a survival skills program for young people. Onoda died in Tokyo on January 16, 2014, at the age of 91.

the Imperial Rescript to Soldiers and Sailors. This lengthy document, first issued by the Japanese emperor in 1882, served as Japan's official military code of ethics. Its main concept was the requirement for absolute loyalty to the emperor, but it also advised military personnel to admire valor, be dutiful, avoid politics, be frugal, practice simplicity, and respect civilians. One of its well-known tenets was that "duty is heavier than a mountain; death is lighter than a feather."

> "We rely upon you as Our limbs and you look up to Us as your head. . . . The soldier and sailor should consider loyalty their essential duty."
>
> —[Japanese] Imperial Rescript to Soldiers and Sailors, 1882

These Japanese soldiers captured by the Chinese in Burma were blindfolded before being led away. Others were not so fortunate and died on the battlefield.

# The British Return to Burma

FACING ANOTHER DEADLY ONSLAUGHT, THE JAPANESE RETREATED IN SOUTHEAST ASIA.

Burma, rich in petroleum and strategically situated between China and India, had been a pawn in the Pacific since December 1941, when it was invaded by the Japanese. The country got caught up in maneuvering again in March 1944, when the British stationed forces along the border with India, leading the Japanese to use Burma to launch a preemptive strike against India. The initiative ended in defeat for the Japanese, costing 50,000 lives and more than 100,000 casualties. It also left Japanese forces in Burma undermanned and undersupplied, although fighting there continued.

After being named Supreme Allied Commander in Southeast Asia in 1943, Britain's Louis Mountbatten assumed the task of recapturing Burma, a former British colony, for the Allies. By October 1944, the British 14th Army had crossed the Chindwin River in northwest Burma, close to the border with India, and then pushed on into central Burma. The next Allied objective was the Burma Road. Japanese control of that strategic land route had forced the Allies to fly supplies into China.

## The Burma Road

The 717-mile Burma Road stretched from Lashio, a town near the center of Burma, to Kunming in southwest China. It was the major supply line linking northern portions of the country with China. In January 1945, the Allies wanted to retake the route as a strategic component of their invasion plan.

## Battle for Burma

Allied forces mounted attacks from the northern and eastern borders of India and finally reached Rangoon, Burma's capital.

### Lord Mountbatten: A Royal Commander

Louis Mountbatten (1900–1979), the fourth child of Prince Louis of Battenberg and Princess Victoria, the granddaughter of Queen Victoria, had several other royal relatives. He was a second cousin to King George VI, an uncle of Prince Philip, and a second cousin once removed to Queen Elizabeth II. When the war broke out, Mountbatten commanded a British destroyer, which German bombers sank in 1941 off the coast of Crete. He survived the attack, swam to shore, and managed the rescue of the ship's sailors. In October 1943, Mountbatten was named Supreme Allied Commander of Southeast Asia. There, he proved himself on the battlefield as a courageous soldier and a competent, charismatic commander.

In February, American soldiers fired a 77 mm howitzer at Japanese troops who were stationed along the Burma Road near the town of Namhkam in northeast Burma near the Chinese border. Removing the enemy opened up a major Allied supply route into the country.

As the Allies, led by Field Marshal Sir William Slim, and the British 14th Army advanced, they seized control of the road's terminus at Lashio. The maneuver allowed Slim to cut off the remaining Japanese supply lines and to proceed with the next phase of the takeover.

As a diversionary tactic, Slim sent one group of soldiers south toward Mandalay, the old royal capital in north-central Burma and the main Japanese base, while the rest of his troops followed a roundabout route to Meiktila, a town some 100 miles south of Mandalay that served as a Japanese communications center. On March 3, with Japanese forces fighting the troops heading toward Mandalay, Slim launched a surprise attack on Meiktila. His troops successfully held the city against several counterattacks, and on March 20, they also took Mandalay. Deprived of critical supply lines, the Japanese had little choice but to fall back some 350 miles to the city of Pegu (present-day Bago) near the southern tip of Burma.

▶ This section of the Burma Road in China was best known for its treacherous switchbacks up and down rough mountainsides.

▲ William Slim, Chief of the Imperial General Staff, was held in high regard by soldiers under his command.

## Sir William Slim: Retaking Burma

General William Slim (1891–1970) was born in England and served with British troops during World War I. He was badly wounded during the attack on Gallipoli, but after recovering was able to rejoin his old battalion. When Slim was wounded a second time, he went to India, then a British colony, to recover. In 1919, Slim transferred to the Indian Army and served in a series of military posts in both Britain and India.

In March 1942, Slim gained command of the Burma Corps, part of the Indian Army comprised of British and Indian troops responsible for defending Burma. The assignment was challenging, as the corps was in full retreat from the advancing Japanese at Rangoon. Slim brought the exhausted survivors to India. He had gained a reputation for boosting troop morale, and in May, as the commander of the new British 14th Army in India, he began preparing his troops to retake Burma.

During the next three years, Slim led his troops to several victories in the country. In 1945, "Uncle Bill," as he was fondly called, successfully led the recapture of Rangoon, and with it, Burma. Louis Mountbatten called Slim "the finest general World War II produced." Slim, who retired after the war, was appointed governor-general of Australia, a British colony, in 1953.

Indian forces included mounted Sikh cavalry who fought with British forces in Burma.

▲ Ghurkas, soldiers from Nepal, joined with British and Indian troops to free Burma from Japanese control. These paratroopers were boarding a plane to Rangoon, where they would drop behind enemy lines.

# On to the Capital, Rangoon

FACING A WEAK AND WAVERING ENEMY, THE ALLIES REGAINED BURMA.

The next major objective in the Burma campaign was to recapture the capital city of Rangoon in southern Burma from the Japanese. It was May, and monsoon season was approaching. Once the torrential rains came, it would be impossible to move troops and equipment, and the Allies knew they had to take the city quickly.

Slim ordered his men south toward Rangoon, some 330 miles from Mandalay, in two lines. One division from India entered the capital on May 1 and met little opposition. Nor could the Japanese send reinforcements to Burma; by this time, they were crippled with severely limited air and naval power. By May 2, Burma was in Allied hands.

▲ After Allied bombardment and Japanese defensive campaigns, Rangoon lay in ruins.

# THE USO BOOSTS MORALE

**A patriotic organization lifted the spirits of hundreds of thousands of U.S. soldiers, sailors, and airmen.**

The United Service Organization, or USO, formed in 1941 as a joint effort by several civilian organizations to lift the spirits of American troops by sending "camp shows" to U.S. forces in Europe, Africa, and the Pacific. The USO was presenting up to 700 shows a day worldwide by V-E Day. As American forces island-hopped across the Pacific toward Japan, USO troupes featuring movie and radio stars, dancers, and singers followed them and performed for battle-weary GIs and wounded soldiers.

Audiences from a dozen to several thousand gathered, at times in the scorching sun or hammering rain, and laughed at comedians and cheered for the performers. The effect on the troops was immediate, and the memories helped get them through the final months of the war.

During the summer of 1945, USO camp shows touring the South Pacific included one led by actor Eddie Bracken that visited military bases and hospitals on Guam and several other islands. Comedian Bob Hope led another USO troupe to locations such as the Solomon Islands. By way of thanks, the airmen stationed there named a B-24 aircraft "Bob's Hope," staying up all night to paint the name on the plane in time for Hope's arrival.

While touring on what was known as the "foxhole circuit," entertainers used whatever kind of stage they could find. Singer Bing Crosby once performed for the troops from the back of a truck. In addition to Crosby and Hope, other famous Americans who volunteered for these shows included the singing trio the Andrews Sisters, actresses Marilyn Monroe and Marlene Dietrich, actors Gary Cooper and Humphrey Bogart, and bands led by Glenn Miller and Duke Ellington.

Bob Hope once recalled, "I still remember fondly that first soldier audience. I looked at them, they laughed at me, and it was love at first sight." Even after the war's end, the USO sent almost 200 camp shows to those waiting to return home. And Bob Hope continued to perform for the troops for 50 years.

▲ Bob Hope entertained the troops abroad, usually with other entertainers such as singer Frances Langford, shown here.

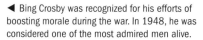
◄ Bing Crosby was recognized for his efforts of boosting morale during the war. In 1948, he was considered one of the most admired men alive.

"America means freedom and there's no expression of freedom quite so sincere as music."

—Glenn Miller

▲ In 1942, Bob Hope made his first overseas trip to entertain the troops, and in 1944 he logged over 30,000 miles, giving more than 150 performances. In 1997, Congress named him an honorary veteran for his services to the U.S. Armed Forces. He is the only person to have earned this honor.

▲ Hope and his troupe often visited wounded soldiers.

◄ Band leader Glenn Miller joined the army and then was transferred to the air force, where he formed the Army Air Force Band. He died in a plane crash while flying from Britain to Paris.

# 7 | TARGETING JAPAN'S HOMELAND

THE ALLIES UNITED IN THEIR GOAL TO FORCE THEIR LAST
WORLD WAR II ENEMY INTO UNCONDITIONAL SURRENDER.

American B-29 Superfortresses flew past Mount Fuji
in Japan during a bombing run to Tokyo.

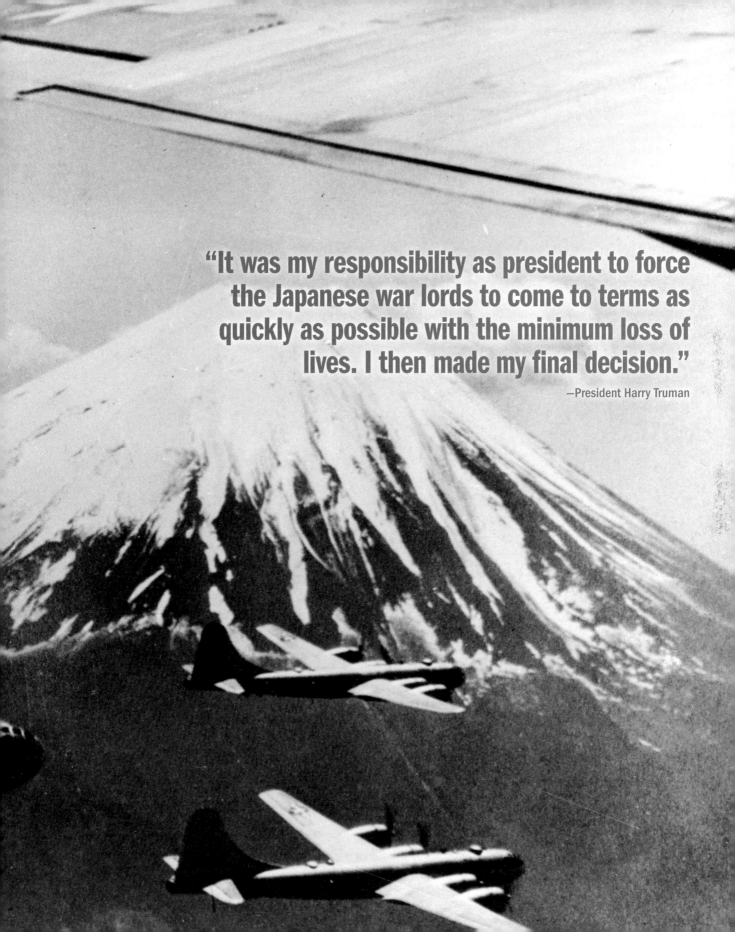

"It was my responsibility as president to force the Japanese war lords to come to terms as quickly as possible with the minimum loss of lives. I then made my final decision."

—President Harry Truman

▲ In a bombing raid on Kobe, 500 B-29s targeted the city's docks. Pilots continued their mission in spite of smoke that obscured their view.

# A Nation Under Siege

FOR THE FIRST TIME, ALLIED BOMBERS BROUGHT
THE WAR DIRECTLY TO THE JAPANESE HOMELAND.

As the Allies moved closer to Japan's home islands, they were fighting a desperate, battle-hardened foe. Although the Japanese war machine had faltered, its military forces had no intention of surrendering. The country's troops were crusading for the emperor, for their nation and culture, and for personal honor.

The Allies were equally determined to force Japan into unconditional surrender. By early 1945, the United States had enough air bases in range of Japan to make good on its promise to wage absolute warfare. In January, the military began a relentless bombing assault, targeting cities large and small on every island.

## Nagoya

With a population of about 1.5 million, Nagoya was one of Japan's largest cities. It was also home to the country's second-largest port and produced nearly half of the country's combat aircraft and airplane engines. On the night of January 3, the Allies initiated a firebombing campaign against the city that would continue for several months. The next strike came less than two weeks later when the Allies attacked Nagoya's Mitsubishi military plant, the largest manufacturing facility in the country and by some accounts, the second-largest factory site in the world. Even then, the Allies were not finished. The B-29s returned again in March, April, and May. In all, the aerial assaults and ensuing firestorms killed about 4,000 people, demolished over 100,000 buildings, and left nearly one-half million residents homeless. Over 40 percent of the city was completely leveled.

## Kobe

Like Nagoya, Kobe was a large industrial port and home to a large shipbuilding industry. With factories that produced steel, machinery,

▲ During the night bombing of Osaka on March 13, American B-29s dropped some 1,700 tons of explosives on the city. The fires from the burning wood-framed buildings could be seen for miles.

and ordnance, it was also central to Japan's war-making capability and thus a prime target for the Allies' bombing initiative.

During the first week of February, 70 B-29s flew over Kobe. They released bombs made with napalm, a chemical gasoline gel developed during the war that helped ignite structures on contact. These new weapons proved to be incredibly efficient; they created firestorms that destroyed wood homes, shops, and many other buildings in the city. A month later, the Allies struck again, this time in a far more deadly raid that obliterated a major shipyard and burned almost half of the city's factories, most of which produced war matériel. In addition, the fires severely damaged approximately one million houses, leaving most city residents homeless. About 500 American bombers returned to Kobe in May and again in June,

reducing what little remained of the metropolis to rubble.

### Osaka

On the night of March 13, more than 270 B-29s zeroed in on Osaka, a city of some three million people located southeast of Tokyo on Honshu, Japan's largest island. The three-and-a-half-hour assault, one of the deadliest of the war, targeted heavy industries, including shipbuilding, iron, steel, and ordnance factories. The low-flying, heavy planes dropped incendiary cluster and napalm bombs in densely populated residential areas, with horrendous results. Nearly 4,000 Japanese citizens lost their lives and another 700 were missing. The Americans returned to Osaka again in June, July, and on August 14, the last day of the war. All told, the raids killed about 10,000 Japanese residents and razed one-third of the city.

## Japan Weakens

The months leading up to Japan's surrender were marked by ferocious battles.

**1945**

**MAR**

**APR**

**MAY**

**JUN**

**JUL**

**AUG**

**SEPT**

**MARCH 9–10** American B-29s dropped napalm bombs on Tokyo, destroying 16 square miles of the city.

**JUNE 18** Military advisers briefed Truman on their plans to invade Japan.

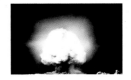

**JULY 16** The U.S. Army successfully tested the atomic bomb in New Mexico.
**JULY 26** The Allies issued the Potsdam Declaration.

**AUGUST 6** The *Enola Gay*, a specially modified B-29, dropped the atomic bomb over Hiroshima.
**AUGUST 8** The Soviet Union declared war on Japan.
**AUGUST 9** The United States hit Nagasaki with an atomic bomb.
**AUGUST 15** Emperor Hirohito announced that Japan would capitulate.

**SEPTEMBER 2** Japan formally and unconditionally surrendered to the Allies.

▲ Curtiss Hellcats played a major role in the bombing of Tokyo. This 1945 Japanese screen print captured the scene when as many as 1,000 Allied bombers operated together, dropping their payloads on the city.

# Devastating Tokyo

AMERICAN BOMBERS RAVAGED JAPAN'S CAPITAL. WHEN THEY FINISHED, LITTLE REMAINED.

Japan's capital, the home of its emperor and military leaders, was a natural target for the Allies. In the first attacks in February, over 2,000 American and Japanese airplanes engaged in a vicious dogfight that claimed about 500 Japanese planes and 80 American ones.

The battle resumed the following month. American general Curtis LeMay announced Operation Meetinghouse, or the Great Tokyo Air Raid, to his pilots, telling them: "You're going to deliver the biggest firecracker the Japanese have even seen."

Starting the night of March 9, some 300 B-29 warplanes began carpet-bombing Tokyo. The raid, which blanketed the city with nearly 2,000 tons of incendiary explosives, was catastrophic. It devastated about 16 square miles, killed or wounded an estimated 130,000 to 200,000 citizens, and destroyed more than 250,000 homes and buildings.

"The city was as bright as at sunrise; clouds of smoke, soot, even sparks driven by the storm, flew over it. That night we thought the whole of Tokyo was reduced to ashes."

—a Japanese newspaper writer, March 20, 1945

The residents had no way to defend themselves, and when masses of people tried to escape the inferno, there was no place to flee. In contrast, American losses were relatively light: The United States lost 14 bombers and 243 airmen.

The bombing runs continued. On April 3, B-29s struck an aircraft factory and the Tokyo suburbs. On the 13th, more than 300 U.S. planes targeted military facilities in the region, and two days later another 109 bombers pounded areas on the city's perimeter. On the 26th, more than 450 B-29s battered the region south of the Imperial Palace, an assault that the Americans repeated in May. Despite the devastation to the capital, the Japanese refused to come to the negotiating table.

### Allied Bombers Targeted Cities Throughout Japan

The Allies targeted not only large industrial cities but towns of every size, on every island in Japan. Cities along the coastlines were hit more frequently than those inland, but no town was out of reach, and few civilians would be spared the fear of the American B-29s that seemingly flew night and day unopposed.

Yutaka Akabane, a senior level Japanese civil servant who survived the war, later observed that "it was the raids on the medium and smaller cities which had the worst effect and really brought home to the people the experience of bombing and a demoralization of faith in the outcome of the war. . . . It was bad enough in so large a city as Tokyo, but much worse in the smaller cities, where most of the city would be wiped out. Through May and June the spirit of the people was crushed."

▲ A single B-29 bomber could carry 40 bombs, each weighing 5,000 pounds. Flying together, as they did during this daylight attack on Yokohama on May 29, 400 B-29s let loose hundreds of incendiary devices. Seven square miles of the city's industrial center were leveled.

### Curtis LeMay: A Blunt, Efficient Commander

U.S. general Curtis LeMay (1906–1990), who joined the U.S. Army Air Corps in 1928 and trained as a pilot, was known for his gruff, aggressive behavior on the battlefield. During World War II, LeMay flew several bombing runs over Germany and gained fame for his bravery in combat. In 1944, he was transferred to China and then to the Pacific, where he commanded a fleet of B-29 bombers. Following the example of European military leaders, LeMay masterminded the firebombing of key Japanese cities, a campaign that targeted civilians and killed about 330,000 Japanese. He argued that the bombing saved American lives in the long run because the Japanese would surrender before U.S. forces invaded the home islands.

◀ General Curtis LeMay led U.S. airmen in the bombing of cities throughout Japan.

"Killing Japanese didn't bother me very much at that time . . . I suppose if I had lost the war, I would have been tried as a war criminal. . . . But all war is immoral and if you let that bother you, you're not a good leader."

# THEN AND NOW

**JAPAN**

Tokyo

## TOKYO, JAPAN

*From ashes and rubble to a modern-day metropolis, Tokyo has rebuilt itself, and in terms of population has become one of the largest cities in the world. Its economy is also one of the strongest. Tokyo today is striving to become the "world's best city."*

The city of Tokyo, which was originally called Edo, was founded some 400 years ago. By the mid-1700s, the growing city boasted a population of about one million. In 1868, Tokyo was named Japan's capital and continued its amazing expansion; in 1940, the population surpassed six million.

Almost half of those citizens were killed or forced to move away during the war. By October 1945, the city's population numbered about 3.5 million. But out of the ruination left behind by 100 bombing raids, Tokyo slowly began to rebuild itself. With the help of U.S. occupying forces that remained in Japan until 1952, the city fostered new industries. The population also rebounded. By 1962, Tokyo had ten million residents. The expansion has continued: Today, more than 13 million people reside in the city center, and another 23 million live in the surrounding metropolitan area.

Tokyo has the world's busiest mass transit system, carrying over 3.2 billion people each year on 200 miles of track. The city's economy places it among the world's top ten powerhouses, and its stock exchange is the third largest in the world. Several million tourists visit the city each year. Some come to shop in the exclusive Ginza district, home to designer boutiques, upscale department stores, and restaurants and cafes. Kabukiza, the kabuki theater in this downtown district, is another draw, and its traditional facade is now topped with a towering skyscraper. Other visitors flock to the Akihabara district, a center for global electronics trade and technology. Akihabara is also home to a variety of shops dedicated to anime, manga, and retro video games.

◄ **THEN** Entire city blocks were leveled during the Allied air raids.

▼ **NOW** High-rise apartment buildings, skyscrapers, and a bullet train have filled the open spaces and created a modern downtown for the once-devastated city.

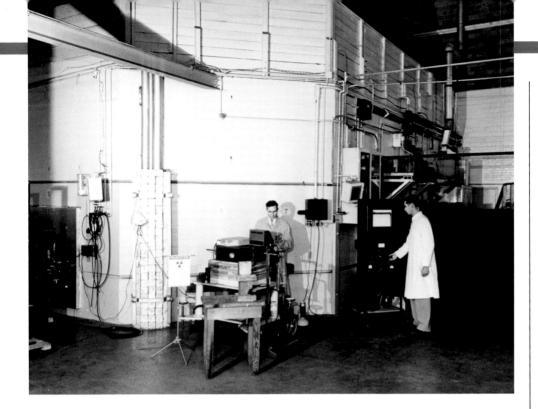

◄ This nuclear reactor, built under the stands of an old football field at the University of Chicago, is where physicist Enrico Fermi, one of the Manhattan Project's leaders, and his team produced the first controlled, self-sustaining nuclear chain reaction. Today, the site is a national historic landmark marked by a Henry Moore sculpture titled "Nuclear Energy."

# The Manhattan Project

THE UNITED STATES OPENED THE DOOR TO THE ATOMIC AGE.

In 1932, a group of British physicists succeeded in breaking atoms apart, a process called fission that produced energy. As word of the discovery spread, physicists in several countries began similar experiments on the atoms of different materials to see how the energy could be harnessed and if it might be used to create a weapon. In America, while war began to rage abroad, scientists were enlisted by the government in a top-secret effort to build the first bomb using the radioactive mineral uranium. Although President Franklin Roosevelt was initially skeptical, this secret program, code-named the Manhattan Project, was launched in 1939. Roosevelt decided that the United States had to compete with the Germans, who had a similar effort underway.

U.S. researchers were dispersed throughout the country, working at several universities and at different sites in New York City, including secret laboratories, warehouses that held uranium, and docks where stevedores offloaded ore. Scientists worked feverishly throughout 1940 and 1941 and made several key discoveries showing that a fission-based weapon was feasible. In January 1942, Roosevelt approved the development of an "atom bomb" that would eventually cost $1.9 billion, or $20 billion in today's dollars.

The Army Corps of Engineers, with over 100 years' experience in complex construction projects, was given responsibility for this new effort. In August 1942, the Corps established the Manhattan Engineer District (MED), the military team tasked with construction. In September, they chose Colonel Leslie Groves to run the operation, which would eventually employ about 130,000 people at several locations. Groves was quickly promoted to general.

### Los Alamos Scientific Laboratory

Located on a secluded mesa in northern New Mexico, about 30 miles northwest of Santa Fe, Los Alamos Scientific Laboratory was known as "site Y" during the war. Fences surrounded the secret research complex, and U.S. Army guards patrolled the site in jeeps and on horseback. Workers had to show their passes at the main gate in order to enter.

Lie detector tests were administered during the job application process, and all employees were sworn to secrecy: They could not tell their families or even other colleagues about their work. To ensure that secrecy prevailed, each person's mail was routinely screened. Only a few top people were privy to the big picture; most workers knew only their specific, assigned task.

Scientists, as well as their families, lived in the undisclosed community. The highly classified facility did not appear on any map. Numerous four-family apartment buildings quickly sprouted up to handle the influx of more than 5,000 residents, and a single post office box served as everyone's home address. Orders for a dozen baby bassinets to be delivered to the same address startled deliverymen: That single box number also appeared on the birth certificates of babies born there.

◀ Guards checked the passes and identification of all who went through the gate into the secret facility.

▲ Fermi traveled from his home in Italy to Stockholm to receive his Nobel Prize in 1938. He was accompanied by his wife Laura, who was Jewish, and their children. Afterward, the family did not return to Italy, where anti-Semitism was becoming rampant, but instead moved to the United States.

Groves's main job was to improve the coordination and efficiency among the various research groups and also to oversee the construction of massive and highly classified research facilities to be built at Oak Ridge, Tennessee; Hanford, Washington; and Los Alamos, New Mexico. In October 1942, on the recommendation of a military committee charged with selecting candidates, Groves named University of California, Berkeley, professor Robert Oppenheimer to head the Los Alamos facility, where the main weapons research would be conducted. Oppenheimer at 38 was a brilliant physicist and one of the few people who understood the potential power of atomic energy. He was already leading a research group analyzing the amount of fissionable material a bomb would require.

Oppenheimer recruited some of the top physicists in the world to come to the United States to help him develop the bomb. Among them were German-born Hans Bethe, who had emigrated to England in 1933 and gained recognition for discovering how stars produce energy, for which he would later win the Nobel Prize; Edward Teller, who was born in Hungary and had become a U.S. citizen,

▲ General Leslie Groves (left) and Robert Oppenheimer (right) had different management styles but worked on the Manhattan Project effectively. Groves was known to be intelligent and demanding, someone who stuck to his decisions. Oppenheimer was a charismatic, gifted leader, a theoretical physicist with little prior administrative experience.

▲ The former private boys' school in the foreground was the original building at Los Alamos. In 1947, the Atomic Energy Commission took ownership of the property, which sprawled across a mountain plateau, demolished many of the World War II–era buildings, and began building a modernized town.

and who was highly regarded for his studies of subatomic particles; and Italian-born Enrico Fermi, a naturalized American citizen who had won the 1938 Nobel Prize for his work on radioactive elements.

On December 2, 1942, as preparations at the Los Alamos laboratory began, a group of scientists led by Fermi used a reactor built on a squash court at the University of Chicago to demonstrate the world's first controlled nuclear chain reaction. The scientists observing the test broke out in a round of applause. The low level of energy it produced could not have powered a lightbulb, but it was a milestone that proved that an atomic bomb was possible and that the government's investment could bring victory. That day, Roosevelt received a coded message: "The Italian navigator has just landed in the new world."

## General Leslie Groves: Eye on the Bomb

Leslie Groves (1896–1970), who ran the military team tasked with building the atom bomb, was a practical, decisive manager who worked well with his colleagues. A 1918 graduate of West Point, Groves was commissioned by the Army Corps of Engineers during World War I and served in France. Over the next two decades, he held various posts of increasing responsibility in Washington, D.C., and in 1942, was named temporary brigadier general to oversee the Manhattan Project.

As head of the Manhattan Project, Groves decided the research directions to pursue, recruited staff, obtained materials and equipment, selected laboratory sites, and oversaw the construction of facilities. He had a good working relationship with the researchers, but noted the contrast between the military and scientific cultures, sometimes complaining that the scientists "preferred to move at a pipe-smoking academic pace."

Groves continued as chief of the Manhattan Project until 1946 and became chief of the Army's Special Weapons Project in 1947. He retired from the military the following year and joined the Sperry Rand Corporation, where he helped develop business uses for the UNIVAC computer until his retirement in 1961.

# BOMBERS: A KEY TO VICTORY

The United States produced massive, powerful bombers that battered Axis countries and helped turn the tide of war.

**B-24 Liberator**
Wingspan: 110 feet
Length: 68 feet
Engines: 1,200 horsepower
Ceiling: 28,000 feet

The military use of aircraft became widespread during World War I, when biplanes were used for reconnaissance missions and were also developed as fighters and bombers.

Early fighter planes were relatively lightweight. They were equipped with machine guns and built for maneuverability, which enabled them to engage in aerial combat and strafe enemy ground positions. Bombers were designed to carry heavy weapons and inflict serious damage on the ground, but their targeting technology was limited. The aircraft were unable to accurately pinpoint a mark, and instead, a two-man crew manually ejected single bombs as best they could. Bombers were relatively slow, weighed down by the onboard explosives, and they were vulnerable to enemy attack.

World War II triggered a rapid evolution in the design of combat aircraft. Bombers and fighters were produced rapidly to meet war needs, and numerous changes were made to improve them, even while manufacturing continued. America's first long-range bomber, the B-17 Fortress, was introduced in 1938; it went from design board to aerial flight testing in less than one year. This plane was soon followed by the B-24 Liberator and then the B-29 Superfortress. Unobstructed by geography or enemy troops, the new planes were faster and could reach altitudes unattainable by World War I–era aircraft. They delivered powerful explosives to level military and industrial sites and to destroy essential war resources.

## B-24 Liberator

The B-17, used by the British during the first years of the war, could travel at 287 mph and had a range of 2,000 miles. But designers of the B-24 Liberator, which went into production in 1941, made improvements: They extended the range by 100 miles, increased the weight of bombs the planes could carry to 8,000 pounds, and equipped the aircraft with ten defensive machine guns. The Liberator was used to carry out the more damaging air assaults on Germany and other Axis targets in Europe; its longer range and greater speed were also used to advantage in the Pacific.

Several American companies including Consolidated, Ford, and Douglas Aircraft produced the Liberator and struggled to keep up with demand. Sometimes, the flight crew even stayed at the factory so they could get used to the new plane as soon as it came off the production line. Nicknamed the "Flying Boxcar" due to its flat-sided fuselage, the B-24 Liberator became the most produced U.S. bomber during the war. In all, more than 18,000 B-24s were built; the plane was retired in 1945.

## B-29 Superfortress

The B-29 Superfortress, introduced in 1944 and designed to fly to Japan from air bases on Pacific islands, was larger and faster than the B-24. This new plane could fly 3,250 miles without refueling, could travel 357 mph, and it had more than double the bomb-carrying capacity of its predecessor—20,000 pounds. The bomber also contained pressurized crew areas and 12 remote-controlled machine guns. The sophisticated aircraft could fly above 30,000 feet, putting it out of reach of antiaircraft fire and most enemy fighters.

Huge formations of 300 or more B-29s carpet bombed Japanese cities, dropping payloads of conventional and incendiary bombs and causing greater devastation than ever seen before from air attacks. The planes also performed reconnaissance missions and dropped mines in Japanese harbors to disrupt enemy shipping. In all, almost 4,000 B-29s were produced during the war, and the planes remained in use until 1960.

The B-29s' most famous missions were delivering the Little Boy atomic bomb to Hiroshima and Fat Man, the weapon dropped on Nagasaki. Today, the *Enola Gay*, the B-29 Superfortress that dropped Little Boy, is on display at the Smithsonian Museum's Steven F. Udvar-Hazy Center in Chantilly, Virginia.

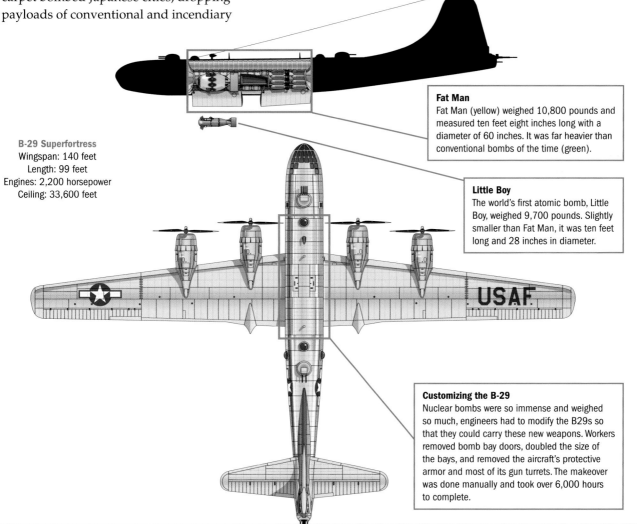

**B-29 Superfortress**
Wingspan: 140 feet
Length: 99 feet
Engines: 2,200 horsepower
Ceiling: 33,600 feet

**Fat Man**
Fat Man (yellow) weighed 10,800 pounds and measured ten feet eight inches long with a diameter of 60 inches. It was far heavier than conventional bombs of the time (green).

**Little Boy**
The world's first atomic bomb, Little Boy, weighed 9,700 pounds. Slightly smaller than Fat Man, it was ten feet long and 28 inches in diameter.

**Customizing the B-29**
Nuclear bombs were so immense and weighed so much, engineers had to modify the B29s so that they could carry these new weapons. Workers removed bomb bay doors, doubled the size of the bays, and removed the aircraft's protective armor and most of its gun turrets. The makeover was done manually and took over 6,000 hours to complete.

► In 1941, U.S. Secretary of War Henry Stimson (right) was appointed to the group who controlled the Manhattan Project. In that role, it was his job to report on the project to President Roosevelt, and following his death, to President Harry Truman (left).

# Destination Japan

PRESIDENT HARRY TRUMAN LEARNED OF THE BOMB AND DECIDED TO USE IT.

Upon taking office on April 12, President Harry Truman did not know about the Manhattan Project. Shortly after he was sworn in, however, Secretary of War Henry Stimson briefly mentioned the ongoing work, and two weeks later, Stimson and Groves gave Truman a full briefing. Truman agreed that the project, which was close to reaching a test detonation, should continue.

That same month, a committee, headed by Groves and composed of both Manhattan Project and Army Air Force representatives, began a series of meetings to determine the best drop sites for the bomb. On May 9 and 10, they decided on the criteria for selecting the target cities and identified Kyoto, Hiroshima, Yokohama, and Kokura, home of the Kokura Arsenal, a large military-industrial complex and one of the largest arsenals in Japan. In late May, the committee agreed on Kyoto, Hiroshima, and Niigata, and the plan was put in motion.

Truman reviewed the committee's plan and understood the consequences of using the new weapon, but he also considered other issues. He wanted to end the war in the Pacific quickly, with as little loss of life to American troops as possible. He wanted to show the Soviets that the United States would be the leading superpower after the war. Another factor was retribution: Truman was adamant that Japan would pay for its actions at Pearl Harbor. On July 25, Truman approved a directive issued by Stimson and General of the Army George Marshall, ordering the use of the "special bomb . . . as soon as weather will permit."

## FACES *of* WAR

### APRIL 22, 1904–FEBRUARY 18, 1967

# J. ROBERT OPPENHEIMER

*General Leslie Groves recruited the theoretical physicist to serve as director of the Los Alamos laboratory because of his deep understanding of atomic energy.*

In some ways, theoretical physicist J. Robert Oppenheimer was an odd choice to lead the research into the world's first atomic bomb at Los Alamos, New Mexico.

Born into a wealthy New York family, Oppenheimer had impeccable academic credentials, having attended Harvard University in Boston, Cambridge University in England, and Göttingen University in Germany. But as a young man, Oppenheimer, who was of Jewish descent, was disturbed by the rise of Nazism and its anti-Semitism. He contributed to anti-Fascist organizations and sided with the republicans in Spain, who represented workers and peasants. Oppenheimer also supported several left-leaning groups, including some associated with the Communist Party. Nevertheless, Groves, who recruited Oppenheimer, considered him a "genius" who understood the potential of atomic energy. In 1942, he handed Oppenheimer the reins to Los Alamos, where the physicist gathered brilliant colleagues, managed several thousand workers, and oversaw the successful Trinity test in 1945.

After the war, Oppenheimer was appointed chair of the U.S. Atomic Energy Commission. He advocated for international oversight of atomic energy and voiced his opposition to the development of the hydrogen bomb.

Hydrogen, or thermonuclear, bombs used extreme heat to fuse atoms instead of split them, and they were far more powerful than atomic bombs.

Because of his outspokenness and the growing anti-Communist sentiment in the country, the Atomic Energy Commission in 1953 revoked Oppenheimer's security clearance, shocking most of his scientific colleagues and casting a shadow on the rest of his career.

▲ Robert Oppenheimer, 1945

**"[W]e have made a thing, a most terrible weapon, that has altered abruptly and profoundly the nature of the world."** —January 1946

▲ In 1963, Oppenheimer (left) traveled to the White House where President Lyndon Johnson presented him with the Enrico Fermi Award. The prize is one of the most prestigious honors for work in science and technology, particularly for the development, use, and production of energy.

▲ Physicist Norris Bradbury, shown here, was in charge of assembling the nonnuclear components of the Trinity Gadget, the device created to test the atomic bomb. The Gadget could not be deployed as a weapon, and due to the secrecy issues, it was never called a bomb. Bradbury went on to serve as director of the Los Alamos National Lab, a post he held for 25 years.

▲ The Trinity nuclear test site and base camp in the Jornada del Muerto desert valley are surrounded by mountains. Today, both lie within the White Sands Missile Range and are open to the public only one day a year.

# Alamogordo

THE FIRST TEST OF A NUCLEAR BOMB TOOK PLACE AT A REMOTE DESERT SITE.

Researchers working at Los Alamos created two types of atomic weapons. One bomb contained uranium, a dense, heavy radioactive material and a source of concentrated energy, with a gun-type trigger mechanism to cause the explosion. Scientists code-named this device Little Boy. Only one uranium bomb was produced, due to the limited amount of weapons-grade uranium. Scientists were confident enough in its design that they did not test it. On July 14, 1945, they sent its components, some by ship and some by plane, to Tinian Island, where Little Boy would be assembled.

Researchers were less certain that the bomb code-named Fat Man would work. It contained plutonium, which had to be produced from uranium, and used a more complex method of implosion, or compression, to make it unstable and produce an explosion. Several plutonium-based bombs were already in production, and that was the type the researchers decided to test.

## The Trinity Test

The date for the plutonium bomb test, code-named Trinity, was set for July 16 at Alamogordo Bombing Range, about 200 miles south of Los Alamos. No one knew exactly what to expect when the bomb detonated. Some scientists thought the device, suspended from a 100-foot steel tower, might not explode at all. Others believed the radioactive fallout from the

The test tower, and every living thing within a mile of it, was incinerated during the blast. After the test, a Sherman tank lined with two inches of lead, needed to protect the men inside, was sent out to explore the site.

explosion would drizzle down on nearby population centers. Teams dispatched to local communities to measure radiation levels after the test were also prepared to evacuate residents if necessary.

In the predawn morning of July 16, about 20 people including Oppenheimer and a group of scientists crowded into three different observation bunkers covered with earth, each about five miles from the test site. Groves stationed himself farther out, at the base camp ten miles away. Other researchers were assigned to watch from different sites in case of an accident.

Then the countdown began. At exactly 5:30 AM, a blinding burst of light filled the dark sky. People saw the flash in the New Mexico cities of Albuquerque and Santa Fe; in El Paso, Texas; and as far as 200 miles away. The fireball became a mushroom-shaped cloud that rose more than 40,000 feet into the air. Seconds later,

a powerful shock wave and blast of heat shot out across the desert. The explosion vaporized the tower and formed a crater 1,200 feet wide.

Some witnesses reacted with elation and relief, exchanging congratulations and slaps on the back; others, with awed silence. Groves could not contain his excitement when he told Stimson: "At 0530, 16 July 1945, in a remote section of the Alamogordo Air Base, New Mexico, the first full-scale test was made of the implosion type atomic fission bomb. For the first time in history there was a nuclear explosion. And what an explosion!"

Others were less sure. "We knew the world would not be the same," Oppenheimer remembered later. "A few people laughed, a few people cried, most people were silent. I remembered the line from the Hindu scripture, the Bhagavad-Gita. . . . 'Now, I am become death, the destroyer of worlds.'"

▲ When Groves (right) and Oppenheimer (left) inspected the Trinity site, they found the melted tower base and the stumps of its legs. They also discovered that the intense heat from the blast had fused the sand around the tower into green, glasslike cinders.

▲ Although the test was kept a secret, residents of Albuquerque saw the bright light and felt the shock waves. Windows in Silver City, New Mexico, some 120 miles from the detonation site, were shattered by the blast.

▲ At Potsdam, Russian leader Joseph Stalin (left), Truman (center), and British prime minister Winston Churchill (right) frequently found themselves at odds, expressing differences that would lead to dissension after the war.

▲ At some of the Potsdam meetings, Stalin wore his full military uniform as marshal of the Soviet Union. During Potsdam, a new military rank was created just for the Russian leader, generalissimus of the Soviet Union. Stalin refused to sign the decree creating it, later stating that the Soviet army had only marshal as its highest rank.

# The Potsdam Conference

THE BIG THREE MET AGAIN TO DECIDE THE FATE OF THE POSTWAR WORLD.

The day after the Trinity test, the leaders of the Big Three nations met at Potsdam, a town just outside Berlin, to continue the planning begun at Yalta for a postwar Europe. The goals of organizing the administration of a defeated Germany, setting postwar borders in Europe, and determining war reparations took center stage.

Truman, Russian leader Joseph Stalin, and British prime minister Winston Churchill were joined by Clement Attlee, Britain's deputy prime minister and a Labour Party member of Churchill's Conservative Party's coalition government. He and Churchill were waiting for results of the recent British election, an unexpected development given Churchill's wartime popularity. When the results were announced on July 26, Attlee became prime minister, and Churchill left the conference.

Attlee, Truman, and Stalin each had different goals regarding reparations. Stalin was focused on the monies promised to the USSR at Yalta, which was half of the total amount available. Truman and U.S. secretary of state James Byrnes sought to avoid a replay of the end of World War I when the Treaty of Versailles required extremely high payments, or reparations, from Germany, ultimately sowing the seeds of World War II. Attlee agreed with the American position.

Though the USSR already controlled

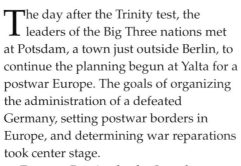

▲ Clement Attlee, Labour Party politician and British prime minister

## Clement Attlee: Labour Leader

Prime Minister Clement Attlee (1883–1967) brought great internal changes to his country and oversaw the independence of several former British colonies.

Though Attlee came from a prosperous middle-class family, as a lawyer early in his professional career, he began working and living in an impoverished area of London. This experience shifted Attlee's politics to the left, and he joined the Labour Party, gradually rising in the ranks, interrupted only by service in World War I.

Attlee became Labour Party leader in 1935, and in 1942, as part of Churchill's coalition government, he became deputy prime minister. As the end of war approached in 1945, Attlee and others in the Labour Party withdrew from the coalition government, and a general election was called. The party's campaign for broad social reforms appealed to voters and led to a surprising landslide victory. With a huge parliamentary edge, Attlee became prime minister on July 26.

During his six-year administration, Attlee fulfilled many Labour Party promises and oversaw the postwar rebuilding of Britain and Western Europe. His government created various social services, including the National Health Service, and nationalized several industries. It helped organize NATO, the North Atlantic Treaty Organization, to protect Western Europe. Attlee had long supported India's independence movement, and in 1947 his government granted the country its freedom, marking the beginning of a shift from the British Empire to the Commonwealth of Nations.

almost half of Germany and all of Poland, the Baltic states, Hungary, Bulgaria, and Romania, Stalin used the conference to push for an expanded sphere of influence in eastern Europe to serve as a defensive buffer along the USSR's western border. Britain and the United States in contrast sought to encourage new democratic governments. Attlee and Truman, representing Western democracies, felt a growing distrust of Stalin's intentions in eastern Europe, and both feared further Soviet expansion.

▲ The conference opened in a meeting room at the Cecilienhof Palace at Potsdam. Truman (his back to the camera), Churchill (upper left), Stalin (upper right), and their aides sat at a round table as they conferred.

▲ Truman (right) appointed James Byrnes (left) to serve as secretary of state on July 3. Shortly thereafter, the two men traveled together on board the USS *Augusta* to the Potsdam meeting. Byrnes also accompanied President Roosevelt to the conference at Yalta in February.

▼ Truman quickly scribbled this note to himself on the back of a conference photograph. In it, he summarized his July 24 meeting with Stalin. The president noted that during that discussion, he told the Russian leader about the new weapon but did not refer to it as an atomic bomb.

### Postwar Germany

During their meetings at Potsdam, the Allies debated but eventually came to an agreement on a handful of proposals. One of the key accords was that all aspects of German society were to be restructured. The country's military and paramilitary forces were to be disbanded, war criminals tried, and all Nazi-era laws repealed and replaced with new, more democratic measures. In addition, all authoritarian influences would be removed from the judicial and educational systems, and the involvement of political parties in local and state governments would be encouraged.

The Big Three agreed that Germany and its capital, Berlin, would be divided into four zones to be governed by the occupation armies of the United States, Britain, the USSR, and France. Each of the four nations would receive war reparations from its occupation zone.

### How to Handle Poland

Another problem facing the Big Three was the future of Poland. How to resolve issues involving that country remained a major source of disagreement for the USSR, Britain, and the United States. In exchange for territory that Poland had lost to the Soviets during the war, Poland was to receive territory in the western portion of the country that had been seized and occupied by the Nazis. During their meeting at Potsdam, the three leaders established Poland's provisional western border; the final demarcation was to be established at a later time.

### The Refugee Crisis

Another of the major difficulties facing the Allies was the refugee issue: The Poles had already begun deporting several million Germans from the western territory, and other eastern European countries were repatriating German citizens as well. The British and the Americans feared the refugees would overrun—and potentially destabilize—the Western occupation zones.

By the time the conference ended, the Allies had not taken any action on the refugee crisis, saying only "any transfers that take place should be effected in an orderly and humane manner." They also asked Poland, Czechoslovakia, and Hungary to temporarily halt any additional deportations.

### Truman's Secret Weapon

On July 16, the day before the conference began, Truman received word that the United States had successfully tested the world's first atomic bomb in the New Mexico desert. He also learned of the Manhattan Project scientists' forecast that within a few weeks, a second and then a third atomic bomb would be ready to use against Japan. Armed with this news, the president became more aggressive with Stalin and sought to push him on several different fronts.

On the evening of July 24, Truman

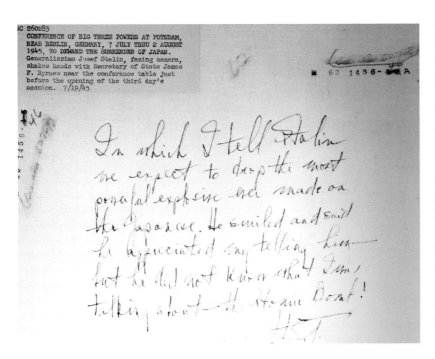

SC 260283
CONFERENCE OF BIG THREE POWERS AT POTSDAM, NEAR BERLIN, GERMANY, 7 JULY THRU 2 AUGUST 1945, TO DEMAND THE SURRENDER OF JAPAN. Generalissimo Josef Stalin, facing camera, shakes hands with Secretary of State James F. Byrnes near the conference table just before the opening of the third day's session. 7/19/45

took Stalin aside without an interpreter to tell the Soviet leader that "a new weapon of unusual destructive force" had been successfully tested, and the United States intended to make "good use of it against the Japanese."

Surprisingly, Stalin seemed unfazed and asked no questions about the weapon or the test, according to an account given by Truman to Churchill. The reason for Stalin's impassiveness would only become known later: Soviet intelligence had two spies working on the Manhattan Project. One of the men, Klaus Fuchs, was a German Communist refugee and British scientist. As part of the project's inner circle, he transmitted weapon design information. The second man, American physicist Theodore Hall, was a Communist who volunteered his services to the Soviets, although he did not supply them with as much information as Fuchs.

▶ The Potsdam Conference was held at the Cecilienhof Palace. Originally built for royalty, the buildings are now open to visitors.

## Harry Truman's Letters

First Lady Bess Truman did not accompany her husband to Potsdam, but the president wrote to her nearly every day of the conference. On July 18, 1945, Truman reported that:

". . . I've gotten what I came for—Stalin goes to war [against Japan] August 15 with no strings on it. He wanted a Chinese settlement [in return for entering the Pacific war, China would give Russia some land and other concessions]—and it is practically made—in a better form than I expected. [Chinese Foreign Minister] Soong did better than I asked him. I'll say that we'll end the war a year sooner now, and think of the kids who won't be killed! That is the important thing."

Then two days later, he sent her the following:

"I have to make it perfectly plain to them [Russia and Great Britain] at least once a day that so far as this President is concerned Santa Claus is dead and that my first interest is U.S.A., then I want the Jap war won and I want 'em both in it. Then I want peace—world peace and will do what can be done by us to get it."

◀ After his presidency ended in 1953, Truman retired to his hometown of Independence, Missouri, with his wife, Bess. There he enjoyed being "Mr. Citizen," as he said in his memoir.

### A Final Decree

Truman and the other Allies agreed to give the Japanese one final opportunity to end the war and signed the "Potsdam Declaration." Among other things, the decree called for the "prompt and utter destruction" of Japan if it did not immediately capitulate. The declaration also reminded the Japanese of what had happened in Germany: "The full application of our military power backed by our resolve, will mean the inevitable and complete destruction of the Japanese armed forces. . . . "

Finally, the Potsdam Declaration also described how the Allies would construct a "new order" in Japan, including meting out justice to war criminals and removing all obstacles to democracy. The declaration gave the broad outline of a new Japanese constitution that would guarantee the Japanese people such basic human rights as freedom of speech, freedom of religion, and universal suffrage.

### No Comment?

When reporters questioned Prime Minister Kantaro Suzuki about his government's response to the declaration, he gave an answer that created some confusion. Because the Japanese government had not yet responded to the ultimatum, Suzuki replied that he was withholding comment. He used the word *mokusatsu*, an ambiguous Japanese term related to the word for "silence."

When translated into English, however, *mokusatsu* has several meanings, and news services reported that the Japanese government considered the declaration "not worthy of comment." For their part, the Allies thought Japan had rejected the plan outright.

Suzuki later gave different versions of what he had meant. He first said he used *mokusatsu* to be a simple "no comment." He later said that the drafting of such a declaration by the Allies meant that "circumstances have arisen that force them [the Allies]" to end the war. "That is why they are talking about unconditional surrender. Precisely at a time like this, if we hold firm, then they will yield before we do. . . . [I]t is not necessary to stop fighting . . . I don't think there is any need to stop [the war]."

### Yoshijiro Umezu: Opposed Surrender

After a long military career, General Yoshijiro Umezu (1882–1949) became chief of the Imperial Japanese Army General Staff and a member of the Supreme War Council in 1944. When the country was expecting to be invaded by the Allies, Umezu advised against surrender, arguing that Japan would get better terms if it could inflict additional casualties on the enemy. In 1945, the emperor chose Umezu to be the military representative who signed Japan's surrender document. The general was tried after the war and sentenced to life in prison, where he died in 1949.

◀ Yoshijiro Umezu

### Soemu Toyoda: Naval Chief

Although Admiral Soemu Toyoda (1885–1957) originally opposed entering the war against the United States, once his nation entered combat he embraced

his role. By 1944, Toyoda was commander in chief of Japan's combined fleet, a member of the Supreme War Council, and aggressive in his strategies, many of which resulted in significant losses for the navy. During 1945, Toyoda argued against surrendering or even negotiating, believing that Japan should fight to the last man. In the final weeks of conflict, Toyoda was named navy chief of staff; he continued to argue against surrender even after both atomic bombs were dropped. After the war, Toyoda agreed never again to go into public service and was spared prosecution in the war trials.

◀ Former admiral Soemu Toyoda (right) received a ceremonial sword from Captain Ethelbert Watts (left) during the occupation of Japan.

## FACES *of* WAR

SEPTEMBER 21, 1867–OCTOBER 20, 1950

# HENRY STIMSON

*Stimson's public service career spanned more than three decades, and he served in the cabinets of four presidents. As secretary of war for President Truman, he recommended using the atomic bomb to help end the conflict.*

As the tragedies in Europe mounted following World War I, retired U.S. secretary of state Henry Stimson watched from the sidelines, observing in 1933 that the situation seemed "like the unfolding of a Greek tragedy, where we could see the march of events and know what ought to be done, but seemed to be powerless to prevent its marching to its grim conclusion."

It would be another seven years before Stimson, aged 73, would be asked by President Roosevelt to come out of retirement and join his administration as secretary of war.

The role turned out to be one of the most memorable in Stimson's impressive career, which included a law degree from Harvard, time as a U.S. attorney in New York State, a stint as secretary of war under President

William Taft, and as secretary of state under President Herbert Hoover.

Under Roosevelt, Stimson not only worked to bolster America's military readiness after the assault at Pearl Harbor, he was instrumental in developing the nation's war strategy after the Pearl Harbor attack. In 1941, Stimson became a member of the committee advising the president on the use of nuclear weapons; later, he was Truman's key adviser on the use of the atomic bomb and argued against the nuclear attacks on Japan. At the end of the war, Stimson retired again.

▲ Henry Stimson

**"My chief purpose was to end the war in victory with the least possible cost in the lives of the men in the armies which I had helped to raise."**

—February 1947

▶ In a ceremony held in the White House Rose Garden, Truman awarded Stimson the Distinguished Service Medal on September 21, 1945, his last day as secretary of war.

# Hiroshima

THE UNITED STATES DROPPED THE
WORLD'S FIRST NUCLEAR WEAPON.

Early on Monday morning, August 6, the *Enola Gay*, a B-29 Superfortress piloted by Colonel Paul Tibbets Jr., took off from the Japanese island of Tinian. The plane carried the uranium bomb Little Boy, which weighed 9,700 pounds and packed an explosive force of 15,000 tons of TNT. Six hours later, the *Enola Gay* was high over Hiroshima, the primary

target, and the weather was clear. The city was bustling with activity. People were on their way to work, and soldiers were assembled on a parade field.

At 8:15 AM, the *Enola Gay*'s bomb bay opened and Little Boy dropped from 31,000 feet. Tibbets immediately put the plane into a sharp turn to avoid the shock wave from the explosion. Some 43

◀ After the blast, Hiroshima was no longer recognizable as a city. The few buildings that survived directly beneath the explosion were made of reinforced concrete and did not collapse, but firestorms caused by the bomb gutted their interiors.

seconds later, the bomb detonated 1,900 feet above the center of Hiroshima. Even though the *Enola Gay* was already more than 11 miles away, the blast shook the plane forcefully. Tibbets and his crew looked back at the city. He later described the view: "The city was hidden by that awful cloud . . . boiling up, mushrooming, terrible and incredibly tall."

At ground zero, dust covered the city, and some 70,000 people died instantly. The explosion destroyed almost every house or building within a mile. Birds in the blast area burst into flames. Paper and other combustibles began burning, and many small fires combined into a firestorm that incinerated over four square miles of the metropolis.

**The Smell of Death**
On September 3, Wilson Hicks, the picture editor at LIFE, visited the devastated city. "We saw Hiroshima today—or what little is left of it," he wrote. "We were so shocked with what we saw that most of us felt like weeping; not out of sympathy for the Japs but because we were revolted by this new and terrible form of destruction. Compared to Hiroshima, Berlin, Hamburg and Cologne are practically untouched. . . . The sickly sweet smell of death is everywhere."

 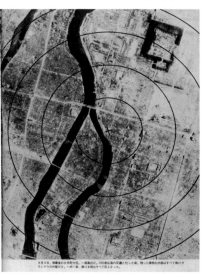

▲ Aerial photos taken before (left) and after (right) the atomic bomb was dropped on Hiroshima show the extensive destruction inflicted on much of the city.

Almost half of the population was dead, and nearly all who remained had serious injuries. All communications were gone, and the Japanese government was unsure of what had happened. It took many hours before relief groups arrived. It was estimated that by the end of the year, at least 30,000 more people died.

On August 9, Truman received a telegram from the Federal Council of the Churches of Christ in America objecting to the use of the bomb and its "indiscriminate destructive efforts." In his reply, the president referred to Japan's sneak attack on Pearl Harbor and stated, "When you have to deal with a beast you have to treat him as a beast."

▲ This massive airfield, home to several hundred B-29s, dominated the tiny island of Tinian.

### Tinian Airbase

The United States launched its atomic bomb attacks on Japan from Tinian, 1,500 miles south of Tokyo, an island the Allies had controlled since 1944. Tinian was also home to the largest airport in the world at the time. The Allies used the runways to launch attacks on the Philippines, Okinawa, and the Japanese home islands. On July 26, 1945, the cruiser *Indianapolis* delivered components of the atomic bomb called Little Boy that would be used to level Hiroshima.

# FACES *of* WAR

## AUGUST 1945

# HIROSHIMA EYEWITNESS

*Those who survived the atomic bombing of Hiroshima and Nagasaki are called the* hibakusha.

At daylight on August 6, Dr. Michihiko Hachiya lay on the floor of his Hiroshima home, recovering from a sleepless night working at the local hospital. Suddenly, a dazzling light exploded above him. Hachiya thought a magnesium flare, used to provide bright light, had ignited. Then he was plunged into darkness and a swirl of dust covered his house. The roof sagged and a support column tilted to one side. "Moving instinctively, I tried to escape, but rubble and fallen timbers barred the way," Hachiya wrote later in his diary. "All over the right side of my body I was cut and bleeding. A large splinter was protruding from a mangled wound in my thigh. . . . My cheek was torn. . . ." Hachiya and his wife managed to get out of their house. With many other injured and burned people, they slowly joined "the dismal parade" walking to a nearby hospital.

Hiroshima's transformation was so profound that it seemed like a hallucination. Hachiya and his wife passed burned and blackened bodies in the streets. The living, in shock and pain, walked like silent ghosts or with arms held out like scarecrows so their burned skin would not rub together. Nothing was left of the city; it had been flattened and looked like a burned field.

Hachiya wrote daily diary entries from August 6 to September 30,

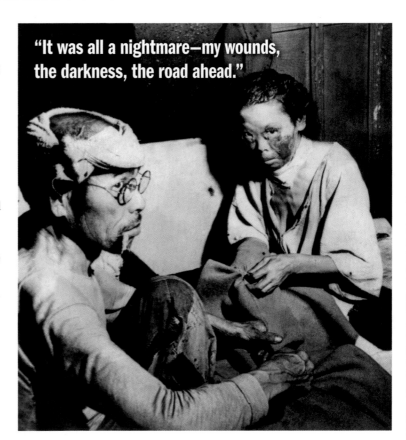

"It was all a nightmare—my wounds, the darkness, the road ahead."

▲ The stories and the images of the survivors were vivid, intense, and unique. Thermal burns and damage to lungs and eardrums, however, were common to all who outlived the blast.

recording his experiences and observations in a one-of-a-kind eyewitness account of the bomb's aftermath. It was published in Japan as a series in a medical magazine, and in 1955 it was translated and published in the United States as *Hiroshima Diary, the Journal of a Japanese Physician.*

"The hour was early; the morning still, warm, and beautiful."

# Official Notifications

THE UNITED STATES ANNOUNCED ITS
ACTIONS AND ITS PLANS TO BOTH THE
JAPANESE AND TO U.S. CITIZENS.

———————

This leaflet, translated into the Japanese language (shown below), was dropped on cities throughout Japan warning civilians about the atomic bomb. The text called attention to the devastation caused by the bomb that had devastated Hiroshima on August 6.

America asks that you take immediate heed of what we say on this leaflet.

We are in possession of the most destructive explosive ever devised by man. A single one of our newly developed atomic bombs is actually the equivalent in explosive power to what 2,000 of our giant B-29s can carry on a single mission. This awful fact is one for you to ponder and we solemnly assure you it is grimly accurate.

We have just begun to use this weapon against your homeland. If you still have any doubt, make inquiry as to what happened to Hiroshima when just one atomic bomb fell on that city.

Before using this bomb to destroy every resource of the military by which they are prolonging this useless war, we ask that you now petition the Emperor to end the war. Our president has outlined for you the thirteen consequences of an honorable surrender. We urge that you accept these consequences and begin the work of building a new, better and peace-loving Japan.

You should take steps now to cease military resistance. Otherwise, we shall resolutely employ this bomb and all our other superior weapons to promptly and forcefully end the war.

**EVACUATE YOUR CITIES.**

## The President Told the World That the United States Had Deployed an Atomic Bomb

In a radio address from the White House at 11:00 AM on August 6, Truman informed the nation that an atomic bomb had been detonated in Japan.

THE WHITE HOUSE
Washington D.C.

### STATEMENT BY THE PRESIDENT OF THE UNITED STATES

Sixteen hours ago an American airplane dropped one bomb on Hiroshima. . . . That bomb had more power than 20,000 tons of TNT. It had more than two thousand times the blast power of the British "Grand Slam" which is the largest bomb ever yet used in the history of warfare.

The Japanese began the war from the air at Pearl Harbor. They have been repaid many fold. And the end is not yet. With this bomb we have now added a new and revolutionary increase in destruction to supplement the growing power of our armed forces. . . .

It is an atomic bomb. It is a harnessing of the basic power of the universe. The force from which the sun draws its power has been loosed against those who brought war to the Far East.

Before 1939, it was the accepted belief of scientists that it was theoretically possible to release atomic energy. But no one knew any practical method of doing it. By 1942, however, we knew that the Germans were working feverishly to find a way to add atomic energy to the other engines of war with which they hoped to enslave the world. But they failed. We may be grateful to Providence that the Germans got the V-1's and V-2's late and in limited quantities and even more grateful that they did not get the atomic bomb at all. . . .

We are now prepared to obliterate more rapidly and completely every productive enterprise the Japanese have above ground in any city. We shall destroy their docks, their factories, and their communications. Let there be no mistake; we shall completely destroy Japan's power to make war. . . .

## FACES *of* WAR

### FEBRUARY 23, 1915–NOVEMBER 1, 2007

# PAUL TIBBETS

*The pilot who was chosen to drop the world's first atomic bomb completed the assignment flawlessly. He later said he was honored to have been chosen for the mission and was awarded the Distinguished Service Cross for the pioneering flight.*

Paul Tibbets never wavered in his belief that dropping the atomic bomb on Hiroshima was the right thing to do, even though the public later questioned the morality of the act and atomic warfare in general. "I was anxious to do it," Tibbets said unapologetically in a documentary that marked the fiftieth anniversary of the Hiroshima bombing. "I wanted to do everything that I could to subdue Japan. I wanted to kill the bastards. That was the attitude of the United States in those years."

Growing up, Tibbets was mesmerized by airplanes and flying. When he was 12, he took a ride in a barnstorming plane, one that toured small towns and rural areas offering flights for a fee. He was hooked. Though Tibbets's father, Paul Tibbets Sr., wanted his son to become a doctor, his mother, Enola Gay Haggard, encouraged the boy to pursue his dream to become a pilot.

In 1937, Tibbets joined the Army Air Corps. When the war started, he led a dozen B-17 Fortresses on the first American daylight raid on Nazi-occupied Europe. Later, the military chose him to command the B-29 unit and train the crews. After Hiroshima, Tibbets was awarded the Distinguished Service Cross, the second-highest award for valor in the Army Air Force. In 1959, he was named brigadier general.

Tibbets always supported the decision to use the bomb. An invasion, he said, would have been more disastrous. "I have been convinced that we saved more lives than we took. It would have been morally wrong if we'd have had that weapon and not used it and let a million more people die."

> "I saw nothing but a bunch of boiling debris with fire and smoke . . ."
> —August 4, 2000

▲ Paul Tibbets

▲ Tibbets named his B-29 after his mother because she had encouraged his desire to be a pilot. Tibbets later said she had been very pleased to be so honored.

> "I didn't bomb Pearl Harbor. I didn't start the war, but I was going to finish it."
> —2002

# Nagasaki

JAPAN'S EMPEROR FINALLY ACCEPTED
SURRENDER AFTER TWO CITIES WERE DEVASTATED.

On August 9 at 3:47 AM, a B-29 flown by Major Charles Sweeney departed from Tinian carrying the plutonium bomb called Fat Man. It weighed 10,800 pounds and packed an explosive punch of 21,000 tons of TNT, 40 percent greater than the power of Little Boy.

At first, war planners did not consider Nagasaki a primary target, even though it was a military port and major shipbuilding city. American planes had already bombed Nagasaki several times using conventional weapons. The next two cities on the target list were withdrawn—Kyoto due to its cultural and religious significance, and Niigata because it was too distant. Sweeney's primary target was Kokura Arsenal, but when his B-29 reached the area, a thick cloud cover prevented the crew from seeing the drop point.

Fuel was running low and antiaircraft fire threatened the plane. Sweeney set a new course for Nagasaki, his secondary target. Again, there was an overcast sky, but a break in the clouds allowed the bombardier to see the city's stadium and drop Fat Boy. At 11:02 AM, the bomb exploded 1,650 feet above Nagasaki.

The destruction was extensive. People within half a mile of ground zero died instantly, and most buildings within that area were completely destroyed. The blast flattened or damaged almost 90 percent of the city's homes. Numerous fires ignited, and water line breaks hampered firefighters. Estimates put immediate deaths at 40,000, with around 30,000 more within six months.

The next day, Emperor Hirohito directed his government to surrender.

"We had a job to do, a war to end."
—Charles Sweeney, November 30, 1998

▲ Military engineers carefully assembled Fat Man, the Nagasaki nuclear bomb, at the Tinian air base.

▲ A Buddhist statue sat amidst the rubble of Nagasaki. The Japanese legislature did not pass a reconstruction plan for the two cities until 1949.

JAPAN

Hiroshima

Nagasaki

# THEN AND NOW

## HIROSHIMA AND NAGASAKI, JAPAN

*These two communities have rebuilt from the ashes of nearly total devastation to become symbols of peace. Hiroshima today is an industrial center and busy port, while Nagasaki's economy centers around trade, fishing, and shipbuilding.*

The destruction wreaked on Hiroshima and Nagasaki was immeasurable. Some estimates put the death rate at Hiroshima at 150,000, and Nagasaki at 75,000. Hospitals, police stations, government agencies, and fire departments were all destroyed in the blasts, making record keeping difficult.

Today, both Nagasaki and Hiroshima have been rebuilt and are centers of peace. Each year, thousands of people gather at the respective blast sites to honor those who died. Particular attention has always been paid to the *hibakusha*, the people who survived the immediate impact of the blasts, but who over the years have suffered from the effects of radiation sickness, in addition to the loss of family and friends.

Nagasaki is home to colorful Zen temples and the Nagasaki Peace Park, which commemorates the atomic blast. At the center of the Peace Park are the Peace Statue and a black pillar that marks the explosion's epicenter. The city's rebirth has centered on foreign trade, shipbuilding, and fishing. Some of the rubble of the blast remains, serving as a stark reminder of war and peace.

Hiroshima also has a Peace Memorial Park, located in what was the heart of the city's commercial district. The park was built on an open field created by the explosion. Also standing are the skeletal ruins of the former Industrial Promotion Hall, a domed building that was closest to the targeted spot.

◄ **THEN** Only weeks after Hiroshima was leveled by the atomic bomb, an Allied war correspondent viewed the ruins of the Industrial Promotion Hall, where commercial expositions had been held. This area, about 175 yards from the explosion's epicenter, had been a vibrant commercial and residential section of the city.

► **NOW** The Atomic Bomb Dome, which is the renamed remains of the Industrial Promotion Hall, is a landmark in the Hiroshima Peace Memorial Park. The tranquil park contains several commemorative monuments and the Peace Memorial Museum. More than 300 cherry trees there attract many visitors in the spring to view the blossoms.

# 8 | V-J DAY

AMERICANS HAD BEEN FIGHTING A DETERMINED FOE FOR THREE AND A HALF YEARS. THE WAR WAS FINALLY OVER, AND IT WAS TIME TO CELEBRATE.

After Japan's surrender was announced, exuberant London crowds celebrated in Piccadilly Circus.

"This is the day we have been waiting for since Pearl Harbor. This is the day when Fascism finally dies, as we always knew it would."

—President Harry Truman, August 15, 1945

# Japan Considers Its Future

ALLIED OFFENSIVES IN THE PACIFIC FORCED JAPAN INTO NEGOTIATIONS.

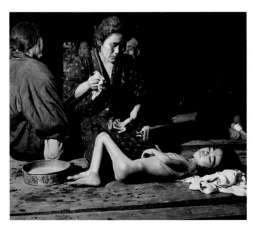

▼ A Japanese mother bathed her ill, malnourished child. Near the end of the war, Japanese civilians suffered widespread food shortages.

After a string of military losses in the Pacific and Southeast Asia, many Japanese leaders understood that surrender was inevitable. The nation lacked vital raw materials, its navy and air force were crippled, and its people had little food. Anticipating defeat at the hands of the Allies, the Japanese hoped the Soviets would help them end the war with terms as favorable as possible, and the government began secret communications with the USSR. In April and May, Japan also worked through emissaries from the neutral countries of Sweden and Portugal to learn what peace terms the Allies might offer, while making it clear that the American insistence on unconditional surrender was unacceptable.

In June and July, the United States began to intercept Japanese messages indicating that the Japanese position was softening and that some in the government were advocating a negotiated truce. Yet even as U.S. bombers pounded Japan's cities into rubble and crushed its industries, Emperor Hirohito refused to recognize that Japan's quest for an empire was coming to an end.

## A Nation Seeks an End to the War

Hardship ruled Japan's home islands as the Allied troops closed in. But even as Japanese leaders reached out to negotiate peace terms, the country defied the Allied order to surrender. After Nagasaki and Hiroshima were hit with atom bombs, the emperor finally conceded defeat, ending the war in the Pacific.

**MARCH** Japan began to move troops from Manchuria to defend the home islands and fight in the Pacific Theatre.

**APRIL 5** The Soviet Union informed Japan that it would not renew the Soviet–Japanese Neutrality Pact.

**JUNE** Japanese officials approached the Soviets, asking them to negotiate a peace settlement favorable to Japan.

**MARCH** • • • • • • **APRIL** • • • • • • • **MAY** • • • • •

▲ Japanese families struggled to find shelter amid the rubble of bombed-out cities.

**JULY 24** The Soviet Union brought its embassy staff and families stationed in Japan home.

▲ **JULY 26** The United States, Britain, and China issued the Potsdam Declaration, ordering Japan's unconditional surrender.

**AUGUST 6** The United States dropped an atomic bomb on Hiroshima.

**AUGUST 8** The Soviet Union declared war on Japan.

**AUGUST 9** The United States dropped an atomic bomb on Nagasaki. Soviet forces invaded Japanese-occupied Manchuria.

**AUGUST 14** Japan surrendered unconditionally.

**AUGUST 15** The Allies announced V-J Day.

**AUGUST 18** Soviet forces landed in Korea, Sakhalin, and the Kuril Islands.

▲ **AUGUST 29** U.S. troops landed in Japan, ready to begin the occupation.

**SEPTEMBER 2** Officials from Japan and the Allies signed the formal surrender agreement ending the war.

**JUNE** · · · · · · **JULY** · · · · · · · · **AUGUST** · · · · · · · **SEPTEMBER**

▲ After the Soviets declared war on Japan, Red Army tanks moved across the Greater Khingan mountain range in an invasion of Manchuria dubbed Operation August Storm.

# The Soviets Declare War on Japan

THE USSR ATTACKED MANCHURIA, KOREA, AND THE NORTHERN JAPANESE ISLANDS.

Even though the USSR and Japan had signed a neutrality pact in 1941, Russian premier Joseph Stalin had agreed at the Yalta Conference in February 1945 that the Soviets would enter the war against Japan. In exchange, Stalin asked that the USSR be able to expand its influence in Manchuria, a Japanese-occupied area in northeast China that had been a source of conflict between Russia and Japan for decades.

When a victory in Europe was within reach, Stalin kept his promise. On August 8, 1945, the Soviets revoked their neutrality pact and declared war on Japan. The next day, over one and a half million Russian troops launched a strategic offensive and invaded Manchuria from three directions—east, west, and north.

The assault surprised the outnumbered and poorly equipped Japanese occupation forces, but they tried to hold their ground. Their task was especially difficult because many troops had been recalled from Manchuria to Japan in order to protect the home islands. Many of the remaining 600,000 soldiers had limited, if any, battlefield experience.

▲ Soviet forces assembled Japanese prisoners of war at Tungliao railroad station in southwestern Manchuria for transport to confinement facilities.

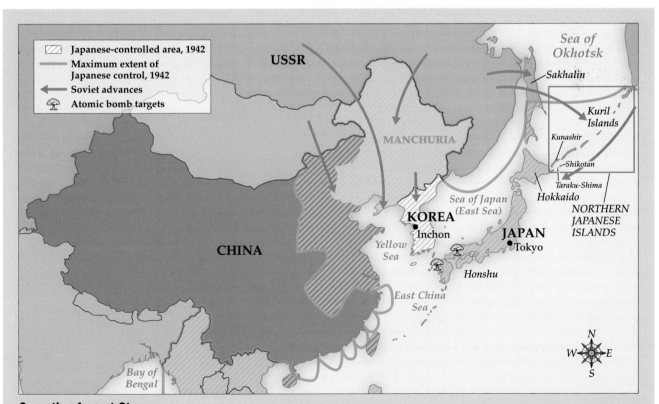

## Operation August Storm

Soviet forces commenced a three-pronged attack into Japanese-controlled Manchuria on August 9, 1945. Air support bolstered their ground troops' efforts, causing the collapse of Japanese resistance. The Soviets continued the campaign for postwar political gains after Japan communicated its acceptance of the surrender terms.

▶ During the war, Emperor Hirohito met regularly with his military advisers to discuss the latest information on campaigns and planned actions.

### Hirohito Acknowledges Defeat

Late on the night of August 9, the beleaguered Emperor Hirohito attended an Imperial Conference, a special joint meeting of the Supreme Council for the Direction of War, the military arm of government, and the Japanese cabinet, the civilian arm. Their vote on whether to surrender or continue fighting ended in a tie, and in an unusual move, Hirohito added the deciding ballot. He agreed to support Prime Minister Kantaro Suzuki's proposal to accept the Potsdam Declaration, and at long last, ordered the surrender.

▼ Soviet motorized troops continued their advance across vast grasslands in Manchuria, quickly wresting control of the entire region from Japanese forces.

"Continuation of the war does not promise successful conclusion no matter from what angle the situation is considered," Hirohito said at the meeting. "Therefore I have decided . . . to order the conclusion of the war . . . I have decided to endure what is unendurable and to accept the terms of the Potsdam Declaration." On August 10, the Japanese government sent a formal declaration of surrender to the Allies, conditional upon the emperor remaining the head of state.

In spite of the surrender, Japanese troops stationed in the occupied region of Manchuria remained committed to fighting the Soviet invaders. The battles there continued another ten days until the Russians seized control of several Manchurian cities and captured the Manchurian emperor. By the time the Japanese on the ground received a cease-fire order, the Soviets had taken the territory they wanted.

The Russians continued their offensive, and on August 18, advance troops landed in northern Korea, in Sakhalin, and in Japan's northern Kuril Islands. Two days later, Soviet forces landed on several other nearby islands; but when Hirohito surrendered, Stalin abandoned plans to invade Hokkaido, Japan's northernmost island.

## FACES *of* WAR

**APRIL 29, 1901–JANUARY 7, 1989**

# EMPEROR HIROHITO

*Born into the imperial family of Japan, Hirohito began his rule as a divine emperor, witnessed his nation's crushing defeat, and was forced to become a constitutional monarch.*

Michinomiya Hirohito, the Japanese ruler who finally surrendered his country to the Allied forces, at times strained against the deeply traditional culture that believed the emperor had divine powers.

Born in Tokyo in 1901 to an ancient royal family, Hirohito became the first Japanese crown prince to travel beyond Japan's borders when he toured Europe in 1921. He later said that he especially enjoyed England, where he was free from the constraints imposed by the Japanese royal court; but when Hirohito tried to incorporate more informal activities into his home routine, he was censured by his elders. In 1926, he was installed as emperor, a role that gave him supreme authority over the nation.

Historians disagree about Hirohito's role in Japanese aggression during the 1930s and '40s. Some claim that he objected to Japan's alliance with the Axis powers and had doubts about war with the United States, but that he went along with the powerful militarists in the government. Others say that he helped plan Japan's military expansion, beginning with the invasion of Manchuria in 1931 and continuing until August 1945. What is not disputed is his decision to accept surrender when his council was divided between fighting to the death or acknowledging defeat.

When the postwar constitution was adopted, Japan became a constitutional monarchy. Stripped of his divine status, Hirohito lost most of his powers in government affairs. He moved away from some long-standing traditions of the royal family, such as keeping a distance from the Japanese people. He allowed journalists to write about his family and made public appearances. In 1971, Hirohito once again traveled abroad, touring Europe; in 1975, he flew to the United States for a state visit with President Gerald Ford. At his death in 1989, Hirohito had ruled Japan for 63 years, the longest reign of any of the country's monarchs.

▲ Michinomiya Hirohito, Japan's longest-reigning emperor

**"I made efforts to swallow tears and to protect the species of the Japanese nation."**

—Emperor Hirohito, September 9, 1945

◀ Emperor Hirohito inspected Japanese army troops while Japan was at war with China. In his rare public appearances, he usually wore a military uniform and rode a white horse.

▶ Following Japan's surrender, civilians in Nagasaki were better able to go about daily life using paths that had been cleared of debris.

# The United States Accepts the Surrender

### THE JAPANESE WERE STILL FIGHTING, BUT THE NATION HAD CONCEDED ITS LOSS.

On August 12, while the Japanese were still trying to defend themselves against Russian forces in the north, the United States accepted Japan's surrender. On the 14th, Japan communicated its official acceptance of the terms, including the fact that the emperor would only have a ceremonial role in the new government. That same day, American B-29s flew over Tokyo and dropped thousands of leaflets telling the Japanese people of the agreement.

The next day, Hirohito told his subjects in a radio broadcast that he had ordered the government to accept the Allied surrender terms. Reactions ranged from shock to utter disbelief. The majority of the Japanese had never heard the emperor's voice. For many, listening to the divine monarch as he announced surrender was a staggering, unthinkable development.

The Japanese military, which had held great power in the government, was divided in its response. One group of army officers attempted a coup. They invaded the Imperial Palace in an attempt to prevent the emperor's radio broadcast, but the leader's guards repelled the attack. Of those who accepted the situation out of loyalty to the emperor, many committed suicide. In the aftermath, the entire population was forced to embrace a national transformation.

---

### Hideki Tojo: Pearl Harbor Mastermind

General Hideki Tojo (1884–1948) was an accomplished military officer and statesman. At the end of World War I, he served for a short time as a military attaché in Berlin. When Japan decided to invade Manchuria in 1931 to gain access to minerals and other resources for Japanese industry, Tojo was named army chief of staff. He was named vice minister of war in 1938 and became prime minister in 1941.

An aggressive militarist, Tojo was responsible for the attack on Pearl Harbor, and afterward he led Japan's war efforts. In July 1944, Japanese leaders who expected defeat forced him to resign. After the war, the Allies held him accountable for Japanese aggression and for permitting the abuse of prisoners of war. He was hanged on December 23, 1948.

"[I]t is natural that I should bear entire responsibility for the war in general. . . . Now that the war has been lost, it is presumably necessary that I be judged so that the circumstances of the time can be clarified and the future peace of the world be assured."

▲ Kantaro Suzuki, 1944

## Kantaro Suzuki: A Strong Voice

Kantaro Suzuki (1867–1948), who served as prime minister of Japan from April to August 1945, is perhaps best remembered for confusion over his position on the July 26, 1945, Potsdam Declaration. But he also was a strong voice for a negotiated settlement with the Allies.

Suzuki's government career started in World War I when he was named vice minister of the Navy. During the 1920s and '30s, he served as the commander in chief of the combined fleet, then retired in 1937 and became a government adviser.

In 1944, when he was working as an adviser to Emperor Hirohito, Suzuki supported a negotiated peace with the United States. He continued to advocate that position, and when he was appointed prime minister in April 1945, he pushed for a settlement that did not include "unconditional surrender." His views antagonized militarists within the government and resulted in several unsuccessful attempts on his life.

After Japan surrendered, Suzuki resigned but continued as an adviser to the emperor. He cooperated with occupation forces to help ensure a smooth transition for his nation.

> "Merely on the basis of the B-29s alone I was convinced that Japan should sue for peace. . . . The cause was hopeless."
>
> —April 7, 1945

▲ Mitsumasa Yonai, 1940

> "It may be inappropriate to put it in this way, but the atomic bombs and the Soviet entry into the war are, in a sense, God's gifts. Now we can end the war without making it clear that we have to end the war because of the domestic situation."
>
> —August 12, 1945

## Mitsumasa Yonai: Assassination Target

Mitsumasa Yonai (1880–1948), an outspoken critic of an alliance with Germany, had one of the shortest terms as prime minister in Japan's history—from January to July 1940. The onetime admiral and navy minister clashed with military factions over his opposition to entering the war, and they ultimately forced him to resign. Yonai's positions also made him a target for assassination attempts. In 1945, he proposed seeking Soviet help for a negotiated peace, and as the war came to a close Yonai sided with those supporting surrender. After the war, he supervised the dissolution of the Japanese navy.

▶ Surrounded by officers and other military staff, General Douglas MacArthur (seated) signed the Japanese surrender document on Admiral Chester Nimitz's flagship, the USS *Missouri*.

# Surrender Ceremony in Tokyo Bay

JAPAN SIGNED THE OFFICIAL SURRENDER DOCUMENTS ABOARD THE USS *MISSOURI*.

**Surrender Souvenir**
Everyone on board the USS *Missouri* received a wallet-sized card certifying their presence at the "formal surrender of the Japanese Forces to the Allied Powers." The card carried the signatures of MacArthur, Nimitz, and Admiral William Halsey.

The Allies chose September 2 as the date for the formal surrender ceremony; the delay gave representatives from all of the Allied nations enough time to travel to Japan. On that overcast Sunday morning, more than 250 Allied warships joined the battleship USS *Missouri* in Tokyo Bay.

With the flags of Allied nations flying above the *Missouri*'s decks, Japanese representatives signed the Instrument of Surrender, which the U.S. War Department had prepared and President Harry Truman had approved. It consisted of only eight paragraphs, beginning with "We, acting by command of and in behalf of the Emperor of Japan . . ." The document further stated, "We hereby proclaim the unconditional surrender to the Allied Powers of the Japanese Imperial General Headquarters and of all Japanese armed forces and all armed forces under Japanese control wherever situated." Foreign Minister Mamoru Shigemitsu signed for the Japanese government, and General Yoshijiro Umezu signed for the armed forces.

General Douglas MacArthur, who had been appointed supreme commander of the Allies to head the occupation of Japan, inscribed his signature as the representative for the Allied powers. He then handed the first pen he used to General Jonathan Wainwright, MacArthur's replacement in the

> "Today the guns are silent, a great tragedy has ended, a great victory has been won, the skies no longer rain death, the seas bear only calmness, men everywhere walk upright in the sunlight, the entire world lies quietly at peace, the whole mission has been completed."
>
> —General Douglas MacArthur, September 2, 1945

<u>Translation.</u>

H I R O H I T O ,

By the Grace of Heaven, Emperor of Japan, seated on the Throne occupied by the same Dynasty changeless through ages eternal,

To all to whom these Presents shall come, Greeting!

We do hereby authorise Mamoru Shigemitsu, Zyosanmi, First Class of the Imperial Order of the Rising Sun to attach his signature by command and in behalf of Ourselves and Our Government unto the Instrument of Surrender which is required by the Supreme Commander for the Allied Powers to be signed.

In witness whereof, We have hereunto set Our signature and caused the Great Seal of the Empire to be affixed.

Given at Our Palace in Tōkyō, this first day of the ninth month of the twentieth year of Syōwa, being the two thousand six hundred and fifth year from the Accession of the Emperor Zinmu.

| Seal of the Empire |

Signed:  H I R O H I T O .

Countersigned:  Naruhiko-ō
Prime Minister

▲ This letter, signed by both Emperor Hirohito and Japan's Prime Minister Naruhiko Higashikuni, confirmed the country's surrender to the Allies.

▲ Mamoru Shigemitsu, minister for Foreign Affairs, served time in prison for his actions during the war.

## Mamoru Shigemitsu: Coming Full Circle

Mamoru Shigemitsu (1887–1957), Japan's minister of Foreign Affairs, signed the surrender documents for Japan aboard the USS *Missouri*. He had been a longtime government official, starting in 1911, and had held various embassy positions in Poland and Germany. He became Japan's minister to China in 1931 and later held the same posts in the USSR and Britain in the years before the war.

As minister of Foreign Affairs near the end of the war, Shigemitsu had urged Japanese officials to make concessions in order to achieve an earlier peace, but his efforts were unsuccessful. After the war, he was found guilty of war crimes and sentenced to seven years in prison.

In 1950, Shigemitsu was paroled, and he soon became active in Japanese politics. Four years later, he came full circle and once again served as minister of Foreign Affairs.

Philippines who had survived the Bataan Death March and spent over three years in a Japanese prison camp. Admiral Chester Nimitz then signed for the United States. Additional signers represented the other Allied nations—China, Britain, the USSR, Australia, Canada, France, the Netherlands, and New Zealand.

Both MacArthur and Nimitz made brief statements to honor the Allied dead and the sacrifices made by the living to achieve victory. Nimitz commented that "the long and bitter struggle, which Japan started so treacherously on the seventh of December, 1941," had come to an end. MacArthur summed up the desire of all who had survived those painful years when he said, "It is my earnest hope and indeed the hope of all mankind that from this solemn occasion a better world shall emerge out of the blood and carnage of the past." Immediately following the 20-minute ceremony, hundreds of U.S. Navy Corsairs and Hellcats flew in thunderous formation over the battleship, followed by a flyover by B-29 bombers.

# V-J Day Celebrations

FESTIVITIES AROUND THE WORLD MARKED THE END OF SIX YEARS OF WAR.

On August 14, an estimated two million New Yorkers gathered in Times Square, impatiently awaiting word of the war's end. The editors of the *New York Times* had promised to flash news of Japan's capitulation as soon as they received official notification, and the crowd fixed its gaze on the paper's news ticker. At 7:03 PM, the lightbulbs in the Times Square sign lit up: OFFICIAL— TRUMAN ANNOUNCES SURRENDER. The sound of the roar that exploded from the crowd was broadcast by radio networks set up for the event and the voices carried far beyond Times Square.

Americans from coast to coast expressed their relief and joy in celebrations that began as soon as the announcement was made. Men, women, and children poured into the streets, some shouting, some crying. From the windows, confetti, bits of paper, and even popcorn floated onto the throngs. People danced and exchanged both hugs and kisses. Thousands filled churches for prayers of thanks. Enlisted men at air bases, naval stations, and on ships at sea let off steam in impromptu parties. As beer flowed, laughter replaced the long months of tension and battle fatigue.

The United States, Britain, Australia, New Zealand, and several other countries declared a two-day holiday. Other nations named August 14 as V-J Day, but Truman later declared September 2, the date the surrender was signed, as Victory over Japan Day in the United States.

### American Cities Erupt in Revelry

"There were no strangers in New York yesterday," wrote one *New York Times* journalist. LIFE photographer Alfred Eisenstaedt's picture of a sailor kissing a nurse in New York's Times Square became an iconic image of the day. Confetti five inches deep covered the streets around the square, and in the garment district, workers created a colorful snowstorm when they threw cloth scraps onto the sidewalks and streets below.

In Washington, D.C., civilians, soldiers, and sailors spontaneously formed an exuberant conga line in Lafayette Square Park. Happy hordes gathered at the White House gates and chanted, "We want Harry!" The president eventually came out to greet them and said, "This is a great day for democracy."

▼ Celebrations continued late into the night after military personnel and civilians learned the Japanese government had accepted an unconditional surrender.

In Chicago, multitudes surged into the city's main thoroughfares, laughing, singing, and blowing party horns. A front-page newspaper photo showed an ocean of people waving flags and newspapers with the headline "It's Over." Exuberant throngs filled the boulevards of New Orleans, formed spontaneous parades, and people waved their hands forming the *V* for victory. Spectators said it was just like Mardi Gras, but one with a sense of incredible relief.

On the West Coast, servicemen and civilians in Los Angeles formed gleeful processions, and some climbed atop cars to ride through the streets. In San Francisco, GIs and civilians lit a bonfire on Market Street. Pent-up emotions ran high, and with the flow of alcohol came some raucous behavior. The city called up thousands of off-duty police, and the navy dispatched extra shore patrolmen to prevent property damage.

In Pearl Harbor, Hawaii, a military newspaper printed the banner headline "WE DID IT AGAIN!" That night, skies blazed, not from a sneak attack, but with celebratory star shells and flares normally used to illuminate battlefields. On this day, those flashes proclaimed victory.

▲ At Pearl Harbor, people gathered to commemorate those who lost their lives and to celebrate the hard-won victory.

◀ A sailor gave a very surprised nurse a kiss during one of the street celebrations in New York City.

▶ Crowds flocked to Queen Victoria's Monument in London for a glimpse of British Prime Minister Clement Attlee, who was en route to meet with the king.

### The British Commonwealth Marks the Victory

On a rainy August 15, masses of Londoners gathered in Piccadilly Circus to listen to the news of Japan's surrender. As the announcement was made, the crowd came to a standstill, then erupted in cheers and rejoicing. Office workers flung open windows to release fluttering paper bits onto the crowds.

Coincidentally, it was the start of a new session of Parliament, and thousands came out to see King George VI and the queen in a carriage that carried them to the opening ceremonies. Later, the entire royal family stepped out onto the balcony of Buckingham Palace to wave to their subjects, and princesses Elizabeth and Margaret walked among the people gathered outside. In a radio broadcast to the people of the British Commonwealth, the king summed up the mood, commenting, "Our hearts are full to overflowing, as are your own." That evening, floodlights beamed on historic buildings throughout London.

Elsewhere in the Commonwealth, jubilant crowds lit bonfires, danced, and set off fireworks. In Birmingham, England, more than 100,000 people watched a parade so large that it took an hour and a half to pass by. Children perched in windows and on tree branches for a better view of the proceedings. Men and women stood on roofs and on top of city bus shelters.

In Sydney, scores of Australians danced in the streets, kicking up their heels and waving flags to the sounds of honking horns. Across New Zealand, sirens sounded and factory whistles blew continuously as everyone swarmed into the avenues. Bands played for joyful dancers, while those who were watching scattered confetti.

▼ Military personnel and civilians alike joined in a victory march through Martin Place in the center of Sydney, Australia.

## Europe Rejoices

Many of the American servicemen who were in Paris when the surrender was announced gathered on the square called Place de l'Opéra, eagerly reading the details in newspapers with the headline "Japan Capitulates." American GIs, officers, and members of the Women's Army Corps started a parade featuring jeeps, trucks, and hundreds of walkers. The throng moved snake-like through the city boulevards, sharing the news with cheers and shouts, and waving newspapers with the gigantic banner headline "PEACE."

## No One Was Forgotten

In Leyte Gulf, the U.S. Navy fleet marked the surrender with a grand flourish. Where Allied artillery fire had blasted the beach less than a year earlier, the ships lit up the night sky with a huge fireworks display. Later, when the navy liberated a POW camp near Yokohama, Japan, the starving prisoners marshaled enough energy to cheer and wave improvised flags of the United States, Great Britain, and the Netherlands.

Gradually the celebrations quieted, and the revelers returned to their homes. Thoughts of those who hadn't come home made the day bittersweet. People around the world had fought, worked, and sacrificed to win the war. They had endured hardships and privation, but the long struggle was finally over. As Truman acknowledged, the surrender marked a great day for democracy.

▲ Allied prisoners of war who had just been liberated from the Japanese Aomori internment camp near Yokohama waved flags to celebrate their release.

▲ Nearly 3,000 men lined the decks of the USS *Cristobal*, eager to return home and reunite with their families.

# Operation Magic Carpet in the Pacific

HUNDREDS OF SHIPS BEGAN BRINGING THE BOYS HOME.

On October 1, the United States organized a massive effort dubbed Operation Magic Carpet to repatriate soldiers, sailors, and airmen from the Pacific Theatre, even while the task of bringing back troops from Europe continued. The navy used battleships, aircraft carriers, and assault transports that originally had moved landing crafts for amphibious assaults. The vessels had to be quickly converted for this new function. Aircraft carrier crews installed three- to five-tiered bunks on hangar decks to make room for thousands of servicemen. In some cases, hundreds of folding cots that stood nearly edge to edge covered the hangar deck.

In six months, the Magic Carpet fleet transported 1.3 million men from the Pacific to the United States. Activity peaked in December, when almost 700,000 troops returned home. The operation ended in April 1946, after bringing more than eight million Americans home from Europe, Asia, and the Pacific.

▶ Military personnel who had served in the China-Burma-India campaign cheered as their homeward-bound ship, the USS *A. W. Greely*, pulled into a dock in New York City in late September.

61ST RAILWAY OP'NG. CO.

14TH AIR FORCE
10TH AIR FORCE
1st 2ND AIR Commando SQUADRONS

A.T.C.
A.A.C.S.
Mars TASK FORCE

MERRILL'S MARAUDERS
Army ENGINEERS
O.S.S.

S.O.S.
COMBAT CARGO
NURSES · MEDICS · A.R.C.

first C.B.I. VETERANS HOME SINCE "V-J" DAY

# 9 | THE POSTWAR WORLD

HAVING SECURED VICTORIES IN EUROPE AND JAPAN, THE ALLIED POWERS TURNED THEIR FOCUS TO REBUILDING SHATTERED ECONOMIES AND TO BRINGING WAR CRIMINALS TO TRIAL.

The United Nations, headquartered in New York City, was founded in 1945 to maintain international peace and promote human rights.

"The structure of world peace cannot be the work of one man or one party or one nation. It must be a peace which rests on the cooperative effort of the whole world."

—Franklin Roosevelt, March 1, 1945

# The War's Aftermath

THE WORLD NOW HAD TWO SUPERPOWERS, THE UNITED STATES AND
THE USSR. THE COLD WAR BETWEEN THEM WOULD LAST FOR DECADES.

The end of the war left some 60 million people dead and entire nations in ruins. Not only was agricultural production in shambles, supply lines from rural areas to cities and towns had been destroyed. Infrastructure and industrial centers had been shattered and economies left in total disarray. Survivors in war-torn areas lacked basic necessities, yet the extensive destruction made it nearly impossible to deliver desperately needed food and other relief supplies.

The widespread population loss affected most of Europe and much of Asia. With so many men killed during the war, fewer workers were available to begin reconstruction projects in urban areas or to join the labor force needed on farms. Countless children were without fathers, and many women were unable to marry to start new families. The millions of people who had fled their homelands became refugees, creating unexpected pressures around the world. Almost every family in battle-scarred countries had experienced the loss of homes, friends, and loved ones.

The years of strife also had irrevocably altered each of the warring nations. Germany, Japan, and Italy were devastated—materially, economically, and socially—as were other Axis nations. Nazi occupation had weakened the French economy, and collaborators were treated with disdain, eroding the country's social fabric. Britain's finances had been depleted by the war, and much of London had been reduced to rubble. Swaths of

Russia, too, were left in ruins. Americans who lost loved ones during the war struggled to cope, even as the nation's economy expanded and the United States became the world's leading economic and political power.

In the aftermath of the conflict, the balance of power shifted among the winners and losers. Instead of several major nations dominating international affairs, the globe transitioned to a place divided between two major opposing philosophies: democracy and communism. Colonialism drew to an end, as Japan and Italy were stripped of their territories, and Britain, France, and the Netherlands lost theirs to independence movements. The Soviet Union, with its imposing Red Army, proved that militarily it could hold its own against the United States.

This new world order, in which American interests were pitted against Soviet, gave way to the "Cold War," a legacy that affected the world for decades.

▲ European refugees gathered at a dispersal point in northwestern France for a meal before being transported to their respective countries.

| War Deaths by Country | | |
|---|---|---|
| Country | Military Deaths | Total Civilian and Military Deaths |
| China | 3 million–4 million | 20 million |
| France | 218,000 | 568,000 |
| Germany | 5.5 million | 6.6 million–8.8 million |
| Italy | 300,000 | 457,000 |
| Japan | 2.1 million | 2.6 million–3.1 million |
| Soviet Union | 8.8 million–10.7 million | 24 million |
| United Kingdom | 384,000 | 451,000 |
| United States | 417,000 | 419,000 |

▲ Chiang Kai-shek was leader of the Nationalist Party and president of China when the war ended.

## China: An Allied Power

The Republic of China and Japan had been at odds since 1937, when Japan invaded Manchuria, a Chinese province rich with minerals, timber, and fertile land. During most of World War II, Japanese troops controlled China's coastal areas, industrial sites, and cities. As a result, over 600,000 Japanese soldiers were unavailable for deployment to the Pacific, an important factor in the Allies' eventual victory. China did not officially enter the war until the bombing of Pearl Harbor in December 1941. They joined the Allies, declared war on Germany, and sent troops to join Allied forces in Burma.

Over the next few years, China, ruled by the Nationalist Party, would also face a different set of problems. The Nationalists supported democratic elections and principles, but they had long sparred with an insurgent Chinese Communist Party. As World War II played out, the two factions maintained an uneasy truce. Tensions resumed in 1945, and soon a civil war broke out. In 1949, the Communists defeated the Nationalists and formed the People's Republic of China. The Nationalists moved their government to Taiwan.

◀ Refugees in Italy were granted temporary housing in areas allocated for displaced persons.

# The Partition of Germany

THE ALLIES RESTRUCTURED THE COUNTRY'S GOVERNMENT AND TRIED NAZIS FOR WAR CRIMES.

Following Germany's surrender, civil authority throughout the country broke down and the economy faltered, which resulted in a lack of public services and widespread hunger and homelessness. To restore order and the economy, the Allies instituted plans made at Yalta and Potsdam and established new

## Postwar Recovery

The Allies carried out their plans for the postwar world. They partitioned Germany, occupied Japan, and planned war trials while working to establish democratic governments. War weary but optimistic, 50 nations gathered to create the United Nations.

**APRIL 12** President Roosevelt died of a cerebral hemorrhage, and Truman was sworn in as president the same day.

**MAY 7** Germany surrendered to the Allies, ending the war in Europe.

**JUNE 5** Germany and Berlin were divided into four zones controlled by U.S., British, French, and Soviet military.

administrative and economic systems. They also took steps to remove elements of Nazism from political and social life, and prosecuted those responsible for the horrors of the Third Reich.

## The Berlin Declaration

On June 5, American, British, French, and Soviet military commanders signed the Berlin Declaration of 1945 that split Germany into four occupation zones. Each of the Allies was assigned responsibility for administering one zone. An Allied Control Council, made up of military representatives, was formed and authorized to exercise joint governing power over the country. The council's decisions were supposed to be unanimous, but in cases of disagreement, each zone's military governor could take separate action. The capital city, Berlin, was also divided into quarters because of the way the zones were apportioned.

During the first week of July, American, British, and French troops marched triumphantly into Berlin, joining the Soviet troops who had conquered the city. On September 7, the Allied occupation forces held a victory parade in the German capital. Senior military officers from each of the four powers led a total of 5,000 soldiers, followed by armored divisions. The triumphant group marched past the historic Reichstag, the former German parliament building, and the Brandenburg Gate, Berlin's main entryway.

◀ An American soldier posed with his Soviet counterpart when the Western Allies entered Berlin in July 1945.

▲ Flying kites on the *Teufelsberg*, Berlin

## Devil's Mountain

The *Teufelsberg*, or Devil's Mountain, is the second-highest point in Berlin, rising about 380 feet above sea level. It was created in the aftermath of the war with about 100 million cubic yards of rubble that came from clearing and rebuilding the city, a gigantic project that took about 20 years. Today, the landscaped hillsides are a park where Berliners sled, fly kites, bike, and hike.

Several other cities in Germany are dotted with similar hills. The one in Stuttgart, called *Birkenkopf*, was built with about two million cubic yards of rubble. One piece of the rubble has a plaque reminding people that the mountain stands as a memorial to the victims of the war.

**JULY 17** The Allies met at the town of Potsdam near Berlin to plan for postwar Europe.

**AUGUST 14** Japan accepted surrender terms.

▲ **AUGUST 28** U.S. occupation of Japan began.

**SEPTEMBER 2** Japan officially surrendered; World War II ended.

**OCTOBER 24** The United Nations was established.

## The Berlin Airlift: Operation Vittles

When Berlin was partitioned into four occupation zones, the Soviets took control of the eastern half of the city and the other Allies occupied the western sectors. By late 1947, the British and Americans had merged their zones in an effort to promote economic development, and they were soon joined by the French.

This new Western coalition worried the Soviets, especially the prospect of a unified West Berlin—a capitalist city in the Russian-occupied zone of Germany, just 100 miles from the Russian border. Starting June 24, 1948, the Soviets began sealing off all railway, highway, and barge access to West Berlin, creating a blockade.

The Allies responded swiftly and began to ship supplies to Berlin by airplane. In the initial phase of the Berlin Airlift, Allied planes delivered about 5,000 tons of food and other goods daily. That amount soon increased to 8,000 tons a day. By the time the Soviets ended the blockade on May 12, 1949, and reopened roads, canals, and railway lines, a total of 2.3 million tons of supplies had been airlifted into Berlin on nearly 300,000 flights. The Allies continued to send food and other supplies via plane until September, hoping to create a surplus in case the Soviets decided to reinstate the blockade.

▲ West Berlin children eagerly awaited the planes bringing food. One pilot, the "candy bomber," dropped chocolate bars to them using tiny parachutes made of handkerchiefs.

▲ Members of denazification commissions interviewed witnesses to decide who was punishable and who was eligible for clemency.

▲ The *Tiergarten*, a large park in the center of Berlin, served as a black market where scarce or controlled items were traded illegally. Police officers patrolled suspected markets and sometimes made arrests. Here a posted sign warned Allied soldiers not to sell or barter goods they got from post exchanges.

## Conflict Among the "Big Four"

The joint administration of Germany soon deteriorated into irreconcilable differences. The USSR, which was responsible for a region with agricultural land, was supposed to supply food to the rest of the country in exchange for reparations from the other three zones. When the Soviets failed to meet their obligations, the United States and Britain began sending relief supplies to Germany at their own expense. The aid facilitated the country's return to self-sufficiency, a development the Soviets opposed.

The rift between the USSR and the Western powers continued to widen. Western occupation governments wanted to encourage democracy. In the last half of 1945, they allowed political parties to form in preparation for future German elections. By 1947, the Western powers combined the administrations in their three regions to further encourage economic growth. Russian premier Joseph Stalin, in contrast, wanted to safeguard his regime by controlling neighboring countries, including the Soviet zone in Germany. He and the Soviet occupiers pressured Germany's moderate Social Democrats to merge with

the Communists to ensure a Communist victory in elections held in the Soviet zone. Over time, these developments led to the evolution of two separate German nations—a country that would not be reunited until 1990.

## Denazification of Germany

During the war, many leading industrialists had supported Hitler, and more than eight million German citizens had become members of the Nazi Party. Others had joined, or had been forced to join, related organizations. Sheer numbers made "denazifying" the country a major undertaking.

In September 1945, the Allied Control Council officially abolished the Nazi Party. Beginning in January 1946, the group issued several directives designed to remove Nazis from positions of authority and to eliminate Nazi organizations and their ideas. The Allies also took control of the press, radio, and movies. The Americans closed German schools, destroyed textbooks, removed and retrained teachers, and created new curricula. The next step was to prosecute Nazis who were classified as the war's "major offenders."

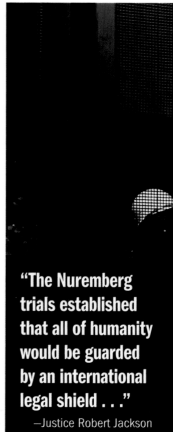

"The Nuremberg trials established that all of humanity would be guarded by an international legal shield . . ."

—Justice Robert Jackson

▲ Nazi leaders were tried in Room 600 of the Palace of Justice. Courtroom proceedings were recorded, and some were broadcast in radio reports. It was the first time most people learned of the Nazi atrocities, the concentration camps, and the gas chambers.

## The Nuremberg War Trials

Even before Germany surrendered, the Allies had planned to establish courts to try Nazi military and political leaders for their actions during the war. On May 2, 1945, President Harry Truman selected Associate Supreme Court Justice Robert Jackson to organize the proceedings and to represent the United States in them.

Jackson started by developing the London Charter, which established the International Military Tribunal and the procedures for the trials. The Allied signatories agreed to hold the trials in Nuremberg, where the Nazis had staged their annual rallies, as the court of record. Much of the city was severely damaged, but the huge Palace of Justice and a prison remained intact.

On November 20, the Nuremberg War Trials began. In the first trial, 22 Nazis faced one or more charges of war crimes, crimes against peace, or crimes against humanity. The defendants included *Luftwaffe* commander Hermann Göring, Hitler's deputy Rudolf Hess, and Hitler's successor Admiral Karl Dönitz. Each morning, guards marched the men from the prison to the courtroom. Over the next ten months, prosecutors offered evidence that included German propaganda movies, films of concentration camp liberations, and physical evidence from the camps, as well as eyewitness testimony. The 250 journalists attending the trials were often heard weeping in the courtroom. On October 1, the court handed down the verdicts. Twelve, including Göring, were

▲ Top Nazi leaders were the first to be tried in the trial of the major war criminals, which lasted ten months. Defendants seated in the dock were, front row (left to right): Hermann Göring (taking notes), Rudolf Hess, Joachim von Ribbentrop, General Wilhelm Keitel; back row (left to right): Admiral Karl Dönitz, Admiral Erich Raeder, Baldur von Schirach, and Fritz Sauckel.

▲ Hermann Göring conferred with his German lawyer.

sentenced to death by hanging. Three received life sentences, four got prison terms of ten to 20 years, and three lesser political figures were acquitted. Between 1945 and 1949, more than 100 other defendants were tried at Nuremberg.

These cases were notable because they attempted to administer justice for the Nazi atrocities and because they established universal standards of human rights and conduct during war. In 1945, the United Nations established the International Court of Justice to decide legal disputes between nations on a voluntary basis. In the years following World War II, the international community would also sign agreements on human rights, genocide, and laws of war.

## Robert Jackson: Work of a Lifetime

Associate Supreme Court Justice Robert Jackson (1892–1954) was an eminent attorney and jurist who left a significant legacy as the architect of the trials at Nuremberg. He was born in Spring Creek, Pennsylvania, and soon moved with his family to Frewsburg, New York. After apprenticing to an attorney and attending one year of law school, Jackson passed the New York State Bar exam. He pursued a successful legal career in Jamestown, Pennsylvania.

President Franklin Roosevelt named Jackson U.S. solicitor general in 1938, and three years later, U.S. attorney general. In 1941, Jackson was appointed to the U.S. Supreme Court, where he served until his death in 1954. Jackson later said that his work developing the International Military Tribunal and its legal precedents was the most important of his life.

◄ In October 1941, Supreme Court Justice Robert Jackson posed for a formal photograph in his new judicial role.

▲ General Douglas MacArthur arrived at Atsugi Air Base near Yokohama on the afternoon of August 30, 1945, to oversee the occupation and transformation of Japan. As he exited the aircraft, greeted by soldiers and reporters, he said, "Melbourne to Tokyo was a long road but this looks like the payoff."

# The Occupation of Japan

MACARTHUR LED THE REHABILITATION OF JAPAN AND THE TOKYO TRIALS.

After Japan surrendered in August, the United States took the lead role for the Allies and put into motion a plan to stabilize the country. The Allies intended to demilitarize their former enemy. They also wanted to create a democratic government, change social and cultural attitudes, and lay the foundation for a strong economy in the country. President Harry Truman named General Douglas MacArthur to serve as the Supreme Commander for the Allied powers, or SCAP, putting him in charge of a large staff of military and civilian personnel who sought to transform the island nation.

MacArthur's first challenge was to address Japan's severe postwar food shortage, and the United States responded with millions of dollars in food aid. Several private relief agencies soon joined the effort to supply food and clothing to Japan. MacArthur then began to plant the seeds of democracy with a series of reforms. In October 1945, he issued a directive that ordered the Japanese government to ". . . remove restrictions on political, civil and religious liberties and discrimination on grounds of race, nationality, creed or political option . . ." and to release political prisoners. He also launched a censorship campaign to eliminate both racial and nationalistic attitudes in the media.

Other changes soon followed. SCAP barred career military and extreme nationalists from public office, disbanded the Japanese army and navy, destroyed military equipment, and abolished national control of education and of the police. To encourage a free-market capitalist economy, the Allies instituted a labor union law and placed restrictions on large industrial conglomerates. Allied occupation staff also shifted the focus of industrial manufacturing from war matériel to consumer goods. Agricultural reforms dissolved concentrated land ownership and helped former tenant farmers buy land.

As a result of these reforms, Japan's political landscape changed dramatically. In January 1946, Emperor Hirohito formally disavowed his divinity, which left him with no governmental power. Political parties such as the Japan Socialist Party, the Japan Progressive Party, and the Liberal Party, which were relatively inactive during the war, reappeared. The Liberal Party won the first postwar election in 1946. Shigeru Yoshida became prime minister, and served in that position five times.

◀ Workers distributed Allied food shipments of wheat flour and rice to Japanese civilians. The food had to be rationed to ensure that everyone received enough to survive.

▲ U.S. Army surplus food was sent to Japan during 1945 and 1946. The shipments not only provided relief, they helped further the democratic goals of the occupation.

▲ When Emperor Hirohito and his wife toured Japan, they broke with ancient traditions by interacting with the Japanese people.

## The Emperor's Transformation

As emperor, Hirohito had little contact with his subjects, who had long regarded him as a descendant of the gods. Photographs from early in his career showed him as an unsmiling military man in uniform, often astride a white horse. But after the Allies created a new constitution for Japan, stripping Hirohito of his imperial powers, the leader appeared transformed. He began attending public events, often with his wife and children.

As Japan's constitutional monarch, he toured the country to view reconstruction projects and to promote the imperial family. During these trips, Hirohito wore a suit and hat, waved his hat as he greeted the crowds, and stopped to shake hands and chat with the people. He made several trips abroad to meet foreign leaders, including Britain's Queen Elizabeth II and several American presidents, before his death in 1989.

▶ Under Japan's new constitution, women could vote for the first time.

▼ The National Diet Building in Tokyo took 17 years to build and was completed in 1936. The central tower, at almost 215 feet, made it the tallest building in Japan at that time. The building survived the war intact.

## A New Constitution

In SCAP's view, for Japan to be successfully democratized, it had to replace the 1889 Meiji constitution, which granted almost complete control of the government to the emperor. It had vested him with the power to appoint the prime minister, to command the army and the navy, and to name members of the house of nobles, the upper chamber of the country's bicameral legislature, called the Diet.

In February 1946, after four months of work, the Japanese presented MacArthur with their draft of a new constitution. But the general quickly rejected it as a refashioning of the Meiji charter. He then charged his own staff with studying the founding documents of other countries and coming up with an alternative in just a week's time.

The new draft, based largely on the U.S. Constitution, was built around the idea that "sovereign power resides with the people." It stripped the emperor of his executive power in the Diet and converted the nation into a constitutional monarchy. Both houses of the Diet were to be elected, and the right of universal adult suffrage was established. The new constitution also granted civil rights to Japanese citizens similar to the liberties in the Bill of Rights. The Allies considered Article 9 of the new constitution, the "no war" clause, the most important item. It outlawed the creation of any armed forces and forbid the nation from threatening or waging war.

In March, Japanese officials requested a few minor changes to the document. Then on April 10, the Japanese people voted in their first postwar election and chose legislative representatives to the Diet. Female candidates won 39 of the 464 seats. In October, both houses of the Diet passed the bill proposing enactment of the constitution. The emperor agreed, and it became effective in May 1947.

> "The adoption of this liberal charter . . . lays a very solid foundation for the new Japan."
>
> —Douglas MacArthur

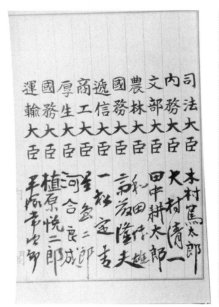
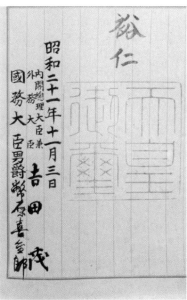

▲ The signatures of Prime Minister Shigeru Yoshida (right) and those of cabinet ministers (left) were inscribed on the signature page of the new constitution.

### Shinto

The Shinto religion, which originated in Japan, involves traditions and beliefs deeply rooted in Japanese life. It is centered around *kami*, sacred spirits of things in nature or creation forces as well as the spirits of ancestors. In the late 1860s, the Japanese government established Shinto as the state religion, and as a result its priests became government officials. In December 1945, MacArthur issued the Shinto Declaration, which separated the Shinto religion from the state and barred the government from providing it with financial support.

◄ Toshogu Shrine, near the city of Nikko, is composed of 55 historic buildings decorated with brightly colored lacquer and religious carvings.

▶ The Tokyo War Trials lasted more than two years, and all of the defendants were found guilty. Seven received death sentences, and 16 were sentenced to life in prison. MacArthur reviewed the decisions, upheld the verdicts, and praised the tribunal's work.

▲ Japanese defendant Lieutenant Kei Yuri listened to a question from his American defense attorney during his trial. He was accused of ordering guards to bayonet to death an American soldier in front of U.S. Army officers.

## The Tokyo War Crimes Trials

The Potsdam Declaration, which outlined terms for Japan's surrender, also required "stern justice" for war criminals. To fulfill that requirement, in January 1946, MacArthur began assembling the International Military Tribunal for the Far East to prosecute Japanese offenders. The tribunal was authorized to review a range of atrocities dating back to 1931, when Japan invaded Manchuria.

MacArthur appointed judges from the ten Allied nations that had signed Japan's surrender document, and each of those countries named prosecutors. The court charged 18 military leaders and nine politicians with war crimes, crimes against peace, and/or crimes against humanity. The tribunal's indictments included specific charges such as mass murder, rape, pillage, torture, forced labor, and the mistreatment and murder of prisoners of war. The emperor and the imperial family were not included for pragmatic reasons: Their support of the occupation was important to aid Japan's transition.

The Tokyo War Crimes Trials began in May 1946 and continued until November 1948. Some of the evidence presented in court shocked the Japanese people; many had not known of the atrocities committed by their troops in Manchuria and the Pacific.

Prosecutors convicted and executed two former prime ministers, Hideki Tojo and Koki Hirota, as well as five generals. Other defendants were also convicted and received prison sentences. Trials took place in other Japanese cities to prosecute "lesser" criminals. Other countries, including China and the Philippines, prosecuted another 5,000 defendants. More than half received life sentences, and around 900 were executed.

▲ Workers at a steel manufacturing facility helped rebuild the nation's industries.

▲ This tin toy was produced in Japan during the 1950s.

## Made in Occupied Japan

During the occupation, Japan was allowed to export goods to help rebuild its economy. Most items were inexpensive, such as household china, porcelain figurines, and mechanical toys made of tin, often produced by hand. They rarely reflected Japanese culture, but instead catered to European or American tastes. At least half of the merchandise had to be marked "Made in Occupied Japan." Today, these items are popular with collectors and have appreciated significantly in value. A windup toy in its original box that sold for 50 cents in 1950 could be worth as much as $50 today.

## A New Course to Reconstruction

From the early days of the occupation, the Allied occupying forces had sought to break up industrial conglomerates and move the Japanese economy to free-market capitalism. The goal was to return the country's output to prewar levels. But increasing poverty, inflation, and Japan's ongoing dependence on U.S. aid led to what has been dubbed "the reverse course."

Starting in 1948, the Allies embarked on a campaign to rebuild Japan's economy and restore self-sufficiency. Restrictions on industrial conglomerates were relaxed, and tax reforms were instituted. In addition, the United States provided equipment and materials so that Japan could retool its manufacturing base.

This change in economic focus was also tied to the Cold War. At the time, the Communists in China's civil war were moving toward victory, and the

Allies were concerned about the spread of communism in Asia. For the Allies, an economically strong Japan would be less likely to succumb to communism.

Defensive protection for the island nation was necessary as well. In 1950, the Allies permitted Japan to form the National Police Reserve and recruit 75,000 members, all of whom were under the government's civilian control.

▼ A lightbulb manufacturing plant in Tokyo provided jobs for workers on an assembly line.

▲ Gardeners at San Francisco's Golden Gate Park created a special display of flowers to welcome the delegates to the conference.

# Hopes for a Peaceful World

THE UNITED NATIONS PROVIDED A FORUM
FOR RESOLVING INTERNATIONAL DISPUTES.

After years of conflict, devastation, and privation, there was a shared determination to avoid another world war. Gradually, this determination evolved into action. The seeds of the effort dated to August 1941, when Roosevelt and Prime Minister Winston Churchill issued the Atlantic Charter, a statement that listed their postwar goals for international security. These goals appeared again in January 1942, when 26 Allied nations signed the United Nations Declaration, which bound them to a common purpose of victory over the Axis powers and a resolve to protect liberty and human rights. In April 1945, with the end of the war in sight, representatives of 50 nations met at the San Francisco

▲ The title page of the Charter of the United Nations featured the organization's emblem. It is a map of the world with the North Pole at its center, surrounded by a wreath of olive branches, a symbol of peace.

**" . . . to save succeeding generations from the scourge of war . . . to reaffirm faith in fundamental human rights . . ."**

—from the UN Charter

◄ Edward Stettinius, chair of the U.S. delegation to the United Nations conference in San Francisco, signed the UN Charter for the United States while President Harry Truman (second from left) and others looked on.

▲ Secretary of State James Byrnes (right) watched as Truman (left) signed the document by which he ratified the Charter of the United Nations.

Conference to write a charter for the new organization.

The charter established the structure of the United Nations and outlined its guiding principles: to prevent war, to affirm fundamental human rights, to facilitate international peace and security, to promote improved living standards, and to support social progress and economic advancements. The United States, Britain, and the USSR were the primary designers of the decision-making structure. The General Assembly consisted of representatives of all member countries. The Security Council, which was responsible for international peace and security, originally had 11 members, six of which were elected to two-year terms. Five—the United States, the United Kingdom, the Soviet Union, France, and the Republic of China—were permanent members, and each had veto power on Security Council resolutions.

Disagreements based on national interests plagued the discussions at the April conference, but they did not prevent the formation of the United Nations. The USSR insisted on individual memberships for each of the countries along the Soviet border in eastern Europe, in hopes of controlling a bloc of votes. Britain got assurances that due to the principle of self-determination, none of its colonies would be put under UN control. There also was considerable debate about the voting process and veto power in the Security Council. Finally on June 25, the delegates unanimously adopted the charter, and the next day they all signed the document. After the permanent members of the Security Council and most of the other members ratified the charter, the United Nations was officially established on October 24, 1945. The world had entered a new period of international collaboration.

▲ The flags of 51 nations were arrayed on the stage of the War Memorial Opera House in San Francisco for the Japanese peace treaty conference. In spite of objections from some delegations, a substantial majority of the nations represented at the meeting signed the treaty.

# The Peace Treaty with Japan

THE ISLAND NATION WAS READMITTED TO THE WORLD COMMUNITY.

By 1950, when Japan had made significant economic and political progress, the Allies acknowledged it was time to officially end the occupation. Negotiations for a peace treaty between the United States and Japan were initiated and continued for several months. There were numerous drafts of the official document, and they included recommendations from other Western Allies—but there were also major Cold War rifts. The United States and Great Britain, for example, could not agree on which government should represent China in the final proceedings: The United States wanted the Republic of China on Taiwan, but Britain insisted on the People's Republic of China on the mainland. With no compromise possible, when 51 nations assembled in San Francisco on September 4, 1951, to approve the treaty, China was not included.

As a result, only 48 nations signed the treaty on September 8. The Soviet Union abstained because it objected to the exclusion of China and because of the territorial disputes it was having with Japan. Poland and Czechoslovakia also refused to sign. Despite the opposition, the treaty, which abolished Japan's control over territory taken during the war and restored Japan's sovereignty, became effective on April 28, 1952.

On the same day, the United States and Japan signed a peace treaty allowing the United States to keep military bases in Japan to counter Soviet and Chinese power. This new agreement inaugurated a bilateral military relationship between the two nations. Japan became an ally with the right to self-defense, and the United States was allowed to maintain its military presence in Japan and give up any right to war reparations.

▲ The Bilateral Security Treaty between the United States and Japan allowed a continuing U.S. military presence in the island nation and transformed it from a defeated enemy to a military ally.

# HONORING THOSE WHO SERVED

The World War II Memorial in Washington, D.C. is a tribute to all the men and women of the "Greatest Generation" who sacrified to bring victory to our nation.

Sixteen million Americans served in the armed forces during World War II, and on May 29, 2004, a memorial honoring their commitment and sacrifices was dedicated in the nation's capital. The event featured a four-day celebration, with special museum exhibits and services in the National Cathedral.

Almost every feature and detail of the seven-acre memorial, situated in the National Mall, is symbolic. A ceremonial entrance is flanked by 24 bronze bas-relief sculptures that provide glimpses into the American experience at home and on the battlefield. Inside, the memorial is anchored by two pavilions— one proclaiming victory in the Atlantic Theatre, the other success in the Pacific. Fifty-six granite pillars represent the states, federal territories, and the District of Columbia. The columns are linked with bronze ropes to reflect the nation's unity during the war and adorned with two bronze wreaths, one of wheat, representing the United States' agricultural strength, and one in oak, signifying the might of a nation that supplied its own troops and those of its allies.

The site also features the Freedom Wall decorated with 4,048 gold stars, honoring the more than 400,000 military personnel who lost their lives during the war or who remain missing in action. Carved at the bottom are the words: "Here we mark the price of freedom."

Visitors can find hidden treasures in the site, including the famous "Kilroy was here" graffiti that is familiar to every World War II veteran. Also carved into the memorial are these words from President Truman: "Our debt to the heroic men and valiant women in the service of our country can never be repaid. They have earned our undying gratitude. America will never forget their sacrifices."

▲ Four million visitors come to the memorial each year to pay tribute to fallen comrades and to honor all those who sacrificed during the war. Many leave flags and flowers to commemorate the event.

"When it mattered most, an entire generation of Americans showed the finest qualities of our nation and of humanity. On this day, in their honor, we will raise the American flag over a monument that will stand as long as America itself."

—George W. Bush, May 29, 2004

▲ Four eagles sit inside each arched pavilion. Each majestic bird has a wingspan of 11 feet and is perched on its own 18-foot-tall bronze column. The four join together to hold a laurel victory wreath. Carvings at the base of the pavilions list many of the major World War II battlefields and war campaigns.

▲ The Rainbow Pool in the center of the monument's plaza opens to vistas of both the Lincoln Memorial (shown here) and the Washington Monument.

# Index

# Photo Credits

FRONT COVER
Gordon Coster/The LIFE Picture Collection/ Getty Images
BACK COVER: Top: © Bettmann/CORBIS; Middle: Ann Ronan Pictures/Print Collector/ Getty Images; Bottom: © CORBIS
TITLE PAGE: Horace Abrahams/Stringer/Getty Images

p. 2: Top: Frank Scherschel/The LIFE Picture Collection/Getty Images; Middle Top: © Bettmann/CORBIS; Middle Bottom: Keystone-France/Gamma-Keystone via Getty Images; Bottom: © GraphicaArtis/Corbis p. 3: Chapter 1: © Photos 12/Alamy; Chapter 2: © CORBIS; Chapter 3: © Everett Collection Historical/ Alamy; Chapter 4: Francois LE DIASCORN/ Gamma-Rapho via Getty Images; Chapter 5: © Photos 12/Alamy; Chapter 6: Keystone/ Getty Images; Chapter 7: © Bettmann/CORBIS; Chapter 8: Keystone/Getty Images; Chapter 9: Richard Laird/Getty Images p. 4: Left: © Bettmann/CORBIS; Center: Ann Ronan Pictures/Print Collector/Getty Images; Right: © Bettmann/CORBIS p. 5: Left: Photo12/UIG/ Getty Images; Center: Apic/Getty Images; Right: MPI/Getty Images

1: THE WESTERN FRONT

pp. 6–7: Photos 12/Alamy p. 8: © Trinity Mirror/ Mirrorpix/Alamy p. 10: © DIZ Muenchen GmbH, Sueddeutsche Zeitung Photo/Alamy p. 11: Bottom Left: © CORBIS; Top Right: Keystone/ Getty Images; Middle Right: © CORBIS; Bottom Right: © GraphicaArtis/Corbis p. 12: © DIZ Muenchen GmbH, Sueddeutsche Zeitung Photo/ Alamy p. 13: Central Press/Hulton Archive/ Getty Images p. 14: Left: omikron/Getty Images; Right: © Pictorial Press Ltd/Alamy p. 15: Left: © Photos 12/Alamy; Right: © Bettmann/CORBIS p. 16: Top: George Silk/The LIFE Picture Collection/ Getty Images; Bottom: © David Cole/Alamy p. 17: Top: © Photos 12/Alamy; Bottom: US Army/ The LIFE Picture Collection/Getty Images p. 18: George Silk/The LIFE Picture Collection/Getty Images p. 19: Pictorial Parade/Archive Photos/ Getty Images pp. 20–21: © Prisma Bildagentur AG/Alamy p. 22: Top: © Bettmann/CORBIS; Bottom Left: Ulf Andersen/Getty Images; Bottom Right: © Hulton-Deutsch Collection/ CORBIS p. 23: Left: © Prisma Bildagentur AG/ Alamy; Right: © David Cole/Alamy p. 24: © DIZ Muenchen GmbH, Sueddeutsche Zeitung Photo/Alamy p. 25: Top: © Stephen Barnes/ Military/Alamy; Bottom: © DIZ Muenchen GmbH, Sueddeutsche Zeitung Photo/Alamy p. 26: © Hulton-Deutsch Collection/CORBIS p. 27: Left: © World History Archive/Alamy; Right: © Bettmann/CORBIS pp. 28–29: © CORBIS p. 29: © Bettmann/CORBIS p. 30: © Bettmann/ CORBIS p. 31: Top: © Hulton-Deutsch Collection/ CORBIS; Bottom: © Hulton-Deutsch Collection/ CORBIS p. 32: Keystone/Getty Images p. 33: Top Left: Margaret Bourke-White/The LIFE Picture Collection/Getty Images; Top Right: © Pictorial Press Ltd/Alamy; Bottom: Frank Scherschel/ The LIFE Picture Collection/Getty Images p. 34: European/FPG/Getty Images p. 35: Top: Popperfoto/Getty Images; Bottom: © F1online digitale Bildagentur GmbH/Alamy pp. 36–37:

© Pictorial Press Ltd/Alamy p. 37: Holz, Karl: Nationalsozialistische Deutsche Arbeiterpartei (NSDAP), Deutschland pp. 38–39: Top: Horace Abrahams/Keystone/Getty Images; Bottom: © War Archive/Alamy p. 39: © Everett Collection Historical/Alamy pp. 40–41: Top: © Photos 12/ Alamy; Bottom: © Andrew Chapman/Alamy pp. 42–43: Keystone-France/Gamma-Keystone via Getty Images p. 43: © Bettmann/CORBIS p. 44: Authenticated News/Archive Photos/Getty Images p. 45: © Hulton-Deutsch Collection/ CORBIS p. 46: Top: © Mary Evans Picture Library/Alamy; Bottom: © Lebrecht Music and Arts Photo Library/Alamy p. 47: Top: © Pictorial Press Ltd/Alamy; Bottom: Keystone-France/ Gamma-Keystone via Getty Images p. 48: William Vandivert/The LIFE Picture Collection/ Getty Images pp. 48–49: © DIZ Muenchen GmbH, Sueddeutsche Zeitung Photo/Alamy p. 49: © Hulton-Deutsch Collection/CORBIS p. 50: Fox Photos/Getty Images p. 51: Top: Keystone/ Getty Images; Bottom Left: © MARKA/Alamy; Bottom Right: © INTERFOTO/Alamy

2: THE EASTERN FRONT

pp. 52–53: © CORBIS p. 54: Keystone/Hulton Archive/Getty Images pp. 54–55: Keystone/ Getty Images p. 55: Top: © ITAR-TASS Photo Agency/Alamy; Middle: © Pictorial Press Ltd/ Alamy; Bottom: © Hulton-Deutsch Collection/ CORBIS pp. 56–57: Paul Popper/Popperfoto/ Getty Images p. 57: Sovfoto/UIG via Getty Images p. 58: Left: WOJTEK RADWANSKI/ AFP/Getty Images; Right: © ITAR-TASS Photo Agency/Alamy p. 59: Top: © CORBIS; Bottom: Margaret Bourke-White/The LIFE Picture Collection/Getty Images p. 60: Hulton Archive/ Getty Images p. 61: Top Left: © Maurizio Borgese/Hemis/Corbis; Top Right: Gavin Hellier/Getty Images; Bottom: Jacek Kadaj/ Getty Images p. 62: © CORBIS pp. 62–63: Slava Katamidze Collection/Getty Images p. 63: © DIZ Muenchen GmbH, Sueddeutsche Zeitung Photo/ Alamy p. 64: © Everett Collection Inc/Alamy p. 65: © Everett Collection Inc/Alamy p. 66: © DIZ Muenchen GmbH, Sueddeutsche Zeitung Photo/Alamy pp. 66–67: © ITAR-TASS Photo Agency/Alamy pp. 68–69: © DIZ Muenchen GmbH, Sueddeutsche Zeitung Photo/Alamy p. 70: G. Melnik/Slava Katamidze Collection/ Getty Images p. 71: Top: © Pictorial Press Ltd/ Alamy; Bottom: © Berliner Verlag/Archiv/dpa/ Corbis p. 72: Imagno/Getty Images pp. 72–73: John Phillips/The LIFE Picture Collection/ Getty Images p. 74: © Pictorial Press Ltd/ Alamy p. 75: Top: © Yevgeny Khaldei/Corbis; Bottom: © Daniel Gerd Poelsler/imageBROKER/ Corbis p. 76: © Yevgeny Khaldei/Corbis p. 77: Top: © Hulton-Deutsch Collection/CORBIS; Bottom: © Stuart Black/Robert Harding World Imagery/Corbis p. 78: © DIZ Muenchen GmbH, Sueddeutsche Zeitung Photo/Alamy p. 79: © Hemis/Alamy p. 80: © Yevgeny Khaldei/ Corbis pp. 80–81: Universal History Archive/ Getty Images p. 81: Galerie Bilderwelt/Getty Images p. 82: © Berliner Verlag/Archiv/dpa/ Corbis p. 83: © Yevgeny Khaldei/Corbis p. 84: Top: Sovfoto/UIG via Getty Images; Bottom: © Hulton-Deutsch Collection/CORBIS p. 85: Top: © Everett Collection Historical/Alamy; Bottom:

© eye35.pix/Alamy p. 86: Keystone-France/ Gamma-Keystone via Getty Images p. 87: Top: Hulton Archive/Getty Images; Bottom: William Poulson/Keystone/Getty Images pp. 88–89: © DIZ Muenchen GmbH, Sueddeutsche Zeitung Photo/Alamy

3: MOVING TOWARD PEACE

pp. 90–91: © Everett Collection Historical/ Alamy p. 92: © Bettmann/CORBIS pp. 92–93: © Bettmann/CORBIS p. 93: Top Right: © Austrian Archives/CORBIS; Bottom Left: Popperfoto/ Getty Images p. 94: Top Left: © Everett Collection Inc/Alamy; Top Right: © Everett Collection Inc/ Alamy p. 95: © Hulton-Deutsch Collection/ CORBIS; Bottom: © Pictorial Press Ltd/Alamy p. 96: Top: Anthony Calvacca/The LIFE Images Collection/Getty Images; Bottom Left: Alfred Eisenstaedt/The LIFE Picture Collection/Getty Images; Bottom Right: Alfred Eisenstaedt/The LIFE Picture Collection/Getty Images p. 97: Fox Photos/Getty Images p. 98: Keystone/Getty Images p. 99: © CORBIS p. 100: Left: © CORBIS; Right: © Hulton-Deutsch Collection/CORBIS p. 101: © str/AP/Corbis

4: LIBERATING THE CAMPS

pp. 102–103: Francois LE DIASCORN/Gamma-Rapho via Getty Images p. 104: ERIC SCHWAB/ AFP/Getty Images p. 105: US Army/Getty Images p. 106: David Scherman/Keystone/ Getty Images p. 107: Left: Galerie Bilderwelt/ Getty Images; Right: ERIC SCHWAB/AFP/ Getty Images p. 108: © imageBROKER/Alamy p. 109: Top: Popperfoto/Getty Images; Bottom: Gjon Mili/The LIFE Picture Collection/Getty Images p. 110: Top Right: Keystone-France/ Gamma-Keystone via Getty Images; Bottom Left: © CORBIS p. 111: Top: Bernard Gotfryd/ Getty Images; Bottom: © JASON REED/Reuters/ Corbis p. 112: © Photos 12/Alamy pp. 112–113: © DIZ Muenchen GmbH, Sueddeutsche Zeitung Photo/Alamy p. 113: © Everett Collection Historical/Alamy p. 114: © Pictorial Press Ltd/Alamy; Right: Apic/Getty Images p. 115: Galerie Bilderwelt/Getty Images p. 116: Keystone-France/Gamma-Keystone via Getty Images p. 117: Andreas Rentz/Getty Images p. 118: Top Left: Hulton Archive/Getty Images; Bottom Left: Galerie Bilderwelt/Getty Images; Bottom Right: © Kazimierz Jurewicz/Alamy pp. 118–119: Galerie Bilderwelt/Getty Images p. 119: Top Left: Sovfoto/UIG via Getty Images; Top Right: Hulton Archive/Getty Images; Bottom: Photo12/UIG/Getty Images p. 120: Top: © Pictorial Press Ltd/Alamy; Bottom: © VPC Travel Photo/Alamy p. 121: Left: George Rodger/The LIFE Picture Collection/Getty Images; Right: Keystone-France/Gamma-Keystone via Getty Images p. 122: © Pictorial Press Ltd/Alamy pp. 122–123: Abrahams/Getty Images p. 123: Top: © Mary Evans Picture Library/Alamy; Bottom: © Kevin Galvin/Alamy p. 124: © dpa/Corbis p. 125: Top: © INTERFOTO/Alamy; Bottom: Werner Forman/Universal Images Group/Getty Images p. 126: Dennis K. Johnson/Getty Images p. 127: Top: Lasting Images/Getty Images; Bottom Left: Dennis K. Johnson/Getty Images; Bottom Right: Johannes Simon/Getty Images